Overview of Vocational and Applied Technology Education

John L. Scott
Michelle Sarkees-Wircenski

AMERICAN TECHNICAL PUBLISHERS, INC.
HOMEWOOD, ILLINOIS 60430

1 2 3 4 5 6 7 8 9 – 96 – 9 8 7 6 5 4 3 2 1

Printed in the United States of America

ISBN 0-8269-4014-5

CONTENTS

INTRODUCTION

Vocational and applied technology education is the primary system through which youth and adults are prepared to enter competitive employment and continue lifelong learning. Vocational and applied technology education programs are designed to assist individuals in exploring career options and developing the academic and occupational skills required for competitive work for all segments of the American society. Vocational education prepares students for over 400 occupations that require education and training below the baccalaureate level. Vocational and applied technology education programs are offered in over 26,000 high schools, community colleges, and technical institutes. Vocational and applied technology education programs are created from a federal-state-local cooperative effort in which federal, state, local, and private funds are combined to support local vocational institutions.

Since the dawn of civilization, a primitive form of vocational education has existed in the form of mothers and fathers teaching their children how to provide the necessities of life. From this primitive form of work preparation, workers invented the age-old institution of apprenticeship and eventually vocational schools to prepare individuals for work and living. The current system of vocational education in the United States is the product of an extended period of experimentation and development through an evolutionary process spanning thousands of years. Vocational and applied technology education as we know it today has been shaped by philosophical, educational, economic, and societal forces and these forces continue to impact all of education.

A review of the history of vocational education is an exciting study, one that will help those involved in it to understand more fully the inter-workings of vocational and applied technology education today. An understanding of the past of vocational education will help those engaged in it today to have an improved sense of purpose and be more informed to deal with present and future issues confronting the field.

This book provides a broad-brush overview of the history and development of vocational and applied technology education including a brief account of the origin and early forms of education for work, the various experiments for including education for work into the schools of Europe, the introduction of apprenticeship into colonial America, the development of education for work in the schools of America prior to the passage of the Smith-Hughes Act of 1917, and the evolution of federal legislation which has shaped vocational and applied technology education, with an emphasis on legislation for special populations. and an overview of vocational student organizations which are an essential component of each of the vocational and applied technology education programs.

Shortly after vocational education programs became operational under the Smith-Hughes Act of 1917, vocational educators recognized the need to provide some type of organized clubs that would motivate students to take full advantage of their vocational education opportunity while providing them with social and recreational activities and opportunities to showcase their skills. A number of local student organizations developed and as vocational education became more widespread, each major service area followed the lead of agriculture in establishing a national vocational student organization to serve their students. Vocational student organizations have come to be perceived as an integral component of a quality vocational education program that enhances and supplements regular instructional activities to better meet the career and leadership skill needs of all students.

The Authors and Publisher

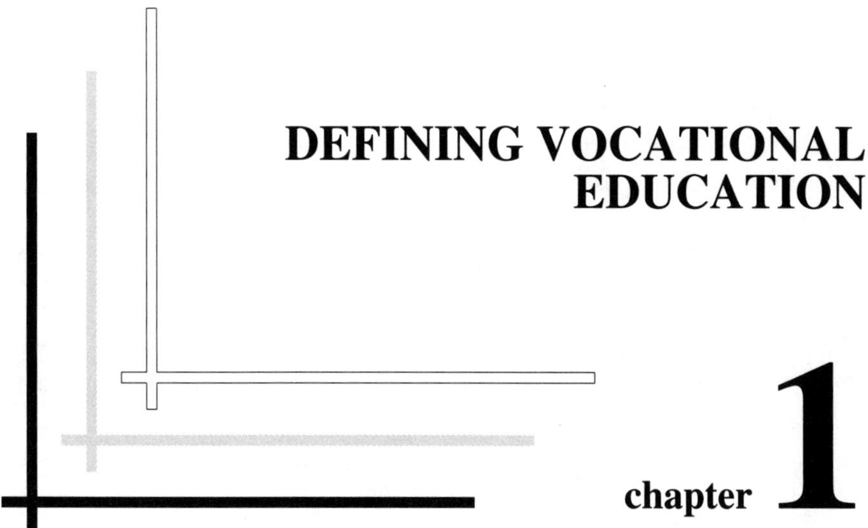

DEFINING VOCATIONAL EDUCATION

chapter 1

INTRODUCTION

Vocational and applied technology education is an important component of the American education system which serves the purpose of providing learning experiences that help students explore career areas and prepare for employment and independent living. Vocational and applied technology education curricula include materials that focus on the development of foundational skills such as basic skills, thinking skills, and personal qualities, as well as a common core of workplace competencies and specific skill competencies required for each chosen occupational area. Vocational and applied technology education programs make use of real-life situations in classrooms and laboratories as well as through supervised work experience in internships, practicums, cooperative education, and apprenticeships in actual worksites which provide meaningful opportunities for learners to realize the value of academic and technical skills and to apply them. Vocational and applied technology education programs are offered in many different forms at the secondary and postsecondary levels with some prevocational programs provided in some school systems at the middle school or junior high school level.

OBJECTIVES

After completing this chapter the reader should be able to:

1. Define vocational and applied technology education.
2. Describe the purposes of vocational and applied technology education.
3. Describe the various vocational program settings.
4. Identify three divisions of secondary vocational curriculum used by the National Center for Educational Statistics.
5. Describe the secondary vocational curriculum for a typical vocational student.
6. Describe components of secondary vocational education instructional programs.
7. Identify the ASTD and SCANS skills.
8. Describe Tech Prep Programs as established by the Carl D. Perkins Vocational and Applied Technology Act of 1990.
9. Describe youth apprenticeship programs.
10. Describe cooperative education programs.
11. Explain the purposes and operations of internships and practicums.

DEFINING VOCATIONAL EDUCATION

Vocational education is a large and diverse educational enterprise, spanning both secondary and postsecondary education. Vocational education encompasses a tremendous number of programs designed to prepare students for employment and for living. Most people identify vocational education at the secondary level with courses in one of the seven specific labor market program areas; agriculture, business, family and consumer sciences (formerly home economics), marketing (formerly distributive education), health, trade and industry (T&I), and technical/communications. Technology education (formerly industrial arts) is sometimes viewed to be a service area of vocational education but it is more appropriately viewed as a vital part of general and academic education. Business and T&I courses are the most popular, with business enrolling over one-half of all vocational students and T&I enrolling one-third. Enrollment in the other service areas is roughly equal. Examples of courses in the service areas include: agricultural science, carpentry, accounting, word processing, retailing, fashion, practical nursing, respiratory therapy, child care, electronics, computer programming, and food and nutrition (NAVE, 1994).

The vocational education curriculum appeals to a diverse group of students with almost every high school student earning at least some credits in vocational education courses. Vocational courses are also very popular at the postsecondary level with nearly two-thirds of all students enrolled in less than baccalaureate institutions enrolled in vocational programs. The majority of secondary students preparing for college have taken at least one vocational course other than keyboarding. Almost 14,000,000 students participate in vocational programs that assist them to explore career options and develop occupational skills for the workforce. Vocational programs are offered by approximately 26,000 high schools, community colleges, and technical institutes and are available in most school districts in the country (American Vocational Association, 1993). Individuals from all racial-ethnic backgrounds and all levels of ability and socioeconomic status take vocational education courses (NAVE, 1994). In addition, millions of adults enroll in vocational programs to acquire basic skills for employment or to retrain for new jobs and keep up with the changing technological requirements of the workplace (American Vocational Association, 1993).

Traditionally, vocational education has been viewed solely as a program for preparing individuals for work, but many educators and policy makers believe it has a broader mission: to provide a concrete, relevant context for learning and applying academic skill concepts, to prepare people for participation in the family and community, and to prepare for college and other types of postsecondary learning (NCES, 1992).

The Carl D. Perkins Vocational and Applied Technology Education Act of 1990 defined vocational education as "organized educational programs offering a sequence of courses which are directly related to the preparation of individuals in paid or unpaid employment in current or emerging occupations requiring other than a baccalaureate or advanced degree. Such programs shall include competency-based applied learning which contributes to an individual's academic knowledge, higher-order reasoning, and problem-solving skills, work attitudes, general employability skills, and the occupational-specific skills necessary for economic independence as a productive and contributing member of society." This definition encompasses a wide variety of classes teaching academic skills, work habits and attitudes, general employability skills, and occupationally specific skills (American Vocational Association, 1990).

VOCATIONAL PROGRAM SETTINGS

Most secondary vocational education occurs in vocational programs in comprehensive high schools which offer academic, personal use, and vocational classes. Programs of secondary vocational education may be found in a variety of settings at the local school level in general high schools, vocational high schools, and secondary area-vocational centers or area vocational schools.

Area vocational schools and centers provide vocational instruction typically for half a day to students who are bussed in from comprehensive high schools or general high schools. Area vocational schools are more likely to be located in suburban than in urban and rural areas. A small number of students are served in all-day vocational schools which are usually located in urban areas. These vocational high schools deliver essential academic courses as well as vocational courses. Vocational education for adults is also carried on during evening hours in some of these secondary vocational schools (Adams, 1993).

Postsecondary vocational education programs are conducted in community colleges, private proprietary schools, area vocational schools also serving postsecondary students, technical institutes, specialized postsecondary schools, adult education centers, skill centers, correctional institutions and four-year colleges and universities. Most postsecondary vocational (occupational/technical) education is provided by community colleges, with the second largest provider being private proprietary schools followed by technical institutes and area vocational schools serving postsecondary students. A dwindling number of four-year colleges continue to offer vocational education programs (Adams, 1993; NAVE, 1994).

Vocational education programs are also found in middle schools and junior high schools in the form of prevocational education designed to orient students to the world of work, to make them aware of career and occupational options, and to give them opportunities to try out a variety of jobs in several fields and at several levels. There are prevocational programs in all seven of the vocational service areas including technology education. These programs assist students in selecting secondary and postsecondary vocational programs, provide opportunities for students to apply academic skills to concrete occupational situations, and motivate students to exert more effort and to stay in school.

SECONDARY VOCATIONAL EDUCATION PROGRAMS AND CURRICULUM

The National Center for Educational Statistics (1992) divided the secondary school curriculum into the three parts of academic, personal use, and vocational. The vocational curriculum was divided into the three curricular areas of: (1) consumer and homemaking education, (2) general labor market preparation, and (3) specific labor market preparation. Consumer and homemaking courses provide training and skills that are necessary for individuals to function in the family and community outside of the paid labor force and include such subjects as child development, clothing, basic food preparation, and home management. The general labor market preparation area consists of classes such as beginning typing/keyboarding, technology education, work experience, career exploration, business math, and business English, all of which are designed to impart knowledge and skills that can be applied in a variety of personal and occupational settings. The general labor market preparation area was earlier called "practical arts" or programs that prepare one for the practical aspects of life but not directly for employment. The specific labor market preparation area consists of introductory, advanced, and elective courses in the seven vocational areas of agriculture, business, family and consumer sciences, marketing, health, trade and industry, and technical and communications. There are also several emerging vocational fields including public services, technology education, and special needs as well as special programs such as cooperative vocational education and apprenticeship (NCES, 1992).

The vocational curriculum at the secondary level consists of regular academic classes and sequenced, introductory, advanced, and elective classes in occupational areas. Vocational programs, such as those in trade and industrial education, may be arranged in cluster programs or occupational specific programs. An example of a cluster program is the construction trades which consists of carpentry, electrical wiring, plumbing, and masonry but could also include specialty areas such as cabinetmaking, concrete form construction, and the like. Cluster programs provide students with a wider opportunity to explore different occupations and an opportunity to see how these areas are interdependent in business and industry.

Secondary Vocational Education Instruction

A wide variety of instructional delivery systems are used in secondary vocational programs. In general, vocational instruction consists of classroom teaching, laboratory applications, supervised work experience, and vocational student organization activities. Vocational classes are typically offered in one-hour, two-hour, and three-hour blocks of time. The basic component of instruction is the classroom where students learn concepts and theories dealing with a wide spectrum of vocational education topics from basic career awareness to highly technical, job specific content. The lessons learned in the classroom form the basis for other types of instructional experiences. Classroom work is followed by supervised laboratory instruction where the concepts and theories are applied in typical job applications. Laboratory instruction is characterized by problem-solving and "hands on" experiences that ensure that skills learned are practical and usable in future work tasks.

Vocational teachers use real-life situations to reinforce classroom and laboratory learning to develop realistic on-the-job skills. These real-life experiences may be live-work tasks that occur in the laboratory or take the form of supervised work experience in internships, practicums, cooperative education, and apprenticeships in an actual worksite. Real-life experiences are not just work experience but are experiential, requiring students to reflect on what happened during their experience by evaluating it, writing or orally presenting what they learned, what worked and did not work, what knowledge or skills they applied, what they need to do to become a better future employee, and what they liked and did not like about the experience (Leske, 1994). Finally, vocational teachers use vocational student organization activities as an integral, intracurricular component of their vocational programs to teach leadership and occupational skills. The structured activities and incentives provided by the awards programs of vocational student organizations leads to improved student performance and future leaders.

COMPETENCIES REQUIRED FOR WORK

Many vocational and applied technology education programs at the secondary and postsecondary levels have revised curriculum and instructional programs to include the competencies identified in the American Society for Training and Development (ASTD) report *Workplace Basics: The Skills Employers want* (1988) and the Secretary's Commission on Achieving Necessary Skills (SCANS) Report *Learning a Living: A Blueprint for High Performance* (1992). Both of these reports identify basic foundational skills needed to learn the specific skills required for the high-performance workplace. Technical changes on most jobs have drastically changed the basic skill requirements and are increasing the range of skills needed to work in an increasing technological work environment. High performance workers must have a solid foundation in the basic literacy and computational skills, in the thinking skills required to apply knowledge at the worksite, and the personal qualities that enable workers to function in an increasingly team oriented environment and to become dedicated and trustworthy workers.

The seven skill groups comprising the workplace basics identified in the ASTD report are:

1. Foundation–Learning to Learn
2. Competence–Reading, Writing, and Computation
3. Communication–Listening and Oral Communication
4. Adaptability–Creative Thinking and Problem-solving
5. Personal Management–Self Esteem, Goal Setting/Motivation, and Personal/Career Development
6. Group Effectiveness–Interpersonal Skills, Negotiation, and Teamwork
7. Influence–Organizational Effectiveness and Leadership

The workplace know-how of the SCANS report is made up of a three-part foundation of skills and personal qualities and five competency areas that comprise the skills needed for effective job performance. These foundational skills and workplace competencies are as follows:

Foundations Skills

- Basic Skills–reading, writing, arithmetic, and mathematics, speaking, and listening
- Thinking Skills–the ability to learn, to reason, to think creatively, to make decisions, and to solve problems
- Personal Qualities–individual responsibility, self-esteem and self-management, sociability, and integrity.

Workplace Competencies

- Resources–know how to allocate time, money, materials, space, and staff
- Interpersonal Skills–work on teams, teach others, serve customers, lead, negotiate, and work well with people from culturally diverse backgrounds
- Information–acquire and evaluate data, organize and maintain files, interpret and communicate, and use computers to process information
- Systems–understand social, organizational, and technological systems; monitor and correct performance; and design and improve systems
- Technology–select equipment and tools, apply technology to specific tasks, and maintain and troubleshoot equipment.

Tech-Prep Programs

Tech-prep programs were established by the Carl D. Perkins Vocational and Applied Technology Act of 1990 (PL 101-392) as a national program designed to offer strong comprehensive links between secondary schools and postsecondary institutions to prepare students for high-skill technical jobs in business and industry. Tech-prep is defined as a sequence of study beginning in high school and continuing through at least two years of postsecondary occupational education designed to prepare students for high-skill technical occupations" (National Tech Prep Network, 1992).

Tech-prep programs span the last two years in high school and the first two years of postsecondary education, leading to an associate's degree or certificate. The curriculum for tech-prep programs is jointly planned between secondary and postsecondary institutions resulting in an articulation agreement which spells out a sequence of academic and vocational/technical courses to be taken while in high school and a sequence of courses to be taken at the postsecondary institution. These programs are intended to build student competence in mathematics, communications, science, technology, and occupational skills through integration of academic and vocational education (NCES, 1992).

Apprenticeship Programs

The apprenticeship method of instruction–structured learning on-the-job under the tutelage of a journeyperson–is the oldest method of formal instruction and is still used to prepare workers in the building trades, machine trades, and a variety of other trade areas. Only a small portion of American workers are prepared through formal apprenticeship programs, and until recently, apprenticeship was not viewed as a viable training for teenage youth since the average age of beginning apprentices is twenty-five. Beginning in the late 1970s, the U.S. Department of Labor funded eight demonstration youth apprenticeship programs which established apprenticeship as a workable training option for young people in certain occupational areas. According to the U.S. General Accounting Office (1991), there are approximately 400 school-to-apprenticeship programs serving over 3,500 students with nearly half of these youth apprenticeship programs in machine trade occupations.

Youth apprenticeship or school-to-apprenticeship programs are based on an employer-school partnership that integrates academic instruction, structured vocational training, and paid workplace experience. In the school-based component of apprenticeship, apprentices receive classroom instruction in academic and vocational subjects leading to a high school diploma and a certificate of competency. At the job-site, apprentices receive on-the-job training including technical knowledge and skill, work attitudes and work habits, employability skills, writing and speaking skills, and reasoning and problem-solving skills. The expected program outcome is for youth apprentices to continue their vocational education in a postsecondary institution or continue in apprenticeship leading to journeyperson status and permanent employment.

Cooperative Education Programs

Cooperative education (co-op) is the oldest and most commonly available option for work-based learning in the United States. The cooperative education program was initiated by Herman Schneider, a University of Cincinnati professor of engineering, in the 1930's and quickly found its way into secondary schools. There was a need then, as there is now, to provide programs that will help students earn money in jobs that enrich their educational experience, increase work-related competence, and improve their general employability rather than have students engaged in part-time jobs that do not relate to their school experience or prepare them to enter full-time employment in a meaningful way.

Cooperative education received categorical federal support through the Vocational Education Amendments of 1968 (PL 90-576) which expanded the number of cooperative education programs nationwide.

Cooperative education is defined in the Carl D. Perkins Vocational and Applied Technology Act of 1990 (PL 101-392) as "a method of instruction of vocational education for individuals who, through written cooperative agreements between the school and employers, receive instruction, including required academic courses and related vocational instruction by alternation of study in school with a job in any occupational field. Such alternation shall be planned and supervised by the school and employers so that each contributes to the student's education and to his or her employability. Work periods and school attendance may be on alternate half days, full days, weeks, or other periods of time in fulfilling the cooperative program."

A U.S. General Accounting Office (GAO) report (1990) indicated that over 430,000 high school students were enrolled in co-op programs which is estimated to be about 8% of junior and seniors which are the grade levels students are most likely to be involved in co-op education. Today, less than 4% of high school students, as a whole, are enrolled in co-op education programs and less than 3% of community college students are enrolled in available co-op programs in their institutions. The 1990 GAO report called for expanding cooperative education as a viable school-to-work transition program.

Cooperative education is a planned program which combines classroom study with arranged periods of paid, career related work. Cooperative education is part of the school curriculum, and students receive grades and earn credit toward graduation for their co-op work experience as well as their related classroom instruction. A cooperative education coordinator, usually with a vocational background, provides classroom instruction in generally related information about work and assists students to obtain specific information related to the jobs they are performing at the work site. A training plan is prepared cooperatively by the co-op coordinator and work station supervisor (mentor) identifying the competencies needed on the job and the general and specific information that is to be provided for a co-op student. Co-op students usually attend school in the morning and go to the training station (work site) in the afternoon. Students generally are required to work a minimum of 15 hours per week and are periodically visited by the co-op coordinator to ensure that the training plan is being followed so that students are receiving instruction in the many aspects of an occupation.

Internships and Practicums

Internship and practicum programs are offered in some vocational schools to provide students with opportunities to polish their skills developed in the laboratory and to develop additional technical competencies in a chosen work setting. Internships and practicums generally allow students to observe and participate in daily work routines, and to experience direct contact with job personnel where they can ask questions about a particular career and perform appropriate tasks to see how they like a certain type of work and to further develop their employability skills. A school worksite coordinator or a vocational teacher periodically visits and observes students at work and discusses the internship or practicum experience with the worksite mentor and intern to ensure a quality internship or practicum experience is being provided. The major focus of internships and practicums is to experience firsthand all aspects of an occupation and not to develop mastery-level job skills.

Internships and practicums are designed as a type of "capstone experience" which usually occurs near the end of an instructional program that provides an opportunity for students to practice what they have learned in school through direct application under the close supervision of a workplace mentor and the school's internship or practicum coordinator. Internships and practicums are usually of short duration and participants are generally not paid for their work productivity other than through receiving a quality work-related experience.

SELF ASSESSMENT

1. What is vocational and applied technology education?
2. Where are vocational and applied technology education programs found?
3. How is the vocational education curriculum determined?
4. What are the purposes of vocational and applied technology education at the secondary and postsecondary levels?
5. How are secondary and postsecondary vocational and applied technology programs alike and different?
6. How is instruction delivered in secondary vocational and applied technology education programs?
7. What is a tech prep program?
8. What is an apprenticeship program?
9. What is a cooperative education program?
10. What are internships and practicums?

ASSOCIATED ACTIVITIES

1. Contact the State Department of Education and obtain a copy of the State Plan for Vocational and Applied Technology and other materials describing vocational education programs such as Tech Prep, apprenticeship, and programs for special populations.

2. Visit work-based education training sites such as cooperative education, apprenticeship, internships, and practicums to observe firsthand on-the-job instruction.

3. Contact the State Occupational Information Coordinating Council in your state and obtain copies of the computerized State Training Inventory which lists where occupational programs are offered in your state.

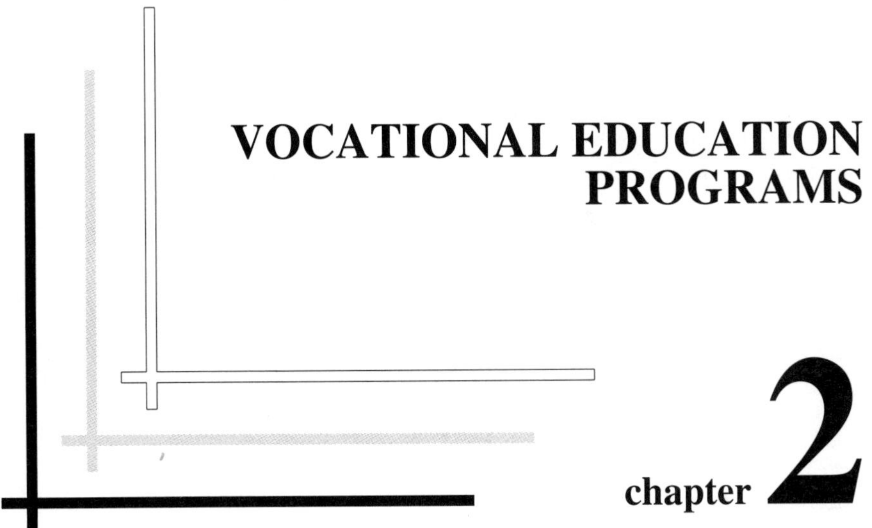

VOCATIONAL EDUCATION PROGRAMS

chapter 2

INTRODUCTION

Vocational and applied technology education is delivered through a variety of specific labor market programs at the secondary and postsecondary levels including agriculture, business, family and consumer science, marketing, health, trade and industry, and technical/communications. Each of the vocational and applied technology education programs provide a wide variety of specific program areas and courses for those who plan to enter a specific labor market field. Vocational and applied technology educators are prepared through vocational teacher education programs in selected public and private four-year colleges and universities. Vocational and applied technology educators are professionals who belong to the American Vocational Association which has as its mission to provide educational leadership in developing a competitive American workforce.

OBJECTIVES

After completing this chapter the reader should be able to:

1. Describe the major program areas of vocational and applied technology education–agricultural, business, family and consumer sciences, health occupations, marketing, technology, technical, and trade and industrial education.

2. Discuss the role of vocational special needs personnel in vocational and applied technology education.

3. Describe some special programs in your state which provide support services for vocational students from special populations.

4. Describe postsecondary vocational-technical programs and curriculum.

5. Describe the instructional delivery system for a typical postsecondary vocational-technical area.

6. Describe the preparation of vocational and applied technology education teachers.

VOCATIONAL EDUCATION PROGRAMS

Agricultural Education

"Agriculture is the broad industry engaged in the production of plants and animals for food and fiber, the provision of agricultural supplies and services, and the processing, marketing, and distribution of agricultural products. Agricultural education generally refers to the curriculum or program in agricultural education designed to offer students at the secondary level the opportunity to explore and prepare for agricultural occupations. Also, postsecondary and adult programs are recognized as legal components of agricultural education" (Herren & Donahue, 1991).

Agricultural education is an integral part of a comprehensive educational program designed to provide students with the knowledge, skills, and attitudes to make them aware of and to be prepared for the world of work in agriculture. Sometimes agricultural education is defined as "providing instruction in and about agriculture." Agricultural education serves three major purposes in American education. First, it provides knowledge and skills required to enter and advance in agricultural careers. Second, it gives students a broad understanding of the important role agriculture plays in our world and provides them with essential knowledge that is needed to function as informed citizens in today's society. This second purpose is called agricultural literacy (Lee, 1994). Third, it provides opportunities through Future Farmers of America (FFA), the secondary vocational student organization of agricultural education, for leadership and personal development. Postsecondary agricultural students also have a nationally recognized vocational student organization, the National Postsecondary Agricultural Students (PAS) that provides similar activities as those offered through FFA. In addition, the National Young Farmers Educational Association (NYFEA) provides opportunities for young adult farmers to develop leadership skills and enhance their knowledge and skills in agriculture after they have left formal educational programs. Many former agricultural education graduates are now in leadership positions in government agencies, education, business, and industry as a result of the leadership training they received in vocational student organizations and the agricultural education program.

Agricultural education has consistently changed its instructional programs to meet the needs of a dynamic, rapidly changing industry of agriculture. Agriculture is becoming highly scientific and technical in such new frontiers as biotechnology which deals with genetic engineering and tissue culture. Agricultural education is responding with new programs like agriscience which consist of a series of laboratory courses which emphasize the basic biological and physical science principles and practices associated with agriculture (Georgia Department of Education, 1994).

Agricultural programs are increasingly being planned to prepare students for a wide range of career options when they complete the instructional sequence of courses. Like other areas of vocational and applied technology education, more attention is being given to integrating academic subjects such as communications, mathematics, and science and to the applications of technology. Agricultural education is being offered in grades 7 through 14 in over 7,600 high schools and 570 postsecondary institutions in the U.S. Many students begin career awareness and exploration programs in agriculture in the middle and junior high school years and continue this area of interest in the high school agriculture program. Some students continue their education for two or more years by enrolling in community colleges and four-year colleges or universities where they earn associate's degrees or baccalaureate degrees in agriculture or related areas (Lee, 1994).

The instructional program in agricultural education utilizes three major components: classroom and laboratory instruction, supervised experience, and FFA and PAS–the vocational student organizations. Classroom and laboratory instruction involves teaching students the underlying concepts and principles of agriculture, and providing them with opportunities to apply what they have learned in a "hands-on" environment. Supervised agricultural experiences (SAE) involve structured learning activities which build on what has been learned through classroom and laboratory instruction but are carried out outside the regular class time, providing an opportunity for students to interact with a number of adults and to develop on-the-job skills. The SAE may vary from traditional on-the-farm home projects to entrepreneurship, cooperative work experience in production agriculture or agribusiness, or to projects conducted in land laboratories provided on or near the school's campuses. The FFA is the vocational student organization specifically for agricultural education students which operates as an integral part of the total instructional program. Students are provided with an opportunity to develop personal and leadership skills as well as to practice good citizenship and cooperation. In addition, FFA provides opportunities for students to become involved in a variety of competitive events and professional development activities to expand their learning and to receive recognition for their accomplishments (Lee, 1994).

Agricultural education encompasses a wide variety of programs and courses offered in middle/junior high schools, high schools, and postsecondary institutions. These programs and courses range from traditional production agriculture to agriscience and technology to the emerging field of agricultural biotechnology which involves working with genetically modified plants, feed supplements for animals, and innovative pharmaceuticals. Most states have developed curriculum guides which provide the basic curriculum framework for instructional programs at the local institution level. Basic agriculture programs/courses typically include: (a) agricultural plants and animals, (b) agricultural mechanics, (c) agricultural sales and service, (d) forestry, (e) ornamental horticulture, (f) agricultural products and processing, (g) natural resources, (h) specialty animals, (i) agribusiness, (j) agriscience, and other agricultural specialty areas. See Figure 2-1.

SAMPLE LISTING OF AGRICULTURAL EDUCATION PROGRAM COURSE/TOPICS

- Agricultural Plants and Animals
- Agricultural Mechanics
- Agricultural Sales and Service
- Forestry
- Ornamental Horticulture
- Agricultural Products and Processing
- Natural Resources
- Specialty Animals
- Agribusiness
- Agriscience
- Agricultural Biotechnology
- Entrepreneurship
- Leadership Development
- Employability Skills
- Environmental Management
- Exploring Careers In Agriculture
- Conserving Natural Resources
- Agricultural Economics
- Forest Technology
- Animal and Dairy Science
- Agronomy
- Agricultural Communications
- Agricultural Engineering
- Agricultural Technology Management
- Animal Science
- Botany
- Crop Science
- Poultry Science
- Dairy Science
- Entomology
- Food Science
- Landscape and Ground Management
- Agricultural Ethics
- Plant Pathology
- Environmental Literacy
- Agricultural Diesel Mechanics
- Veterinary Technology

Figure 2-1. A sample listing of program and course topics that are included in agricultural education.

Business Education

Business education is the instructional program that provides education about business and education for those who plan to enter business occupations. It is a program that serves the total school population through a relevant curriculum that provides career direction, a sound foundation for advanced study, and the development of employability and job skills required for productive employment in business occupations. In addition to preparing individuals for employment, business education provides students with the knowledge and understandings needed to conduct personal business affairs and to effectively use the services of the business world as a consumer.

Business education is the most popular occupational program in secondary schools, with over one-half of all students who have taken one or more occupational education courses enrolled in business education. Business education, taught as a general labor market preparation program, provides instruction to help students develop basic literacy in business, economics, and computers. Business education taught as a specific labor market preparation program is the instructional program that prepares qualified individuals for America's businesses. This educational program prepares people for the largest segment of the job market (business occupations) with qualified employees (NAVE, 1994).

Business education, like other occupational programs, has had to continuously change curriculum and instructional practices to keep pace with changes in business, equipment, organization, policy, and market demands. Instruction focuses on skill development with word processors, computers, high-speed copiers, laser printers, and fax machines. Business principles and concepts have also changed focus from secretarial office procedures to management systems and entrepreneurship, from a focus on the local economic community to an international one, and from computer applications to information systems (Phillips, 1994).

Computers, fax machines, electronic mail, and other advances in technology have significantly transformed the manner in which business education is delivered. Business education instructional programs have made dramatic philosophical shifts in educational practice from single learning to multiple learning, rigidity to flexibility, isolated content to interrelated content, memorized responses to problem awareness and problem- solving, national dimensions to international proportions, one career to multiple career preparations, and job-specific skills to broad-based transferable skills. As technology continues to impact this field, new and innovative educational approaches must be established to provide business education students with the enhanced skills and knowledge they will need to participate in the international marketplace (Georgia Department of Education, 1992).

Business education courses, such as keyboarding, are offered in some elementary schools and in many middle/junior high schools as exploratory, prevocational courses to provide students with a broad understanding of business education and career options. At the secondary school level, business education courses can serve two purposes: one as general labor market preparation and preparation for executing personal business transactions, and the other as specific labor market preparation or vocational education. Business education courses for specific labor market preparation are also offered at the postsecondary level in community colleges, technical institutes, and four-year colleges and universities at less than baccalaureate degree programs. Business education programs offer a wide variety of courses or classes including: keyboarding, word processing, spreadsheets, database management, business graphics, and electronic publishing. See Figure 2-2.

SAMPLE LISTING OF BUSINESS EDUCATION PROGRAM/COURSE TOPICS

- Business Communications
- Office Management
- Office Procedures and Technology
- Systems Analysis and Design
- Accounting
- Business Law
- Economics
- Computer Technology
- Speedwriting
- International Business Management
- Banking and Finance
- Keyboarding
- Spreadsheets
- Data Base Management
- Desktop Publishing
- Computer Graphics
- Consumer Economics
- Technology, Life, and Careers
- Exploratory Business
- Leadership Development
- Personal Skill Development
- Cooperative Business Education
- Local Area Networks (LANS)
- Telecommunications/Teleconferencing
- Multi-media Presentations (HyperCard, etc.)
- Information Systems
- Networking
- Voice-Reproduction Systems/Voice-Activated Equipment
- Electronic Mail
- Computer Programming
- Entrepreneurship
- Executive Secretarial
- Business Data Entry/Peripheral Equipment
- Legal Secretarial
- Information and Office Technology

Figure 2-2. A sample listing of program and course topics included in business education.

The business education instructional program consists of sequenced courses ranging from introductory to advanced which are nearly always conducted in a laboratory environment since the use of office equipment is an integral part of most instructional topics. Business education teachers, using modern visual-presentation technology, can deliver instruction to an entire class of students and observe individual student performance on applied academic or business education assignments without moving away from the command center. Introductory courses acquaint students with technological concepts and principles; application courses and experiences facilitate the students' abilities to apply these concepts; and advanced courses emphasize transferability of knowledge and higher order skills such as problem solving and decision making. Business education students are provided with opportunities to engage in participatory activities in school-based enterprises and in real-life situation in the business community through long-term projects, job shadowing, internships, cooperative business education, internships, and youth apprenticeships. Like other vocational program areas, business education students enhance their business skills and leadership skills by participating in Future Business Leaders of America (FBLA) or Business Professional of America (BPA), which are the vocational student organizations for secondary business education students. Postsecondary business education students can participate in Phi Beta Lambda (PBL), the postsecondary vocational student organization (Policy Statements, 1993).

Business education is responding to the demand to assist in preparing a high-skilled workforce so our nation can be competitive in the global marketplace. Business educators at the secondary and postsecondary levels are establishing tech-prep programs consisting of carefully sequenced courses in the last two years of high school and the first two years of postsecondary education. Tech-prep programs are designed to prepare students for highly skilled technical occupations that allow either direct entry into the workplace or continuation in postsecondary education programs leading to certificates or associate degrees.

Business educators are also establishing youth apprenticeship programs that link education with business through a partnership of school-based learning and work-based learning. In youth apprenticeships, students have an opportunity to apply core-subject knowledge, develop workplace readiness skills, and experience significant relationships with skilled adults called mentors (Cassidy, 1994).

Family and Consumer Sciences Education

Family and consumer sciences education is a new name and focus for home economics education which is also called consumer and homemaking education and vocational home economics education. The new, conceptual framework for home economics education was developed and accepted by those participating in the Scottsdale, Arizona Conference of October 23, 1993. This conference was sponsored by the major organizations representing home economics education and was composed of 100 participants selected by these sponsoring organizations. The tripartite mission of family and consumer sciences is: empowering individuals, strengthening families, and enabling communities (American Home Economics Association, 1993). The overriding mission of family and consumer sciences education is to prepare students for family life, work life, and careers in family and consumer sciences by providing opportunities to develop the knowledge, skills, attitudes, and behaviors needed for:

- Strengthening the well-being of individual and families across the life span.
- Becoming responsible citizens and leaders in family, community, and work settings.
- Promoting optimal nutrition and wellness across the life span.
- Managing resources to meet the needs of individuals and families.
- Balancing personal, home, family, and work lives.
- Using critical and creative thinking skills to address problems in diverse family, community, and work environments.
- Facilitating successful life management, employment, and career development.
- Functioning effectively as providers and consumers of goods and services.
- Appreciating human worth and accepting responsibility for one's actions and success in family and worklife (Stewart, 1994).

The unifying focus of family and consumer sciences is an integrative approach to the relationships among individuals, families, and communities and the environments in which they function. Family and consumer science professionals believe in:

1. Families as the fundamental societal unit.
2. Life-span approach to individual and family development.
3. Meeting individual and family needs within and outside the home.
4. Diversity that strengthens individual, family, and community well-being.
5. The right to educational opportunities for all individuals to enhance their intellectual development and maximize potential.
6. Strong subject matter specializations with a commitment to integration.

7. The use of diverse modes of inquiry.
8. Education as a lifelong process (American Home Economics Association, 1993).

Family and consumer sciences education is a term that serves as an umbrella for the profession as a whole, and more accurately reflects what the profession is about. It includes consumer and homemaking education which prepares students for the occupation of homemaker which requires knowledge, attitudes, and skills that are interrelated and necessary to improve the quality of life for individuals and families. It also includes home economics occupations for paid employment which utilizes similar concepts and applications that are basic to consumer and homemaking education but differ in the instructional setting, the instructional objectives, the level of competency, degree of responsibility required, and the scope of the operation. For example, the basic principles of human development apply in child care and elder care services which are occupations the same as they do in caring for the family which is a basic role of the homemaker (Home Economics Education Association, 1991).

Most secondary students enroll in one or more vocational courses before they graduate with nearly half of those in vocational courses enrolled in consumer and homemaking courses. In 1987, 10.6% of high school graduates who completed one or more courses in specific labor market preparation programs were enrolled in occupational home economics (NCES, 1990).

Family and consumer sciences education curriculum is drawn from various disciplines including the social sciences, physical sciences, biological sciences, economics, psychology, philosophy, and the arts. Subject matter is identified from these disciplines to form an integrated curriculum that prepares students for the practical problems of the home family and workplace. Analysis techniques are used to identify the roles, duties, and tasks of homemakers and occupations in family and consumer sciences which provide content topics for the curriculum. Most states now use technical committees to provide input into the development of curriculum guides which provide the basic curriculum framework for instructional programs at the local educational agency level (American Home Economics Association, 1989).

Family and consumer sciences education programs are found in middle/junior high schools, high schools, and postsecondary institutions. At the middle/junior high schools, family and consumer sciences education programs are usually exploratory in nature are designed to prepare students for the occupation of homemaker and to introduce students to the knowledge, attitudes, and skills that will enable them to balance the roles and responsibilities within the home, family, and workplace. Frequently, students explore home economics careers as a part of this program. This may range from the use of individualized chapters and computer programs to group activities providing information and hands-on activities related to specific careers. For example, one state encourages the use of certain career chapters integrated with specific content studied at three levels. At the sixth-grade level, the curriculum usually focuses on self-esteem, self-concept, physical development, social development, interpersonal relationships outside the family, roles and responsibilities as a family member, freedom and responsibility, values clarification, decision making, personal budgeting, communication skills, and leadership development. At the seventh-grade level, the curriculum focuses on the importance of eating a variety of foods, the economic aspect of foods, child safety, babysitting, and consumer home economic careers. At the eighth-grade level, the curriculum focuses on textile and the selection and care of clothing, the use of the sewing machine, mending, management of time, personal energy and money, care and organization of clothing and personal living space, conservation of natural resources, and good consumer practices (Georgia Department of Education, 1993).

Family and consumer sciences education at the high school level (grades 9-12) includes the traditional programs of consumer and homemaking education and occupational home economics with emphasis placed on consumer and homemaking education at grades 9-10 as the basis for specific labor market preparation in occupational home economics in grades 11-12 for those who choose this program. In consumer and homemaking education, values, management, and interpersonal relationships are major curriculum organizers that unify the content of subject matter areas such as: individual, child, and family development; parenting; interpersonal and communication skills; families in today's society; clothing and textiles; consumer education and resource management; food and nutrition; nutrition, health and wellness; housing and management; balancing work and family; employability skills; leadership; entrepreneurship, consumerism; and career exploration. Occupational home economics courses may include child development, child care, elder care, food service, fashion merchandising, culinary arts, and industrial sewing (Home Economics Education Association, 1991). See Figure 2-3.

The instructional programs of family and consumer sciences education consist of classroom and laboratory instruction, supervised experiences in the home or in a real-life situations through cooperative education and other work-based programs, and learning experiences provided by Future Homemakers of America (FHA) and its two chapters, FHA and Home Economics Related Occupations (HERO). FHA is the recognized vocational student organization serving family and consumer sciences education. Classroom instruction includes integration of academic skills with the concepts and principles which form the basis for subjects in family and consumer sciences. Laboratory instruction provides students with opportunities to apply learned concepts and principles in the classroom through problem-solving and hands-on applications related to homemaking and occupational home economic tasks. Supervised experiences are provided through projects which can be completed at home or in real-life situations in the community through cooperative education, internships, or mentoring programs. FHA/HERO activities provide students with opportunities to develop leadership skills and to engage in competitive events and professional development activities which are an integral part of the regular instructional program.

SAMPLE LISTING OF FAMILY AND CONSUMER PROGRAM/COURSE TOPICS

- Housing and Living Environment
- Consumer and Resource Management
- Individual, Child, and Family Development
- Nutrition and Food
- Textiles and Clothing
- Personal Development
- Interpersonal and Communication Skills
- Families in Today's Society
- Parenting
- Nutrition, Health, and Wellness
- Consumer/Resources Management
- Decision Making
- Child Safety/Babysitting
- Identity/Self-esteem and Self-concept
- Career Exploration/Career Development
- Values Clarification
- Consumerism
- Child Care
- Elder Care
- Leadership Development
- Chef/Cook
- Child Development
- Dietetic Assisting
- Clothing/Textiles Management, Production, and Service
- Family/Individual Health
- Family Living and Parenthood
- Food Management, Production, and Service
- Home Management
- Hospitality (Travel and Travel Service)
- Housing, Home Furnishing, and Equipment
- Hotel/Motel Management
- Institutional Management
- Interior Decorating/Design
- Waiter/Waitress
- Culinary Arts
- Employability Skills
- Balancing Work and Family
- Entrepreneurship
- Careers in Family and Consumer Sciences
- Cultural Diversity
- Personal Relationships
- Prenatal/Postnatal Care
- Family Relationships
- Personal/Family Budgeting
- Food Science, Safety, and Nutrition
- Food Biotechnologies
- Food Microbiology
- Toxicology

Figure 2-3. A sample listing of program and course topics included in family and consumer sciences education.

Strong programs of family and consumer sciences education are needed to prepare people for paid employment in critical areas such as child care and elder care, but are needed now more than ever before to stabilize and strengthen the home and to address some of our nation's most pressing social concerns such as malnutrition, child and spouse abuse, break-down of the family, consumer fraud, teenage pregnancy, energy waste, and environmental pollution. The increasing complexity and changing nature of family roles and tasks require that organized opportunities for learning these skills be expanded and enhanced for both male and female students (Home Economics Education Association, 1991).

Health Occupations Education

The health occupations program is designed to acquaint individuals with the career options in the health services industry and to provide the knowledge, skills, and attitudes necessary to succeed in the wide field of health occupations. Health occupations consists of a wide range of job opportunities including registered nurses, licensed practical nurses, nursing aids, physicians, physical therapists, medical technicians, clinical technicians, radiological technicians, clinical laboratory technicians, medical records technicians, emergency medical technicians, medical secretaries, receptionist, dental assistants, dental hygienists, and respiratory therapists. Employment in the health services industry will continue to grow almost twice as fast as total nonfarm wage and salary employment. Demand for health care professionals is spurred by an aging population, new medical technologies that allow treatment of previously untreatable illnesses, and the growth of outpatient and home care. Among the fastest growth areas is home health care services and services provided in offices of physicians (U.S. Department of Labor, 1993).

The health care services include occupations in medicine and health care of humans or animals in the fields of medicine, surgery, and dentistry; and in related-patient care areas such as nursing, therapy, dietetics, prosthetics, rehabilitation, diagnostic imaging, and pharmacy. Included in this industry are occupations in sanitation, environmental and public health, and in laboratories and other health care facilities. Most workers in the health occupations care for, treat, or train people to improve their physical and emotional well-being. They are employed in a wide variety of settings including home health care agencies, hospitals, nursing homes, offices of physicians, rehabilitation centers, health care centers, schools, industrial plants, social agencies, sports clinics, and private homes. Many of the health care jobs require specialized postsecondary education and training. In addition, many of the jobs in the health care occupations require licensing or registration to practice or use a specific title (U.S. Department of Labor, 1991).

Health occupations programs are found at the middle/junior high school, high school, and postsecondary levels. At the middle/junior high school level, students are provided with a broad overview of the health care industry and are given opportunities to explore a number of health care careers. Secondary health occupations programs provide students with opportunities to explore health occupation careers, to gain an understanding of the basic concepts and principles of health care, and to apply these concepts and principles in the health occupation laboratory in simulated life situations. Advanced secondary health occupation students may also gain real job experience in a health care setting through an internship (practicum) or cooperative education option. Most health occupations programs in secondary schools are designed to prepare people to be nurse's aides/assistants and patient care workers.

Postsecondary health occupation students are usually enrolled in special health care programs such as practical nursing, medical assisting, ophthalmic dispensing, respiratory therapy, physical therapy, dental assisting, dental hygiene, dental laboratory technician, surgical technology, radiological technology, emergency medical care, and patient care assistant. These programs range from less than one year for some certificates to two-year associate degree programs. Postsecondary health occupations programs require admissions tests and other entrance requirements. Registered nursing programs range from two to four years in length and bachelor degree programs are available to prepare people for leadership positions in the health care industry.

The health occupations instructional program at the secondary level consists of classroom instruction delivered in sequenced courses covering technical content related to a wide variety of health care topics, followed by laboratory work which provides students with opportunities to apply what they have learned in the classroom. See Figure 2-4.

Secondary students may have the opportunity to further develop their knowledge and skills in a practicum or real-life health care setting under the supervision of a clinical instructor. Health occupation students can develop leadership skills and enhance their personal skills through participation in the Vocational Industrial Clubs of America (VICA) or the Health Occupations Students of America (HOSA), two vocational student organizations (VSOs) serving secondary and postsecondary students. These VSOs offer a number of activities for leadership development, professional development, and skill development through individual and group competitive events.

Health programs are very popular at the postsecondary level with over 22% of all vocational students enrolled in this growing program (NAVE, 1994). Health occupations instructional programs at the postsecondary level consist of a number of sequenced academic and technical courses in a specialized health care field designed to provide a variety of techniques and materials necessary to assist students in acquiring the essential knowledge and skills required to give competent care. Examples of academic core courses include English, mathematics, and basic psychology. Fundamental occupational courses may include medical terminology, anatomy and physiology, and nursing fundamentals. Specific occupational courses may include medical surgical nursing I and medical surgical nursing II practicum. Classroom instruction is followed with laboratory practice and a variety of clinical experiences or practicums in health care settings that are organized so that theory and practice are integrated under the guidance of the clinical instructor.

SAMPLE LISTINGS OF HEALTH OCCUPATIONS PROGRAM/COURSE TOPICS

- Emergency Medical Care
- Medical Assisting
- Medical Laboratory Technology
- Medicine and Premedicine
- Respiratory Therapy
- Home Health Aids
- Licensed Practical Nursing
- Nurse Practioner
- Nursing Assists
- Registered Nurses
- Personal Services
- Nursing Science
- Pharmacology
- Basic Nutrition
- Human Anatomy and Physiology
- Human Development
- General Psychology
- Chemistry
- Dental Assisting
- Dental Hygiene
- Dental Laboratory Technology
- Physical Therapy Assisting
- Recreational Therapy
- Surgical Technology
- Medical Research Aids
- Microbiology
- Radiological Technology
- Physician Assistant
- Clinical Practice
- Biomedical Equipment Technology
- Health Care Assisting
- Medical Secretary
- Occupational Therapy Assisting
- Medical Records Technology
- Optometric Technology
- Nurse Anesthetist
- Nurse-Midwife
- Magnetic Resonance Imaging Technology
- Exercise Physiologist
- Music/Art/Dance Therapists
- Dialysis Technician
- Nuclear Medical Technologist
- Hypnotherapist
- Psychiatric Technician
- Health Care Receptionists
- Sports Medicine
- Medical Terminology
- Veterinary Assisting

Figure 2-4. A sample listing of program and course topics included in health occupations education.

Marketing Education

Marketing education is the instructional program designed to prepare individuals for the major occupational areas within marketing and management. Marketing, simply defined, is the selling of ideas, products and services of all kinds to identified and qualified markets. Marketers manage the massive system of distribution that brings goods and services to industrial users and consumers worldwide. Marketing involves information gathering, recruiting, image building, promoting, training, campaigning, financing, lobbying, researching, and communicating. It borrows heavily from the disciplines of psychology, sociology, and economics. Marketing is a process that can be adapted to virtually every economic, social or public activity, and is an essential ingredient in making our free enterprise system work (DECA Inc., 1992).

Marketing programs are based on the discipline or subject matter of marketing and provide instruction in basic academic skills, business foundations, economic foundations, and the marketing functions of: (a) distribution, (b) financing, (c) management of marketing information, (d) pricing, (e) product planning of goods and services, (f) promotion, (g) purchasing, (h) risk management, (i) selling, (j) management, and (k) entrepreneurship. Marketing programs in local secondary and postsecondary schools are designed to match the diversity of marketing needs in their geographic regions but they all include instruction in the principles, concepts, attitudes, and skills necessary to prepare individuals for work in retail, service, and manufacturing environments from the entry level job of a new employee to leadership positions in technical areas and management (Marketing Education Resource Center, 1987).

Like other major occupational education areas, marketing education can be taught as a general labor market preparation program or as a vocational program for specific labor market preparation. Exploratory marketing programs are offered at the middle/junior high school level to provide students with the basic foundations of marketing and to provide them with an opportunity to explore marketing occupations and careers through job shadowing, field trips, and short-time internships. Marketing programs at the secondary and postsecondary levels consists of sequenced courses such as advertising, sales promotion, job preparation, management, marketing research, sales, transportation and distribution, human relations, purchasing, and entrepreneurship. Some programs may include specialized courses in the areas of hotel/motel marketing, fashion marketing, or establishing small businesses. See Figure 2-5.

SAMPLE LISTING OF MARKETING EDUCATION PROGRAM/COURSE TOPICS	
• Entrepreneurship	• Pricing
• Distribution	• Product/Service Planning
• Market Research	• Sales Promotion
• Fashion Merchandising	• Purchasing/Buying
• Hotel Marketing	• Risk Management
• International Marketing	• Sales
• Real Estate	• Financing
• Advertising and Visual Merchandising	• Management
• Finance and Credit	• Transportation and Distribution
• Food Service Management	• Human Relations
• Leadership Development	• Small Business Management
• Employability Skills	• Insurance
• Career in Marketing	• Organization Management
• Marketing Information	• Behavioral Theory and Marketing

Figure 2-5. A sample listing of program and course topics included in marketing education programs.

Marketing education provides students with the foundation for careers that have a marketing, management, entrepreneurial, or service orientation. While specialization in one area is possible, most marketing education programs are designed to allow students to choose a concentration from among a number of marketing industries and occupations. General workplace skill development is integrated into the marketing education curriculum to provide opportunities for students to develop leadership, team work, participatory skills, applications of technology, and other important workplace skills. Marketing education, like other vocational education fields, is participating in tech-prep programs that help students make the transition from secondary schools to postsecondary schools and into high-paying careers in marketing.

Instructional programs of marketing education are also likely to include a school-based enterprise such as a school store, an on-going project related to marketing in the business community, or a marketing internship (cooperative education) which provides students with an opportunity to experience supervised work in a real-life marketing environment with pay. Cooperative education, which is a combination of planned on-the-job training and classroom instruction, has been part of quality marketing education programs from the beginning. Marketing students develop leadership skills and enhance marketing skills through participation in the Distributive Education Clubs of America (DECA), the secondary vocational student organization for marketing students. DECA provides students with a number of programs and activities such as leadership development, professional development, and competitive events to help them with personal development as well as further their understanding of the civic and ethical responsibilities of business. Postsecondary students can benefit from the activities of Delta Epsilon Chi, the postsecondary student organization for marketing education students (Marketing Education and DECA: *Essential Factors in Creating a Quality Work Force*, 1992).

Marketing education is an important part of a comprehensive secondary education. Nearly one-third of our nation's public high schools offer marketing education programs. Recent data regarding the percentage of public high school graduates completing one or more courses in specific labor market programs of vocational education shows that 8.7% have been enrolled in marketing education programs (*Vocational Education in the United States: 1969-1990*). The Bureau of Labor Statistics (1992) estimated that nearly 80% of the nation's work force will be engaged in service sector jobs by the year 2000 and to one degree or another, most of these workers will be involved in marketing. Marketing is a vital part of our economic system and students need expanded opportunities to enroll in marketing programs to prepare for the estimated 15,900,000 jobs projected by the year 2000 (DECA Inc., 1992).

Technical Education

Technical education is the vocational program that prepares people for technical occupations, the fastest growing segment of the work force. Technical occupations are defined as occupations that require workers to use higher levels of math, science, and technology to make decisions on the job than is normally required in skilled-trades occupations. Technical education is viewed both as a program and a level of education. Technical education, viewed as a level of education, is provided in other occupational areas such as agricultural education or health occupations and occupies a position in the occupational continuum between skilled workers and craftsmen and professionals such as physicians, engineers, researchers, and managers. One way to delineate between traditional vocational education, technical education, and professional education is to think about the major orientation of each. Vocational education is primarily practice oriented, technical education has a combined theory and practice orientation, and professional education is primarily theory oriented. See Figure 2-6.

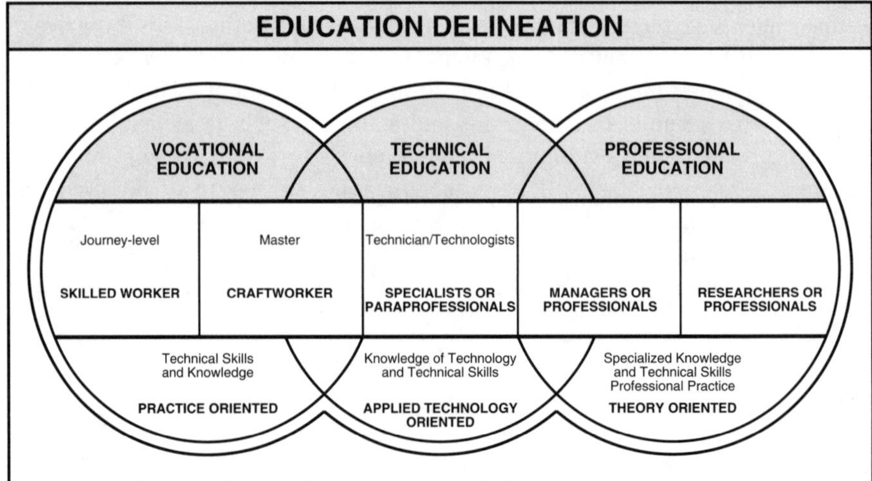

Figure 2-6. Delineation between vocational education, technical education, and professional education.

Technical education, viewed as a program, prepares technicians and technical workers through a curriculum that emphasizes a field of technical specialization including practical skills, supporting sciences, and mathematics. Technicians and technical workers must have functional academic skills, a command of the theoretical principles related to the technology of the occupation, and practical skills and abilities the specialization area requires. The SCANS report (1991) *What Work Requires of Schools* stated that a high-performance workplace requires workers who have a solid foundation in the basic literacy and computational skills, in the thinking skills necessary to apply knowledge to solve work problems, and in the personal qualities that make workers dedicated and trustworthy. Technical workers who have the ability to manage resources, work amicably and productively with co-workers, acquire and use information, master complex systems, and work with a variety of technologies are the kinds of employees needed for the high-performance work force called for in the SCANS Report.

Kenneth Gray (1993) noted a 1980 study by the American Society for Training and Development which identified three types of technical workers: professionals, technicians, and blue-collar technical workers. Professional technicians usually are prepared in a baccalaureate degree program; technicians usually hold associate's degrees or two-year certificates; and blue-collar technical workers–the fastest growing technical area–are high school graduates who usually complete one or more years of postsecondary vocational-technical training. Examples of blue-collar technical workers include electrician, medical technician, air conditioning and refrigeration technician, and automotive service specialist.

All vocational service areas can become involved in producing technical workers through the tech-prep program which is designed to produce highly-skilled and technical workers through a two-year secondary vocational education program: these programs include courses in mathematics, sciences, and communications that are articulated with a two-year postsecondary experience in a community college, technical institute, or through apprenticeship. The NAVE (1994) report indicated that secondary health and technical programs are increasing, which reflects articulation efforts between secondary and postsecondary vocational programs.

The majority of technical education programs are offered at the postsecondary level in public and private postsecondary institutions including community colleges, technical institutes, technical centers, engineering schools, and four-year colleges offering technical programs of less than baccalaureate degree programs. Technical education constitutes 23% of all postsecondary vocational education student enrollment and this percentage is expected to increase as technology continues to make the workplace more technical (NAVE, 1994). See Figure 2-7.

Technical education programs are offered on a full-time or part-time basis and lead to certificates, diplomas, or associate degrees. Technical education programs consist of sequenced courses which contain a number of tasks/competencies which have been validated by technical committees to ensure that they are adequate, relevant, and current. The typical technical education program consists of general core courses that include academic subjects which provide the foundation in the basic skills required in an occupation, fundamental occupational courses that provide the knowledge base and foundation for more highly specialized courses in an occupational area, and specific occupational courses which build upon fundamental occupational courses and provide the basic knowledge and skills required for individuals to function effectively in a chosen occupation. In addition, elective courses are often provided to accommodate the specialized interest of students within the occupational area (Stonehouse, 1993).

Technical education instruction is delivered through classroom presentations that provide students with the basic concepts and principles of an occupational area followed by laboratory assignments that call for students to apply what they have learned in real or simulated work tasks, projects, or situations. Some technical programs include internships or practicums that require students to continue their knowledge and technical skill development in a structured on-the-job training experience. Postsecondary technical students can enhance their personal development through participation in one of the postsecondary VSOs such as Vocational Industrial Clubs of America (VICA) for trade, industrial, technical, and health occupations students; Phi Beta Lambda (PBL) for business education students; Delta Epsilon Chi (DEC) for marketing students; and Postsecondary Agricultural Students (PAS) for individuals enrolled in agricultural education.

SAMPLE LISTING OF TECHNICAL EDUCATION PROGRAM/COURSE TOPICS	
• Automotive Technology	• Computer Operations
• Aerospace Production Planning	• Printing/Graphics Technology
• Aerospace Tool Design	• Computer Programming
• Aircraft Structural Technology	• Construction Management
• Air Conditioning Technology	• Dental Laboratory Technology
• Aviation Maintenance Technology	• Forest Technology
• Avionics Maintenance Technology	• Surgical Technology
• Information and Office Technology	• Veterinary Technology
• Instrumentation Technology	• Electronic Engineering Technology
• Advanced Machine Tool Design	• Environmental Engineering
• Marine Engine Technology	• Industrial Electricity Technology
• Marketing Management	• Industrial Maintenance Technology
• Automated Manufacturing	• Telecommunication Technology
• Biomedical Engineering Technology	• Welding and Joining Technology
• Biotechnology	• Automotive Collision Technology
• Mechanical Engineering Technology	• Drafting and Design Technology
• Medical Assisting	• Robotic Workcell Technology
• Medical Laboratory Technology	• Radiological Technology
• Microcomputer Specialist	• Management and Supervision Development
• Paralegal Studies	
• Business Equipment Technology	• Commercial Plumbing Technology
• Business and Office Technology	• Research Laboratory Technology
• Respiratory Therapy	• Visual Communications Technology
• Civil Engineering Technology	• Electrical Distribution Technology

Figure 2-7. A sample listing of programs and course topics included in technical education.

Technology Education

Technology education (formerly industrial arts education) is the instructional program that acquaints people with their technological environment and provides them with a broad knowledge of the applications of technology in daily life. More specifically, it is a "comprehensive, action-based education program concerned with technical means, their evaluation, utilization and significance within industry, its organizations, personnel systems, techniques, resources and products, and their social and cultural impact" (International Technology Education Association, 1994). The Carl D. Perkins Vocational and Applied Technology Education Act of 1990

(PL 101-392) defined technology education as "an applied discipline designed to promote technological literacy which provides knowledge and understanding of the impacts of technology including its organizations, techniques, tools, and skills to solve practical problems and extend human capabilities in areas such as construction, manufacturing, communication, transportation, power and energy" (American Vocational Association, 1990).

Technology education programs propose to help students:

- Develop an appreciation for the importance of technology in our world.
- Make informed occupational and career choices.
- Apply tools, materials, processes, and technical concepts safely and efficiently.
- Make wise consumer choices.
- Make appropriate adjustments to a rapidly changing environment.
- Recognize and deal with forces and trends that influence the future.
- Apply critical-thinking and problem-solving skills.
- Discover and develop individual talents.
- Apply creative abilities.
- Apply academic skills and the content of other school subjects (International Technology Education Association, 1993).

Most people recognize that technology has changed our world, but few people understand the various aspects of technology and how pervasive technology is in our society. Technology is commonly defined as a discipline or body of knowledge and the application of this knowledge combined with resources to produce outcomes in response to human desires and needs. Technology affects every aspect of our lives, reshaping our homes, education, transportation, entertainment, jobs, and industries. Since technology is so prevalent in our society, it is important for all people to understand technology so they can function effectively in their roles as consumers, workers, employers, and family members. It is the mission of technology education to prepare all individuals with a functional understanding of technology so they can make informed decisions and contribute to our technologically-based society (Savage & Sterry, 1990).

Technology education draws its content from four universal domains: (1) sciences, (2) humanities, (3) technologies, and (4) formal knowledge. The sciences and humanities domains contain all recorded knowledge of the sciences and humanities. The technologies domain, likewise, contains all recorded knowledge related to the types of technology. The formal knowledge domain consists of language, linguistics, mathematics, and logic. Each of these bodies of knowledge are interrelated; each contributes methods and content useful to others. Technology is the study of the people made world; science is the study of the natural world; and humanities/arts is the study of value and the study of human behavior. The primary method of knowing for technologists is discovery through a problem-centered approach to address human needs and wants called the technological method. Technology education uses the technological method and scientific method to help students solve practical problems in the applications of technology. The technology education curriculum is organized around a set of concepts, processes, and systems that are uniquely technological (Savage & Sterry, 1990).

A major goal of technology education is technological literacy or an understanding of technology and its effect on individuals, society, and the civilization process. As a vital part of the school's curriculum, technology education teaches elementary school, middle/junior high school, and high school students to understand, use, and control technology in an experiential, laboratory environment. In the classroom/laboratory, students develop insights into the applications of technological concepts, processes, and systems through structured "hands-on" learning activities using a variety of technological equipment such as computers, computerized machines, audio-video production equipment, and a variety of experiment- oriented learning chapters. Students are taught the application of math and science and to use knowledge of technology to solve practical problems in the broad areas of communications, manufacturing/construction, and transportation/power/energy. See Figure 2-8.

Technology education programs are available at the elementary, middle/junior high school, and secondary school levels. At the elementary school level, the focus is on technological awareness with classroom activities oriented around the development of motor skills and informed attitudes about technology's influence on society. At the middle school level, the focus of technology education programs is on exploring the applications of technology to solve problems and exploring the various technological careers. A wide variety of problem-solving situations are used, giving students opportunities to create and design. Activities are designed to further promote technological awareness and to promote psychomotor development through processes associated with technology. Secondary technology education programs are designed to give students experience related to scientific principles, engineering concepts, and technological systems. Programs can be arranged around the four technical systems of communications, construction, manufacturing, and transportation or can revolve around emerging megatechnologies, technological issues, frontiers of science and technology, and technical adaptive systems. Secondary students experience the practical application of scientific and mathematical principles; gain an in-depth understanding and appreciation for technology in our society; develop basic skills in the proper use of tools, machines, materials, and processes; and solve problems involving the tools, machines, materials, processes, products, and services of industry and technology (International Technology Education Association, 1988).

SAMPLE LISTING OF TECHNOLOGY EDUCATION PROGRAM/COURSE TOPICS

COMMUNICATIONS

- Desktop Publishing
- Photography
- Computer-aided Drafting & Design
- Radio and Television Broadcasting
- Telecommunications
- Acoustic Communications
- Light Communications
- Graphic Communications
- Electronic Communications

MANUFACTURING

- Robotics
- Mass Production
- Computer-aided Manufacturing
- Plastics
- Synthetic Materials
- Manufacturing Inputs and Outputs
- Transformation Processes
- Managerial Processes
- Manufacturing systems
- Manufacturing Materials
- Manufacturing Processes
- Manufacturing Enterprise
- Automating Manufacturing Systems
- Manufacturing Technology

CONSTRUCTION

- Construction Managed Activities
- Construction Production Processes
- Construction Managerial Processes
- Preparing for Construction Project
- Designing and Planning the Project
- Managing Construction Activities
- Building the Structure
- Installing Systems
- Finishing the Project
- Closing the Contract

TRANSPORTATION

- Technological Base
- Acts of Transporting
- Technical Systems
- Environmental Factors
- Internal Combustion Engines
- Electric Motors
- Career in Transportation
- Land Transportation
- Water Transportation
- Air Transportation
- Space Transportation
- Pipeline Transportation
- Conveyor Transportation

Figure 2-8. A sample listing of program and course topics included in technology education.

Secondary technology education students are provided opportunities for leadership development and personal growth through Technology Student Association (TSA) activities. The TSA is the VSO for technology education students. TSA activities are integrated into the regular instructional program and include chapter activities, a non-competitive achievement program designed to motivate students to exert greater effort in their technology program, and a number of individual and team competitive events such as aerospace technology, construction technology, extemporaneous speech, and technical report writing. TSA activities assist students in exploring careers in technology and in making career decisions.

Trade and Industrial Education

Trade and industrial education, often called T&I and referred to in some states as vocational industrial education, prepares individuals for initial employment in a wide range of vocational industrial occupations, assists adults who are already employed to advance in their chosen occupations, and retrains those individuals displaced because of technological developments and organizational changes. The mission of T&I education is to prepare individuals at the secondary and postsecondary levels for skilled occupations and technical work in industrial occupations.

The major goal of T&I education is for students to develop sufficient knowledge and skills to secure initial employment or advance through experiences that: (a) focus on performance skills required in an occupational field, (b) provide an understanding of and use of functional technology related to a chosen occupational area, (c) prepare individuals to deal effectively with personal and group relationship problems, (d) assist individuals in developing desirable work habits, ideals, and attitudes essential to successful job performance, and (e) provide relevant instruction to enable individuals to develop critical thinking and problem solving skills, manipulative skills, safety judgments, technical knowledge, and related occupational information preparing individuals for meaningful, productive employment in vocational industrial pursuits (NATIE, 1994).

Trade and industrial education programs prepare individuals for employment in the diverse industrial and service sectors of our nation's economy. Trade and industrial education includes training for apprenticeable trades, technical occupations, and other industrial and service occupations. Trade and industrial education is considered to be the broadest of all vocational fields, with training programs designed to prepare workers in a wide range of trade and industrial occupations classified on multiple levels of employment ranging from operatives to semi-skilled and skilled craftspersons and technicians of less than baccalaureate degree. Trade and industrial occupations are found in a variety of job categories such as manufacturing, construction, communications, printing, transportation, mining, protective services, visual arts, personal services, and building and grounds service occupations. Occupation in this vocational program involve, by are not limited to, layout, design, producing, processing, assembling, testing, maintaining, servicing or repairing, cooperative programs with industry, middle management and supervisory development, entrepreneurship and other special training for industrial programs which ensure growth and development in the industrial sector, and emergency industrial mobilization training programs and services.

Trade and industrial education programs are found at the secondary and postsecondary levels. Trade and industrial education programs at the secondary level are the second most popular occupational program with 36% of all students who enrolled in labor market preparation areas earning credits in trade and industrial education programs. There are many trade and industrial education programs at the postsecondary level which are usually classified as technical. Trade and industrial education accounted for 15% of postsecondary vocational student enrollment with 23% of students enrolled in technical programs, 29% in business, and 22% in Health (NAVE, 1994).

Trade and industrial education programs reflect the current and projected trends in business and industry through the utilization of functional advisory committees and partnerships. The curriculum for the many trade and industrial education programs, like electronics or automotive technology, are derived from occupational analysis and involve employability skills, technical knowledge, attitudes, job skills, and communication and leadership skills. In addition, the curriculum includes mastery of complementary technology; related mathematics and science; technical communication skills; drawing, art, or design; occupational safety and hygiene; labor, industrial relations, and management; and other directly related and supplementary experiences. Instruction may be full-time or part-time and may be provided in a school, technical institute, or community college setting or cooperatively at the worksite through internships, cooperative education, and youth apprenticeships.

Instructional programs in trade and industrial education are offered in some middle/junior high schools as exploratory courses which introduce students to the many diverse occupations and careers in the business and industrial sector of the economy and provide them with opportunities to engage in basic work tasks in a laboratory environment. These programs are usually delivered in one-hour instructional blocks for part of a quarter or semester, giving students an opportunity to select or be scheduled for several different occupational program areas.

Trade and industrial education programs at the high school level are delivered through specific labor market preparation programs using the cluster approach or single-occupation approach. The State of Georgia delivers most trade and industrial education instruction through the cluster approach with one occupational program preparing students for several jobs. For example, the construction program offers students opportunities to experience instruction in carpentry, masonry, electrical, and plumbing trades. Other states deliver instruction in one occupational area such as a carpentry program. There are many different occupational areas in trade and industrial education. See Figure 2-9. Since trade and industrial education occupations are so diverse, the industrial cooperative

SAMPLE LISTING OF TRADE AND INDUSTRIAL EDUCATION PROGRAM/COURSE TOPICS	
• Machine Trades	• Marine Mechanics
• Automotive Service Technology	• Architectural Drafting
• Collision Repair Technology	• Industrial Maintenance Technology
• Transportation Occupations Cluster	• Technical Drafting
• Metal Fabrication Cluster	• Welding
• Construction Occupations Cluster	• Electronic Products Servicing
• Electro-mechanical Cluster	• Culinary Arts
• Electronics Cluster	• Aviation Maintenance Technology
• Drafting Technology	• Textile Technology
• Cosmetology	• Law Enforcement
• Food Service	• Television Production
• Barbering	• Motorcycle Service Technology
• Electronics	• Robotic Workcell Technology
• Graphic Arts	• Custodial Services
• Carpentry	• Brick Masonry
• Masonry Trades	• Commercial Tile Setting
• Electrical Trades	• Advertising Design
• Air Conditioning & Refrigeration	• Aircraft Structural Technology
• Appliance Repair	• Automated Manufacturing
• Air-cooled Gasoline Engine Repair	• Telecommunications Technology
• Sheet Metal Fabrication	• Heavy Equipment Mechanics
• Residential and Commercial Plumbing	• Computer Assisted Drafting and Design
• Cabinetmaking	• Truck Repair Technology
• Commercial Baking	• Precision Machine Technology
• Commercial Photography	• Plastics Technology
• Diesel Equipment Technology	• Painting and Decorating

Figure 2-9. A sample listing of program and course topics included in trade and industrial education.

education program is provided in many schools to allow students the opportunity to receive work preparation in occupations which are not part of the regular school vocational program or to develop job skills in a real work environment to enhance what they have learned in available trade and industrial education programs.

Secondary trade and industrial education programs, like other vocational and applied technology education programs, provide classroom instruction in applied academics and the basic concepts and principles of an occupation or job, followed by opportunities to apply what they have learned in laboratory projects and actual live-work projects such as repairing other students' cars in an automotive technology program. Advanced students may have an opportunity to develop on-the-job experience through internships, co-operative education, or youth apprenticeship programs. Trade and industrial education students as well as health occupations students, develop leadership skills and enhance job skills through participation in the many activities of the Vocational Industrial Clubs of America (VICA), which is the vocational student organization for both of these vocational programs. VICA activities such as chapter activities, professional development, and competitive events are integrated into the instructional program to motivate students to exert more effort in preparing for occupational careers. The awards associated with VICA activities provide students with recognition for quality effort and work.

Trade and industrial education programs are being certified by industry to ensure that programs meet quality standards set by industry experts. Currently in Georgia, programs are industry certified in the areas of auto mechanics, construction, graphic arts, auto body repair, forestry, and marketing with plans underway to certify programs of horticulture, business education, electronics, food service, health occupations, and metalworking.

Nationwide, trade and industrial educators are anxiously awaiting voluntary skill standards and the opportunity to test their students in relation to these standards so they can obtain a recognized, respected, and portable credential to enhance employment opportunities.

Trade and industrial educators are becoming more involved in tech-prep programs, youth apprenticeship, and other types of work-based programs. Many years before the term tech-prep was introduced, many secondary trade and industrial education teachers had established articulated curriculum patterns with postsecondary instructors to encourage students to continue their preparation for work. Tech-prep programs lead to an articulated curriculum between the last two years of high school and the first two years of postsecondary education or apprenticeship, and encourages the integration of academic skills in mathematics, science, and communication into the curriculum.

Many occupations that use registered apprenticeship programs as a source of highly-trained workers are in the trade and industrial areas which makes the establishment of youth apprenticeship programs easier to accomplish. Apprenticeship is a program that provides comprehensive performance-based training to entry level workers in the theoretical and practical aspects of an occupation. An apprenticeship contract is developed between the high school and an employer which identifies the practical on-the-job training to be provided by a journeyworker with the related instruction to be provided by a competent trade and industrial education teacher who was a former journeyworker. Secondary students attend classes in school part of the day and spend the balance of the day developing job skills at the workplace.

Vocational Special Needs Programs

Since the passage of the Vocational Education Act of 1963 (PL 88-210), federal and state legislation has continued to include provisions encouraging and mandating that vocational education programs serve all students including those who are considered to be "at risk" because of economic, academic, physical, mental, or language disabilities. In response to federal mandates, most states have established a number of programs that provide support services so that individuals from special populations can prepare for and succeed in regular vocational educational programs. For Example, in Georgia in the early 1970's the Coordinated Vocational Academic Education (CVAE) program was established to serve students who are academically and/or economically disadvantaged and are limited in their ability to participate in regular programs. CVAE students receive special support services form a trained vocational special needs teacher in vocational education, communications, computational skills, and employability skills. This program has been highly successful and continues to provide support services to "at risk" students (Georgia Department of Education, 1990).

Another example of a Georgia vocational special needs program is "Project Success" which assists ninth and tenth grade students who have been identified as potential high school dropouts to remain in school. This successful innovative program uses a "school-within-a-school" approach, where a team of vocational and academic instructors are block-scheduled to teach and counsel a select group of participants. This program provides students with the concentrated assistance they need to realize their potential self-worth and learn the basic work-related, employability, and life-coping skills needed to become productive, useful citizens (Georgia Department of Education, 1990).

Vocational special needs personnel provide a wide variety of support services for individuals with special needs through individualized support services provided in vocational classrooms and laboratories. For example, the Georgia Related Vocational Instruction (RVI) program supports the special needs of students with disabilities by providing them with courses and counseling that enable them to acquire entry level job skills. Students are provided instruction in special courses that deliver content jointly planned by the RVI teacher and the vocational teacher, but they also receive special assistance from the RVI teachers during the time they are in the vocational classroom and laboratory.

Vocational special needs personnel at the secondary and postsecondary levels provide a wide variety of support services ranging from coordinating the development of IEPs and ITPs to providing supplemental instruction; from vocational assessment to vocational guidance and program placement; from arranging for additional support from support personnel to obtaining support from community agency service providers; from coordinating the learner's school instructional program to arranging for job shadowing and other work-based opportunities; and from assisting individuals with special needs to obtain job placement to providing the follow-up and follow-through services necessary to help these individual adjust and advance in employment.

POSTSECONDARY VOCATIONAL-TECHNICAL PROGRAMS AND CURRICULUM

Postsecondary vocational-technical education programs are designed to provide adults with high quality, relevant preparation for initial employment, or for additional preparation in the same field, for preparation in another career or occupational field. Postsecondary vocational-technical education (sometimes called technical and occupational education) encompasses a number of program areas and a wide range of course offerings, but 75% of vocational-technical student enrollment is in the three areas of business (29%), health (22%), and technical (23%). An additional 15% is in trade and industrial education with the remaining 11% of enrollment in agriculture (1%), marketing (2%), family and consumer sciences (4%), and other areas (5%). Postsecondary vocational-technical education student enrollment is almost evenly split between part-time (51%) and full-time (49%). There are slightly more females enrolled in postsecondary vocational-technical education (54%) than males (46%). Postsecondary vocational-technical students constitute one-third of all postsecondary student enrollment (NAVE, 1994). In the Fall of 1990, about 6% of the U.S. population between the ages of 18 and 34 were enrolled in vocational-technical courses (NCES, 1990).

Postsecondary vocational-technical programs of less than a baccalaureate degree are offered in public and private two-year colleges, technical institutes, adult career centers, correctional facilities, and in public 4-year colleges that offer vocational-technical programs leading to certificates and associate degrees. The percentage of postsecondary vocational students enrolled in different types of schools in the Fall of 1990 were as follows: public two-year colleges (43%); vocational, trade, technical, or business school (19%); four-year colleges (10%); programs run by employers (5%); and schools run by other providers (24%). Most postsecondary vocational-technical education is provided in community colleges with private proprietary schools the second largest provider, followed by technical institutes and area vocational school serving postsecondary vocational students. These institutions offer programs in the occupational areas of agriculture, business, marketing, health, home economics, computer/data processing, engineering/science technologies, protective services, communications technologies, and trade and industry. Instructional programs range from less than a year to three years with programs lasting less than two years being the most common (NCES, 1990).

The instructional programs in postsecondary vocational-technical education consist of sequenced academic and technical preparation courses taught in the institution by competent instructors with work-based training options such as internships and practicums exercised in some programs–notably health. The common course sequence consists of academic and fundamental occupational courses taught first, followed by specific occupational preparation courses and internships and practicums scheduled when students have advanced to a level that they can profit from work-related experiences. The application of mathematics and science principles are emphasized in postsecondary vocational-technical courses along with higher-order skills such as critical thinking, reasoning, and problem solving. The expected student outcome is a technical worker who can work independently, or with others, in diagnosing and solving work-related problems and contributing to the success of the business or industry in which one is employed.

Postsecondary-technical education curriculum is derived from occupational analysis and validated by technical committees composed of a group of experts representative of the various aspects of an occupational area. The occupational analysis process results in the identification and validation of competencies (skills, knowledge, and attitudes) required in a field along with the tools, equipment, and materials needed to support instruction. Most states have developed curriculum guides (program guides) and standards to ensure that students receive a comprehensive, quality educational experience.

Postsecondary vocational-technical instruction is delivered through classroom presentations which include applied academics and the foundational concepts and principles of an occupational field, followed by applications of this knowledge in well-equipped laboratories that simulate the type of equipment and environment which is found in the workplace. Instructional programs usually last about 6 hours per day for full-time students. Many postsecondary students work and attend school on a part-time basis with a large number attending during evening hours. Postsecondary vocational-technical students have opportunities to develop leadership skills and enhance their occupational and employability skills by participating in the vocational student organizations in their occupational areas such as Vocational Industrial Clubs of America, Phi Beta Lambda, Delta Epsilon Chi, and Postsecondary Agricultural Students.

Vocational Teacher Education

Successful programs of vocational-technical education require teachers who are competent in their occupational field and in pedagogy–teaching skills. Educational reform has initiated a new type of workforce preparation program in which integrated learning and the development of cognitive skills, broad technical skills, and understanding of all aspects of an industry are emphasized. Vocational teachers are required to engage in professional staff development activities which include updating their occupational knowledge and skills as well as their teaching skills in order to maintain their teaching credentials.

Most secondary vocational teachers hold baccalaureate or higher degrees with the exception of trade and industrial (T&I) and health occupation teachers where most state departments of education continue to accept limited professional preparation courses and extensive occupational experience in lieu of a college degree as criteria for teacher certification. The NAVE (1994) indicated that 45% of secondary T&I teachers and 33% of postsecondary T&I teachers have less than a baccalaureate degree.

Vocational teachers receive preparation in public and private four-year colleges and universities offering vocational teacher education programs. Vocational teacher education programs provide students with core academic subjects required for all college students combined with courses in a technical teaching field and in professional education. Students are required to successfully complete a student teacher internship lasting a quarter or semester to help them develop teaching experience under the mentorship of a master teacher. Vocational teachers who are not required to earn a degree are expected to complete a number of specified professional education courses in vocational teacher education programs in order to meet state teacher certification requirements. All vocational teachers are required to complete local staff development activities or college courses periodically to renew their certification.

The NAVE Report, Volume I (1994) recommended that all vocational teachers should obtain a bachelor's degree with preservice training in education for initial certification. In addition, this report affirmed the need for most vocational teachers to have a limited amount of relevant occupational experience as part of teacher certification criteria.

AMERICAN VOCATIONAL ASSOCIATION

The American Vocational Association (AVA) is the national professional organization for vocational and applied technology education professionals with state affiliates representing some 37,177 members composed primarily of vocational and applied technology education teachers, supervisors, teacher educators, counselors, administrators, and special support personnel. The mission of AVA is to provide educational leadership in developing a competitive workforce. The purposes of AVA include:

1. Professional Development–Encourage career development, professional involvement, and leadership among members.
2. Program Improvement–Foster excellence in vocational-technical education.
3. Policy Development–Advocate national public policy to benefit vocational-technical education.
4. Marketing–Market vocational-technical education (American Vocational Association, 1992, American Vocational Association, 1995).

The American Vocational Association encompasses the following divisions:

1. Administration
2. Agricultural Education
3. Business Education
4. Employment and Training
5. Guidance
6. Health Occupations Education
7. Home Economics Education (new name is Family and Consumer Sciences)
8. Marketing Education
9. New and Related Services
10. Special Needs
11. Technical Education
12. Technology Education
13. Trade and Industrial Education.

The leadership of AVA includes: an executive director, a president, vice presidents representing the divisions of AVA listed above, and vice presidents from Regions 1-5. The headquarters of the organization is located at AVA, 1410 King St., Alexandria, VA 22314. The phone number is (703) 683-3111.

Publications of AVA include: the *American Vocational Education Journal*, *Vocational Education Weekly*, *School-To-Work Reporter*, and *Legislative Update*.

SELF ASSESSMENT

1. What is agricultural education and where and how is it delivered?
2. What is business education and where and how is it delivered?
3. What is family and consumer sciences and where and how is it delivered?
4. What is health occupations education and where and how is it delivered?
5. What is marketing education and where and how is it delivered?
6. What is technology education and where and how is it delivered?
7. What is technical education and where and how is it delivered?
8. What is trade and industrial education and where and how is it delivered?
9. How are vocational and applied technology teachers prepared?

ASSOCIATED ACTIVITIES

1. Visit postsecondary institutions and obtain promotional materials describing the various vocational-technical programs offered at the institution.
2. Obtain materials from the American Vocational Association and from the professional associations for each occupational area, such as the International Technology Education Association, as part of your personal professional library.

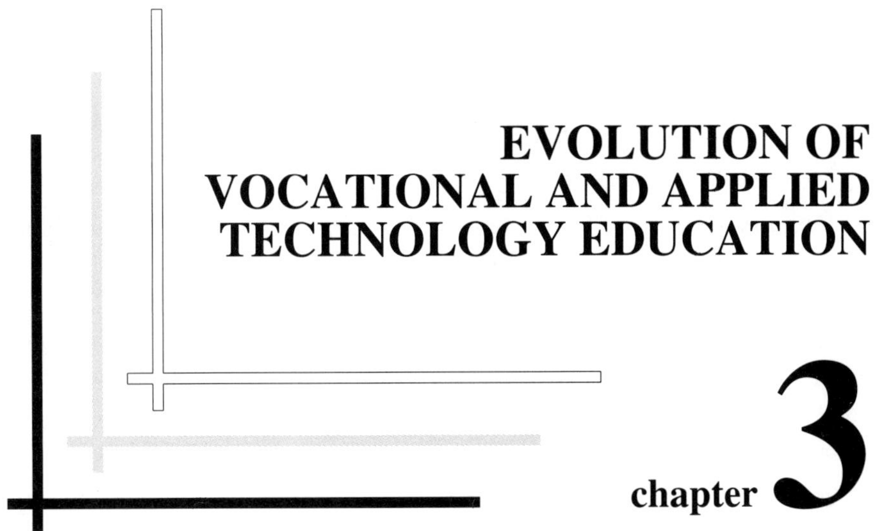

EVOLUTION OF VOCATIONAL AND APPLIED TECHNOLOGY EDUCATION

chapter 3

INTRODUCTION

In order to appreciate the past, understand the present, and to anticipate the future, it is essential to have a knowledge of the significant historical events in an interest area and this is particularly true about education for work. It is interesting to trace how humankind first learned to work by imitation, followed by trial and error, apprenticeship, and organized classroom and laboratory instruction in schools. The evolution of vocational and applied technology education can be traced from the Paleolithic period through the Neolithic period, Agricultural Civilization, Bronze age, Iron Age and Greek Civilization, Roman Civilization, Middle Ages, Renaissance and the Reformation, Industrial Civilization and Power Age to our Post Industrial or Information Age of today. For thousands of years, informal and later formal, apprenticeship was the main means of learning how to work. From the sixteenth century to the present, a number of educational reformers have revealed their ideas about preparing people for work in schools and some even put their ideas to the test through actual experimentation. The experiments of Otto Salomon resulting in the Sloyd system of education and the work of Victor Della Voss resulting in the Russian system of tool instruction have contributed greatly to our system of vocational and applied technology education today. A review of these selected historical events and the people who laid the groundwork for our present system of work preparation education provides valuable insight into our present system of work education – vocational and applied technology education.

OBJECTIVES

After completing this chapter the reader should be able to:

1. Describe the earliest informal forms of education for work.
2. Describe the institution of apprenticeship.
3. Discuss the types of work and tools used during the paleolithic, neolithic, agricultural civilization, and bronze and iron ages of history.
4. Describe the educational systems used in the Greek and Roman Empires.
5. Describe the period of history called the Middle Ages and how learning was preserved.
6. Discuss apprenticeship in the guilds of England.
7. Identify the key concepts and ideas of work education proposed by the early educational reformers of Europe.
8. Describe the Swedish Sloyd System of Work Education.
9. Describe the Russian System of Manual Training.
10. Describe the industrial civilization and how it affected the need for new programs of work preparation.
11. Explain how the power age advanced civilization.

EVOLUTION OF VOCATIONAL AND APPLIED TECHNOLOGY EDUCATION

From the dawn of history to the present time, there has evolved two kinds of education–education for work and education for culture. For many years education for work was carried on almost wholly through practical experiences with tools, materials, utensils, and machines in the home, field, shop, store, or factory and only recently through organized vocational and applied technology education provided in educational institutions. In contrast, education for culture has almost always been delivered through the medium of books and through formalized instruction in the home by private tutors, in church-related schools, private schools, and later in history through public schools.

For centuries, these two types of education were widely separated and students of each type of education differed widely in social and occupational classes. In recent times, however, these types of education are combined and the modern view is that what is needed for today's world is a fusion of the two. In fact, educational leaders are advocating a new pedagogy that combines academic and experiential education in a system of lifelong learning in schools, community, and work.

Although changes resulting in combining these two distinct types of education have been made only in recent times, they have not been the result of a sudden stroke of a pen but rather have been the subject of discussion, controversy, and experiment for hundreds of years.

Early Beginning in Europe and Asia

In order to understand the present and to anticipate the future, it is essential to have a knowledge of the past. Historians, archaeologists, and scientists are using the tools of technology to reconstruct the origins of man and our world. With each new discovery of our ancient world, mankind comes one step closer to a more focused picture of the earliest civilizations. Much of what we know about ancient history is provided through artifacts of the tools and implements used by our ancient ancestors to survive. Very early, people learned that by using their intellect to develop tools, work could be performed more easily and the necessities of life, food, clothing, and shelter could be provided with less effort. The constant search of people for a way to relieve the burden of work and improve living has led to the modern technological world of today.

Individuals have learned to work by various methods, perhaps first by accident, followed by imitation, trial and error, and eventually through planned experiences–apprenticeship being the earliest recorded form of planned learning. The study of history is very much a study of how people learned to work, survive, advance, and the study of tools and implements that were developed along the way to make this work possible and more efficient.

Since the dawn of civilization, a primitive form of industrial education has existed. Parents assumed the task of teaching their children how to use their heads and hands to provide the necessities of life. This parent-child relationship was the beginning of the apprenticeship system which evolved later.

Although this parent-child relationship was an unconscious process of imitative learning, it was very effective, for it enabled primitive people to survive their unstable environment. Later it became an incidental learning and teaching process as people evolved and began the spiral process upward toward civilization and recorded history.

Paleolithic Period

The history of work education (vocational education) is very, very old, perhaps beginning with the use of stone tools in the Paleolithic period (old stone age) about 2,500,000 years ago. Historians believe that modern humans came to be in this period and learned to survive by hunting animals and gathering eggs, insects, and edible plants. Toward the end of the paleolithic period, humans had developed a number of stone tools, learned to use fire, made weapons (bow and arrow, spears), developed bone sewing needles, and invented a crude system of measurement using body parts (hand, cubit). From the different types of stone tools recovered, scientists believe that early humans learned to drill, chop, slice, burnish (sharpen other stone tools), scrape, and saw. The method of education was through fathers and mothers showing their sons and daughters how to perform survival tasks with available tools and materials. The content of early work education was securing food (hunting, fishing, trapping), providing shelter (housing, clothing), and making tools and weapons (*Academic American Encyclopedia*, 1994).

Neolithic Period

In the Neolithic period, which began around 9000 B.C., people learned to improve stone and wood tools and developed insights into animal and plant husbandry. They learned to domesticate animals (camels, sheep, oxen, horses) and to plant and harvest cereal grains in areas where the soil was soft, rainfall was adequate, or bodies of fresh water were near at hand. Artifacts from this period indicate that the crafts of pottery, spinning and weaving, basketmaking, boat and house building, and farming were practiced (*Academic American Encyclopedia*, 1994).

Agricultural Civilization

The agricultural civilization began with the development of the ox-drawn wooden plow in the Middle East in the 4th millennium B.C. The two-phase economy of earlier periods, hunting and gathering, was expanded to include animal husbandry, plant cultivation, and field cultivation. Much of the agriculture activity centered in the rain-sparse river valleys of Mesopotamia, Egypt, and India. During the agricultural civilization, a system of picture writing (hieroglyphics) evolved (later becoming the Egyptian alphabet), an Egyptian calendar was established marking the first recorded event in history, political states came into being, warfare began, and the Bronze age appeared (Roberts, 1971).

Bronze Age

In the early years of the agricultural civilization, people learned to smelt copper and bronze (an alloy of cooper and tin) to form a variety of tools and implements for domestic use and warfare. Artifacts of this period reveal the bronze drill and the bow drilling technique, bronze axes, knifes, files, scraping tools, adzes, and saws. A variety of new crafts developed, and skilled artisans were in great demand (usually captured slaves and free people of low class stature). To make bronze products, ore had to be gathered, fuel had to be developed, molds for castings had to be constructed, and furnaces had to be built. Materials used to manufacture bronze products had to be gathered from distant lands, thereby promoting commerce and sometimes conquest. Bronze weapons were developed and the most powerful weapon of war to that date, the horse-drawn, two-wheeled chariot that carried an archer armed with a compound bow came into being (Roberts, 1971).

During the Bronze age a number of new trades developed including the building trades that resulted in the impressive structures that characterized early cities. In Mesopotamia, molded, kiln-dried bricks were used to build large structures, while in Egypt the favored building materials were quarried limestone blocks that were used to construct the famous pyramids. People learned to use stone and wooden and bronze tools to produce products and construct buildings. They also learned how to transport heavy loads to building sites by barges and sledges. These technological innovations required skilled craftsworkers who had to be trained to perform their work. This training was accomplished mostly through the method of father-to-son, mother-to-daughter passing along of knowledge and skills and through the time-tested method of learning by trial and error. Toward the end of the Bronze period, the first recorded reference to apprenticeship appeared in the Babylonian code of King Hammurabi in 2100 B.C. The Hammurabi code suggested that "If an artisan take a son for adoption and teach him his handicraft one may not bring claim against him. If he does not teach him his handicraft that son may return to his father's house" (Roberts, 1971).

In the later part of the Bronze period, the Egyptians refined their picture writing system into an alphabet consisting of 24 characters or alphabetic signs. They devised a pointed reed for a pen, developed a writing fluid, and learned to split papyrus into thin layers for use as a writing medium (crude paper). The inventions of a written language and writing process lead the way for the establishment of organized schools for scribes between the period 2000 and 1200 B.C. These early schools consisted of a primary stage aimed at helping students to read and write ancient literature, followed by an apprenticeship period in which students were placed with an experienced scribe–usually a government worker. Youth of the nobility and middle class were encouraged to become scribes which was a position of distinction in the society of the day. Scribes recorded their work on paper or on clay tablets. Many clerks were needed to record business transactions resulting from commerce with people from the Nile Valley, and these clerks were trained in schools under the direction of religious leaders (Roberts, 1971).

Iron Age and Greek Civilization

The Iron age began toward the end of the second millennium B.C. with the discovery of iron making which flourished in Greece about 1000 B.C. As a result of agricultural productivity, iron making, and strategic location on the Mediterranean Sea for commerce, Greece became a world power. Early tools made of iron included drills, drill bit holders, gouges, broad axe, knives, skew, hand-made files, scraper, shaper planes, metal-cutting saws, calipers, and dividers. They also developed war paraphernalia from bronze and iron and built a large fleet of merchant ships and war ships (men-of-war). The Greeks developed a form of architecture using stone and wrought iron bars embedded in the stone called post and lintel (column-and-beam) construction. Greek architecture is one of the major accomplishments of the Greek people (Roberts, 1971).

As the two major cities of Sparta and Athens grew, there was an increased need for various craftworkers to do the menial work which led to the development of a caste system. The burden of production and construction fell upon second class citizens, slaves, and the Perioecci which was a group of "dweller about" who were, in a sense, slaves once removed. The Perioecci learned their trades from their fathers and mothers or through apprenticeship. Children of Greek citizens were provided a formal cultural education in institutions (Barlow, 1967).

Two major city/states emerged in Greece, Sparta, and Athens. Citizens were required to attend schools to make them better soldiers and loyal citizens. In Sparta, boys at age seven were placed in public barracks were they received rigorous physical training for war under the direction of professional soldiers. They listened to public discussion as a means of political training and were to engage in music and dancing as a means of mental and moral training. At age 18, they received advanced training for war for two years and were then sent to an army post until age 30 when they were eligible for full citizenship. Women and girls received gymnastics training to make them strong and capable of bearing healthy children (Roberts, 1971).

In Athens, formal education began at age seven, with boys being sent to school and girls educated at home. Boys attended three different types of private, tuition-supported schools: a letter school for reading, writing, and arithmetic; the music school; and the gymnasium school. At the age of 18, boys were examined morally and physically for citizenship, and if found worthy, were assigned to two years of training as a citizen-cadet after which they could become full citizens of Athens (Roberts, 1971).

In the period 479 to 431 B.C., known as the "Golden Age of Greece," education changed with less emphasis on strenuous training and a broadening of the curriculum to include geometry, drawing, grammar, and rhetoric. A system of higher or university education was established by sophists – private teachers who went from city to city to give lectures for youth who had completed grammar school. These sophists organized schools of philosophy or universities which later became public supported. Individuals applying to these universities could study medicine, architecture, engineering, and other professions. Extensive library and laboratory facilities were provided along with a staff of research specialists to enable students to achieve their educational goals. The Greek education system has had a profound effect on the educational systems of many countries continuing even to today (Roberts, 1971).

Romans

Beginning around 1000 B.C., the city of Rome on the Italian peninsula began to flourish, and by 200 B.C. these people had conquered most of the other people around them to become a new world power. They became a rich country from the spoils of war and developed a system of banks, currency, and shares in commercial enterprises. They built an impressive infrastructure consisting of roads, aqueducts, and drainage systems. They mastered the art of arch and vault construction and constructed massive buildings, theaters, and baths. They borrowed heavily from the greek civilization and established codes of law, public administration, and an educational system for Roman citizens. Technical inventions of the Roman empire period included the waterwheel and the development of a heavy iron plow capable of turning the clay soils of Northern Europe. Children of Roman citizens could attend private schools for formal cultural education while those who worked in the crafts and trades were left to the age old father-son, mother-daughter training method and apprenticeships to receive their preparation for life (Roberts, 1971).

The Roman genius for organization was exemplified in their system of education. They developed an educational system consisting of three levels: elementary, secondary, and higher. At age seven, students entered the elementary school where they studied reading, writing, conduct, and memorization of laws. At age ten, students entered the secondary or grammar school for educational experiences in rhetoric, oratory, and other subjects including mathematics, music, history, and law to prepare them for effective public life. Graduates of the secondary school could obtain higher education by attending one of the Greek universities and later the University of Rome around 75 B.C. At first, education in Rome was available in private schools, but by 75 B.C. the practice of paying teachers of grammar and rhetoric had begun. In the fifth century A.D., the influence of the Roman culture began to wane, teaching in the schools became formal and superficial with little student appeal, and by the sixth century A.D., the universities were closed. It was at this time that Western civilization entered the Dark Ages of the medieval period. It is important to note that the great majority of people, even in the progressive civilizations of Greece and Rome, received no formal schooling and the education they acquired came through their trade or occupation by parents and masters, through social contacts, and through trial and error (Roberts, 1971).

Middle Ages

The middle ages was a period of history for nearly a thousand years beginning around 300 A.D. and extending into the early 1300s. They are sometimes called the "Dark Ages" for the attention of people turned to preparing for the "hereafter" and little progress was made in scientific discoveries, inventions, and culture. It was also a time when barbarian tribes of northern Europe invaded their neighbors, causing chaotic conditions, civil disorder, feudalism, and religious turmoil. The common people were ruled by rich feudal lords who controlled them through ignorance, fear, superstition, and poverty. Christianity had overcome the pagan world in 313 A.D. when the Edict of Milan removed the last obstacles of the Christian church. It was through the establishment of the Christian monasteries and the establishment of a scriptorium which trained monks to copy large numbers of manuscripts and distribute them throughout the Christian world that learning was preserved. Monks were required not only to engage in prayer and academic endeavors, but to perform seven hours of manual labor each day which established manual labor in high regard. They learned to perform the manual labor tasks required to sustain life in the monastery by working as apprentices with more experienced monks and thus kept alive the practice of apprenticeship and the mysteries of the crafts through the dark ages. Unfortunately, early education focused on preparing selected people for service in the church while the majority of people remained illiterate (Barlow, 1967).

In the later middle ages around the eleventh century, people began to flock to towns where merchants engaged in retail and wholesale trade and in commerce with other towns and over the seas. Skilled craftworkers and artisans practiced their crafts and trades resulting in goods and services which they bartered to meet their needs. Merchants formed guilds to protect their economic interests and artisans soon organized into craft guilds to control the quality and quality of production, to keep down competition, and to provide thorough training for those who were accepted as apprentices to the guilds. Guilds of the middle ages were like fraternities and societies formed to further their mutual welfare. These guilds became an important part of the life of cities because they provided services to their members including protection for members, relief for widows of deceased guild members and for families of sick members, and general education and training for work. Education at the elementary level was provided for children of guild members by clergy paid for by guild treasuries while the indentured apprenticeship system provided sons of guild members with the knowledge and skills of the craft and other instruction including moral and religious training (Barlow, 1967).

Apprenticeship in the Guilds

Historical records do not describe much about organized apprenticeship which is considered the earliest form of vocational education, but other types of evidence suggest that apprenticeship was an important part of the educational programs of the early Egyptians, Babylonians, Hebrews, Greeks, and Romans. Apprenticeship was a necessity for the handicraft economy that characterized early cities and towns. Apprenticeship, like other forms of education, was not widely practiced during the dark ages but experienced much growth when it was practiced by the guilds which were formed in small towns and cities. As towns and cities grew, so did the need for workers who could meet the needs of household factories that began to feature products made through the division of labor. These workers were called apprentices, but they were often poorly trained and therefore produced less than quality goods. Guilds very early recognized the need to establish regulations to govern who could enter apprenticeship, how apprenticeships programs would be administered, and what standards of quality would be expected for finished goods.

Indentured apprenticeship programs were established by craft guilds to provide qualified workers for their crafts and to establish guidelines for quality apprenticeships. Some of the regulations for apprenticeships included: (a) forbidding one master from enticing another master's apprentice, (b) providing for written agreements between apprentice and master, (c) prescribing the minimum term of apprenticeship (usually seven years), (d) insuring that only qualified masters could offer indentured apprenticeship, (e) insuring that only apprentices that were approved by their master and members of the craft guild could practice the trade upon completion of the terms of apprenticeship, and (f) forbidding masters from taking more than two or three apprentices unless journeymen were employed to assist in teaching them (Roberts, 1971).

Masters were required to instruct the apprentice in the mysteries and skills of the craft and in citizenship, and to provide him with room, board, clothing, and a set of tools upon completion of the apprenticeship. The apprentice was bound to live with the master the required time, to serve diligently and obey reasonable commands, to remain unmarried, to refrain from immoral practices, and to not be absent from the master's service unless granted permission. Upon completion of the apprenticeship, the workers title was changed to journeyman and work for the master continued for several years for a small wage until the journeyman could attempt to earn the title of master by competing a piece of work known as a masterpiece. If work on the masterpiece was satisfactory to the master and guild committee, the journeyman could assume the title of master, and could begin to take on own apprentices and journeymen (Roberts, 1971).

Masters took on indentured apprentices which in many cases were like adopted sons for several important reasons beside providing service for the craft guild. Some of these reasons were: (a) to have a proxy son in the event that the master had no sons of his own, (b) to carry on the trade secrets of the craft when the master died, and (c) to have someone to honor the master when he died, to bury him and to pay any unpaid debts should they exist.

The guild and apprenticeship flourished in England up to 1562 when the Statute of Artificers was passed, transforming the control of apprenticeship from guilds and local municipalities to government control under a national apprenticeship system. Apprenticeship was established by the guilds as a means of controlling the quality and quality of goods and services. Guilds liked to keep the supply of workers and goods and service low and the prices high. The demand for goods and services was ever increasing and so were the prices. Towns were forced to bring in foreign artisans to meet demands for labor. Faced with competition, masters began to violate the regulations governing apprenticeship set by the guilds. Apprenticeship under the guilds began to get a bad name and by the middle of the eighteenth century, English guilds had all but lost their power to control industry and trade. The guilds served a valuable role in providing a form of general and vocational education for lower and middle-class people at a time in history when all types of education were at a low ebb (Roberts, 1971).

Renaissance and the Reformation

The Renaissance, which began in the fourteenth century and lasted for a period of 250 years, led to the revival of learning and culture for the few, featuring a rediscovery of the literature and culture of Greece and Rome. Attention was directed to the "here and now" instead of the "hereafter" that preoccupied people's minds during the Dark Ages. A new spirit of individuality and the dignity of man emerged and inspired an age of geographical and scientific discovery. During this period, firearms appeared in Europe and bell makers expanded their product line to include iron cannons and catapults. The sailing ship was transformed into galleons armed with hundreds of cannons resulting in the development of formidable naval power. Latin was the language of religion and learning, but common people could neither read nor understand that language and therefore were unable to profit from the education of the day. During the Renaissance, the process of printing was developed and became a common carrier of knowledge. Great works of sculpture and art was produced by Donatello, Cellini, Da Vinci, and Michelangelo. The use of the vernacular spread, and books written in the vernacular were flowing off new printing presses, offering an educational resource for the masses as soon as they learned to read (Barlow, 1967).

During the period of the Renaissance, the means of educating the lower and middle-class citizenry was the same as it had been for centuries–the father-son, master-apprentice system. The Renaissance revitalized commerce, fostered the development of small towns and cities, and led to the establishment of a burger (merchant) class and the establishment of merchant and arts and craft guilds. The common person was able to develop potential from indentured apprenticeship programs that were established by these guilds which provided elementary education as well as preparation for work training (Roberts, 1971).

The Reformation was essentially an extension of the Renaissance, but it did play an important role in speeding up social change in Germany and the Scandinavian countries. Martin Luther, an Augustinian monk and professor of theology at the University of Wittneberg, stirred up the leaders of the Roman Church over his Ninety-Five Theses challenging church doctrine and practices and became the leader for the German people for religious revolt. While Luther was interested chiefly in redirecting theology toward the Bible as the "authority" rather than church doctrine, he did favor a system of educating youth that involved participation in school several hours each day and the rest of the time spent at home learning some trade so that study and work could complement each other. It wasn't until the late 1800s that Luther's idea of combining academic and work education in the schools was attempted (Barlow, 1967).

EDUCATIONAL REFORMERS IN EUROPE

From the sixteenth to the nineteenth centuries traditional ideas about educational theory and practice based on humanism (the teaching of classical literature from a purely grammatical and linguistic point of view) were supplemented by the views and experiments of educational reformers. As literate use of the vernacular spread, the need for a different type of education for the common people received attention primarily from religious leaders. A brief presentation of these educational reformers and their ideas for including preparation for work and life in the schools of Europe follows. These presentation are based on the scholarly work of Charles A. Bennett (1926 and 1937) and Loyd P. Nelson (1981).

Martin Luther (1483-1546)

Martin Luther, a German clergyman, was critical of the type of education given in monastic and ecclesiastical schools and viewed boys in these schools as being in prison. He advocated that education should be a responsibility of the state and that rich and poor, boys and girls should be given the right kind of education, even made compulsory if necessary. He recommended the schooling should be only two hours per day, leaving the rest of the day for ordinary economic duties such as learning a trade at home. Luther advocated a curriculum of Latin, Greek and Hebrew, logic, mathematics, music, history, and science.

Rabelais (1483-1553)

Rabelais, a Roman Catholic priest, was an outspoken critic of the education offered by the church in France. He wrote two novels *Gargantua* and *Pantagruel* in which he presented his ideas of reform. He even advocated that one of his characters in his book should be given some strong medicine that would erase all the knowledge and perverse habits a young person developed in the schools of his day. Rabelais maintained that the abstract and remote could better be attained through the concrete and near at hand. He suggested that students could learn and retain school subjects such as mathematics effectively through games, recreation, and to a lesser degree, manual labor. He advocated that knowledge of handicrafts and industries could be gained by students only through observation. His ideas of learning through natural events and situations of life would be further developed by educational reformers centuries later.

Richard Mulcaster (1531-1611)

Richard Mulcaster was the head master of the Merchant Taylor's School in England. He believed that the hand, ear, and eye were the greatest instruments for receiving learning. He wanted all children to learn to read and write, but was more interested in developing the special abilities of the few. He is believed to be the first to make drawing one of the fundamental studies of the school. With this early beginning, drawing soon came to be an accepted practical course in a growing number of European schools.

Francis Bacon (1561-1626)

Francis Bacon was one of the first educational leaders to use the term "manual arts" in his discussions of how learning could be improved by studying nature and making observations and experiments of concrete, common objects and real world experiences. He became one of the leaders of the realism philosophy.

John Amos Comenius (1592-1670)

In the early 1600s, the educational philosophy of humanism was being replaced by sense-realism which emphasized the teaching of natural phenomena and social institutions. While Francis Bacon was credited for spearheading the realism movement, it was John Amos Comenius who was one of the early leaders of the sense-realism movement which featured the following tenets concerning education:

1. Everything should be taught according to the course of nature.
2. Only one thing of a kind should be taught at one time.
3. Repetition reinforces learning, therefore repeat often.
4. Everything should be taught in the mother tongue first.
5. Teaching should be done without violence; pupils must not fear the teacher.
6. No learning should be done by rote.
7. There should be uniformity in teaching time.
8. The object should be taught first, then the characteristics of the object.
9. All learning should be accomplished through experiences and investigation.

Comenius spent many years developing his pansophic ideas about education–ideas about the organization of all knowledge with educational methods. His educational innovations spread throughout Europe and eventually the world. Comenius's general goals for education were:

1. Simplify content and move gradually to the complex.
2. Teach words by using things.
3. Teach things through the use of words.

He wrote the first illustrated textbook, *Orbis Pictus* in which elementary children were presented with a picture whose parts were numbered and referred to in the text. He later wrote a language textbook, *Janus* in which he attempted to place words carefully in sentences in such a way as to bring significance and understanding to the reader.

Why was Comenius and his educational ideas important to the development of all education and particularly occupational education? It was Comenius who championed the view that all of the senses should be applied to the learning process. He perpetuated the idea that words could be understood when they were linked to objects familiar to learners. In so doing, he introduced a practical method of education. Secondly, Comenius, through his pansophic writings, attempted to organize into an integrated whole all segments of knowledge which were part of the culture of his time. Today, two of the important thrusts of educational reform are to involve learners in authentic learning experiences which require the use of all senses and to develop integrated curricula and teaching methods that bring learning topic into completeness or "wholes" to promote understanding.

Comenius also believed that both girls and boys should receive formal schooling and he proposed a system of education that had been proposed much earlier by the Romans that included (1) an infant school in every home for children up to six years of age, (2) a vernacular school, or public elementary school, in every community for children six to twelve years of age, (3) a gymnasium, or secondary school, in every province, for selected students from twelve to eighteen years of age, and (4) a university in every kingdom or large province, for young men who could continue their education beyond the age of eighteen.

In his infant school, play was utilized as the major method of learning, an idea that Froebel probably borrowed years later for his kindergartens. In the later years of the infant school, children would utilize drawing and writing as a major focus of learning. In the vernacular school students would: (1) learn to read in their mother-tongue, (2) write with accuracy, speed, and confidence in accordance with the rules of the grammar of the mother-tongue, (3) count, (4) measure, (5) sing, (6) learn by heart many psalms and hymns, (7) know the Catechisms and many Bible stories and verses, (8) learn the principles of morality, (9) learn something of economics and politics, (10) learn general history, (11) learn geography, and (12) learn the most important principles of the mechanical arts so that they would not be ignorant of the world around them and so that what they learned may be useful in future live should they need to apply it. Children would attend two hours of school in the morning and two hours after midday. The remaining hours were to be spent at home doing domestic work or in some form of recreation.

Comenius has been called the "father of modern pedagogy" because of his early formulation of principles and methods as well as school structure that would become common in schools years later.

Samuel Hartlib (1600-1670)

Samuel Hartlib was a wealthy English merchant who devoted much of his resources and energy to any question or project promising social improvement. For example, he was the first to conceive the plan for erecting an agricultural college in England. Another scheme of Hartlib's was an "office of address" which was to be useful in helping the poor find employment and to the employers in finding people willing to learn and work. This idea became the forerunner of the government bureaus of education and labor of the present day and gave birth to the concept of a local employment service. Hartlib had a number of distinguished friends that he encouraged to write out their ideals of education, including John Dury, the Puritan preacher; John Milton, the poet; John Evelyn, writer on forestry and gardening; Hezekiah Woodworth, interested in the education of detectives; and Sir William Petty, statistician, political economist, and professor of anatomy at Oxford. These scholars advocated the teaching of things rather than word; facts of nature and of life; real science of every possible kind; and persistent training in virtuous and noble sentiment. Sir William Petty advocated the publishing of great cyclopedias of the arts and sciences and to bring together scholars from throughout Europe to hasten the advancement of learning through discovery, and through more effective methods of education. He also proposed the establishment of a guild for tradeworkers and a literary workhouse for children. Perhaps the most significant idea Petty had was to recommend that industrial education be made an integral part of the school.

Royal Society of London (1648)

The Royal Society of London was founded by a group of famous scholars of that day such as Robert Boyle, chemist and Sir William Petty, to expand and advance realism with its emphasis on methods of research by observation, comparison, and experiment. They even recognized how the method of experiment would advance the manual arts and provide a better method of education. Joseph Moxon, a member of the Society, put together fourteen writings on the unity of the manual arts and the natural sciences into one volume entitled *Mechanic Exercises or the Doctrine of Handy Works*.

The establishing of the Society marked the opening of a great age of scientific discovery in England. For example, Sir Isaac Newton had discovered the law of gravitation and Robert Boyle had invented the air pump. Experimental chemistry, mineralogy, zoology, and botany had been established among the sciences.

John Locke (1642-1727)

John Locke, an English Physician and a member of the Royal Society, became one of the chief proponents of the idea that education should fit a boy for practical life, whether it be a trade or a profession. He advocated a dual system of practical training with poor children to receive occupational training and wealthy children to receive training in management and a form of recreation. In 1697, he advocated a system of working schools for all pauper children between three and fourteen years of age, where they would be taught selected trades. His pedagogy insisted on individual exercise in habits of practical usefulness, and habits of thinking and forming tested judgments as more important educationally than in the established subjects of the schools of his time.

Locke advocated learning the mechanical trades because (a) they afforded good physical exercise, (b) the skills gained were worth having, and (c) they provided diversions or recreations. Locke's *Essays on Human Understanding* is regarded as the "corner-stone of modern empirical psychology."

August Hermann Francke (1663-1727)

August Hermann Francke, a professor of oriental languages and a German pastor, was the founder of a school for poor children, a Latin school for the well-to-do, a seminary for training teachers, and a publishing house especially to print inexpensive copies of the Bible. This institution became the educational center for the Pietist Movement in the Lutheran Church that spread over Germany. He emphasized religious instruction for his students, but he also gave instruction in several manual arts. He felt that children should not work for the making of as many objects as possible for economic reasons, but they should work for their own development. Even the well-to-do children in the Latin school received instruction in painting and handwork primarily as a means of preventing idleness and childish amusements.

Johann Hecker (1707-1768)

One of the teachers in Francke's school, Johann Hecker, recognized the need to expand on Francke's school curriculum and methods of instruction, giving emphasis to science, art, and the trades and industries in a new type of secondary school. This new "realschule" was established in Berlin in 1747 with the purpose of "not teaching mere words, but to teach students realities, explanations being made to them from nature, from models and plans, and of subjects calculated to be useful in after life." The school curriculum included drawing, mathematics, science, history, modern languages and Latin, and a number of manual arts, thus began the non-classical secondary school curriculum in Germany.

Jean Jacques Rousseau (1712-1778)

Jean Jacques Rousseau was born in Geneva, Switzerland. His mother died when he was born and his aunt failed to give him adequate guidance when he was maturing. He lived a restless and unwholesome life, trying a variety of different jobs, until he was 38 years of age. He entered and won a contest for the best dissertation on the subject "*Whether the progress of the sciences and of letters has tended to corrupt or to elevate morals.*" He recognized his talent for thoughtful writing and wrote two other highly controversial books, *The Social Contract* and *Emile*. These two books stirred up so much hatred among Frenchmen that he was forced to leave France and go first to Switzerland and then to England.

In his educational novel *Emile*, Rousseau spoke out against the educational system of France and its classical teaching methods, and recommended that much of education should be taught through nature study and the manual arts. He believed that experience was the best teacher and would have everything possible taught by actions, and say only what could not be done. He stated that "Emile would learn more in one hour of manual training, than in a whole day of verbal instruction." His purpose in having Emile learn a trade was not to earn his living by it, but as a vital part of the process of his education. He advocated that manual arts could serve as a means of mental training and thus showed the way to a new era in education.

Johann Heinrich Pestalozzi (1746-1827)

Johann Heinrich Pestalozzi was born in Zurich, Switzerland where he attended school under the tutelage of teachers who were on the cutting edge of educational controversies and political issues. In this environment, he became interested in readings on social and educational reform. He encountered the writing of Rousseau (*Emile*), a classic work describing the need for reform in the school era of his time. The young Pestallozi chose to devote his career to education with the hope of improving the plight of the poor. Pestalozzi's writing on educational methods became recognized throughout the European continent and were later transported to America by those who had contact with him.

Pestalozzi lived in the era of the early industrial revolution when steam power began to be applied to the production of goods, factories and factory towns sprang up, bringing with them progress on the one hand and devastating outcomes on the other. Some people became wealthy while others became virtual slaves to the new work system. Many worked long hours in crowded, often unsanitary conditions. People became a producer of things and their social well-being became secondary to the production of marketable goods.

Pestalozzi developed a keen interest in industrial education but deplored education that only prepared a person for one factory skill. He favored a type of work preparation that involved a wider range of human education. It was important to him that workers maintain their dignity and humanity rather than simply becoming a producer of goods or the deliver of services related to the materialism of the times. The debate continues even to this day as to whether work preparation education should be specialized in one area or whether it should involve a wider exposure to a variety of areas to prepare more flexible workers.

Pestallozi is generally given credit for first applying psychology to the learning process. He developed a number of educational principles that have common acceptance today. These are:

1. Children are not mere objects onto which adults might impose their image, rather they are persons with personality and intelligence. The purpose of education is to provide stimulation necessary for the development of potential.
2. Education must be sensitive to the nature of the child, taking into account the stage of development of the person. Materials to be learned must be chosen based on the ability and level of the child.
3. Education must be child-centered, and the teacher needs to gain insight into the way the child's mind works and develops. Ideally, teachers should learn along with children.
4. Facts and experiences should be grouped in proper order from the most simple to most difficult and the child should complete the elementary before proceeding to new concepts.
5. Mental training should be the major emphasis rather than a mere knowledge of facts.
6. Teachers should avoid harshness and show love and concern for the child, but discipline to the task is essential to learning.
7. Education should develop mental, moral, and practical potential of the child.

Pestalozzi's method of instruction was characterized by the use of objects, those that came from the natural environment and made objects. He believed that perception was improved by the use of objects, a principle that continues even today. It was this principle that was basic to manual training.

Pestalozzi's most recognized educational writing was in his novel, *Leonard and Gertrude* which conveyed the message that correction of social plight could be found in schools that based instruction on nature, love, and sound pedagogy.

Pestalozzi's ideas came to America through Joseph Neef, one of his students, who first established a school in Philadelphia and later became part of the social experiment of William Maclure and Robert Owens in New Harmony, Indiana.

Pestalozzi's methods and contributions to pedagogy grew out of the following: (a) his intense desire to improve the conditions of the poor in Switzerland, (b) his firm belief that such improvement, to be permanent, must come through education, (c) his stated opinion that the schools should be in closest connection with and prepare for the life of the home instead of leading away from it, (d) his interest in Rousseau's doctrine of education according to nature, (e) his early conviction that, under favorable conditions, the manual labor of children could be utilized to pay for their education, and (f) his repeated successful use of objects and manual labor, both skilled and unskilled, as a means in teaching the traditional school subjects. Pestalozzi emphasized that objects as well as language should be analyzed and placed in order from simple to complex to facilitate learning. The concept of manual labor developed by Pestallozi would later become the basis for the manual labor movement in America.

Johann Herbart (1776-1841)

Johann Herbart, one of the world's great educational philosophers and developer of Herbartian psychology, served as a private tutor for three wealthy students enrolled in Pestalozzi's School at Hofwyl. He was impressed with Pestallozi's methods of instruction and the system of manual arts training which he saw primarily as a means of teaching some of the other school subjects and as a means of discipline. While he did not see all occupations as being instructive, he did recommend that all youth learn to use the recognized tools of the carpenter as well as the rule and compass. He believed that elementary schools should have workshops but they should not be actual technical schools. He recommended that all students should learn to use their hands.

Freidrich Froebel (1783-1852)

Fredrick Froebel was born in Germany to a pastor and his wife in 1782. His mother died when he was a baby and his father and four brothers raised him until his father remarried. His stepmother rejected him as he grew older and he was taken into the home of his uncle who cared for him and paid for his education. Froebel became apprenticed to a forester for two years where he learned to love nature and expand his knowledge of plant life. He was a deeply religious young man who constantly sought to make connections between facts and events and to understand the harmony and unity that he believed God had intended for the universe. Froebel joined his brother in studies at the University of Jena where he studied life sciences and mathematics. While still in his early twenties, he returned to the vocation of forestry and surveying. He soon decided to go to Frankford to study architecture, but instead became a teacher. He was influenced by the invitation of one of Pestallozi's deciples, a man named Gruner. Before starting to teach at the Frankford Model School, Froebel visited Pestallozi's Institute at Yverdun in Switzerland for two week where he observed the well-know methods of the master and his assistants. Froebel taught at Frankford for a number of years, became a tutor for three wealthy students, and joined these students in study back at Pestallozi's Institute in Yverdun.

During his second stay at Yverdun, Froebel continued to emphasize unity and interconnection as the basic tenet of his educational process and realized the differences he had with Pestallozi's approach. To him, the achievement of unity and interconnection had to involve three elements: reception, reflection, and student response in the form of some type of creative production activity. He believed that Pestallozi emphasized the first element, reception, and did not emphasize the other two enough. Both of these educators used objects as the vehicle for learning, but Froebel though that reception and reflection were interrelated, with understanding coming only when learners made application of what was perceived in the form of some self-activity. He classified the powers of a child in terms of learning components of receptive, reflective, and executive. Receptive powers accumulate knowledge, reflective power classifies knowledge and prepares it for use and the executive powers apply it.

After serving in the military and completing additional study at the University of Gottingen, Froebel published his views on unity and other educational ideas in his book, *The Education of Man* in 1826 which became a classic throughout the world.

Froebel made manual training an important part of his educational method. Like Pestallozi, he believed that manual training should be broad in scope, rather than focused on narrow preparation for some factory skill. He even recommended that all people should have the opportunity to take manual training as part of the self-activity of his plan. He viewed the product developed in the learning experience merely a symbol, with the important product being the learner himself.

Froebel proposed schooling that devoted the forenoon to instruction in the current subjects of school study, and the afternoon to work in the field, the garden, the forest, and in and around the house. He recommended woodworking; weaving; binding; caring for gardens, orchards and fields; caring for animals; preparation of artistic materials; making objects from clay; drawing and painting; and many other diverse subjects.

Froebel reinforced many of the educational ideas and methods of Comenius and Pestallozi and added some of his own, thus extending and enhancing the foundation for a more practical education for the students of his time and future students. His practices led to a wide diversity of mediums in the construction of objects and the selection of these activities according to the ability and interest level of children. He has been called the father of the modern day kindergarten. His educational methods had a profound effect on Cygnaeus, an educator from Finland, who introduced sloyd (woodwork) as an obligatory form of instruction in the schools of his country.

Otto A. Salomon (1874-1907)

Otto Salomon is know as the father of the sloyd system of education, of which he was the main leader in Sweden from 1874 until his death in 1907. It was through his writings, public lectures and teachings in one of the earliest known teacher education institutions that Salomon became the professor of sloyd. A more detailed account of this educational movement is presented here because it later found its way to America during the manual training movement.

Sloyd was a system consisting mainly of woodworking that was introduced into elementary schools to help children develop their mental and physical powers. It was to teach general dexterity of hand and to instill a general love of work. It promoted a respect for rough, honest bodily labor; training in habits of order, exactness, cleanliness, and neatness; developing the habits of attention, industry, and perseverance; developing physical powers; and training the eye and sense of form.

Sloyd grew out of the home industries of Sweden. Because of the geographic location of Sweden, the winters were very dark and long, requiring many hours indoors. It was during these long winters that families worked together to produce implements and objects that they needed for themselves and that could be traded for other objects they needed for survival. Several families would band together to make many different objects that would be needed to get them through the next year, thus promoting skill training but also a form of social interaction that included folk music and dancing along with elaborate tables of food that gave birth to the smorgasbords of today.

Sloyd as home industries began to decline around the middle of the nineteenth century in direct proportion to the increasing progress of factory systems that made available the equipment and supplies needed in rural areas of the country that formerly had to be made by hand. At first, most of the factory system output was military equipment, but as the country disengaged itself from wars, factory output was converted to meeting the domestic needs of the people.

Like other countries in the early and middle 1800s, there were lots of social and economic problems. The Swedes were always known for their appetite for alcoholic beverages and many of them were moved to drunkenness and suffered its adverse social effects. At this time, there was dissatisfaction with the class-structured legislative body and people were rebelling against the dominance of the state-church in favor of forming independent churches. The educational structure that was well organized under the state-church system began to crumble, with many parishes not having an elementary school. In 1842, school reform occurred with the Riksdag (government) passing laws funding a school in every diocese for the training of teachers, and mandating that there should be at least one qualified teacher and school board in each parish.

Some Swedish leaders felt that a restoration of sloyd would be valuable as a means of improving both the economic and moral status of national life. They realized that there was little chance of reviving the home industries of earlier years. Rather, sloyd schools were established and funded by private societies, provincial councils, and individuals. The main purpose of sloyd schools was to prepare students for employment and a constructive life. Private sloyd schools started in the 1840s, and it wasn't until 1872 that they received financial support from government.

Salomon's uncle, August Abrahamson who was a wealthy Gothenburg merchant, purchased Naas, a large estate and established a sloyd school for peasant youngsters in 1872. Otto Salomon was put in charge of this school which differed from other sloyd schools of the time because it had as its main purpose the enhancement of the student's general education rather than being a trade school. Boys were the first students, but a few years later girls were added. The curriculum included arithmetic, Swedish, geography, and drawing, with seven out of every ten hours devoted to sloyd instruction. In 1874, sloyd Teachers Seminary was established with the purpose of preparing people to teach in the independent sloyd schools or in the elementary schools of Sweden. At first, the teacher training was a full-year in length, but the time was shortened after 1882. Only those committed to teaching sloyd were admitted, and their tuition and fees were waived leaving only a modest amount to be paid by the participant for room and board.

Swedish born Gustaf Larson was one of the last members of the full one-year class and later emigrated to the United States where he introduced sloyd methods into the manual training movement in America. Larson wrote that his teacher education curriculum included mathematics, natural science, pedagogies, psychology, school methods, mechanical drawing, Swedish, and physics, along with the sloyd areas of carpentry, turning, carving, and forging. He indicated that instruction was fifty-five contact hours per week. Teachers and administrators came from all over the world to study sloyd at the sloyd Teachers Seminary, thus spreading sloyd methods to many countries. The precedent for preparing teachers rather than employing craftworkers from industry to teach occupational education took root in Sweden.

Aim of Instruction

At the elementary level, sloyd was intended to prepare students indirectly for life with a chief aim to give students formal instruction to develop their mental powers and a secondary purpose to develop dexterity of hand. It was intended to instill a taste and love for work in general; inspiring respect for rough, honest bodily labor; training in habits of order, exactness, cleanliness and neatness; developing the habits of attention, industry and perservance; promoting the development of physical powers; and training the eye in sense and form.

General Instructional Principles

Attendance was voluntary, therefore work was to meet the following conditions. Work must:

1. Be useful.
2. Not require fatiguing preparatory exercises in tool usage.
3. Provide for variety.
4. Be capable of being done by students themselves.
5. Be real work, not play.
6. Not be nick-knacks (articles of luxury).
7. Become the property of students when completed.
8. Correspond to the capabilities of students.
9. Be capable of being completed with exactness.
10. Exemplify neatness and cleanliness.
11. Involve and emphasize thinking powers and not be solely mechanical.
12. Strengthen and develop bodily powers.
13. Assist in developing sense of form.
14. Allow the use of numerous manipulations and usage of various tools.

Teachers

Instruction must be given by trained teachers rather than just a craftworker, and if possible, by the same teacher who instructs in intellectual subjects. Teachers are to introduce, instruct, and monitor the work but are to avoid directly doing the work for students.

Age of Students

Students should have reached the stage of development that usually occurs at age eleven.

continued . . .

. . . continued

Areas of Instruction

Instruction in sloyd should be confined to one branch or craft/trade area because a sufficient number of subjects are already taught in school and every branch of sloyd is a subject in itself. In addition, the time devoted to this work is limited and different kinds of work may cause the student's interest to be diverted. For students age eleven, wood sloyd is the most suitable which includes carpentry, turning, and wood carving. Sloyd carpentry differs from trade carpentry in the following ways: (1) types of objects constructed, with objects usually smaller than those constructed in the trade, (2) tools used in sloyd are not as diverse as those used in the trade, with the most important tool being the sloyd knife, (3) method of work employed where the student performs all the work in sloyd, whereas in the trade a division of labor is used. Turning was usually considered a separate branch of sloyd and therefore taught separately.

Number of Students

Sloyd instruction works best with individual instruction, therefore the number of students taught by one instructor should be limited.

Models

Models should be used rather than drawings to make the instruction more intuitive. The form is to be sketched either directly on the wood stock by placing the model on the wood piece or by means of a diagram with ruler and compass on the wood.

Choice of Models

There were guidelines regarding the type of models to be used in sloyd instruction, including the following:

1. All objects of luxury are to be avoided.
2. Objects made are to be capable of being used at home.
3. Objects should be of the type that can be completed by the student without direct instructor help.
4. Objects should be made entirely of wood.
5. The work is not to be polished.
6. As little material as possible should be used.
7. Both hard and soft woods are to be used sparingly.
8. Turnery and carvings are to be used sparingly.
9. Models are to develop the student's sense of form and beauty, thus requiring examples of form such as spoons, labels, and other curved objects.
10. A series of models need to be selected to teach students the use of necessary tools and to know and carry out all the most important manipulations connected with woodworking.

One of the best descriptions of Swedish sloyd was developed by the school at Naas and was published in 1888. An edited description of this publication follows (Nelson, 1981).

Saloman developed his system of sloyd by incorporating the ideas and works of six earlier educators including Comenius, Pestalozzi, Cygnaeus, and Froebel. He studied under Cygnaeus of Finland and borrowed heavily Cygnaeus's views that physical education and manual training are essential parts of a quality school curriculum. Neither of them felt that school was an appropriate place to train for a trade.

Victor Della Voss (1829-1890)

Victor Della Voss was born in Russia, completed the gymnasium school, and continued his higher education at Moscow University where he completed the candidate's (Masters) degree from the department of natural science of the school of physics and mathematics. He taught mathematical sciences in his former secondary school and later became a lecturer in mathematics in the Lyceum's University courses. While there, he co-authored a physics textbook, studied manufacturing facilities and techniques abroad, and also became familiar with teaching methods in the technical schools of Europe. He served as professor and director of the Imperial Technical School of Moscow. He was instrumental in changing the long-standing trade school into a higher education institution. During the next few years, Della Voss and his staff developed a new system of industrial education which became known widely as the "Russian System" of manual training.

The schools of earlier leaders in manual training such as Comenius, Pestalozzi, Froebel, and Salomon emphasized manual training instruction as part of the students' general education and, to much less of a degree, acknowledged preparation for a livelihood. Victor Della Voss and his associates at the Imperial Technical School of Moscow organized instruction principally with a vocational preparation outcome in mind. Its primary mission was the preparation of mechanical constructors, mechanical engineers, technical engineers, civil engineers, drafters, supervisors, and chemist. The institute was organized into three divisions: special, general, and preparatory and featured high level instruction in each area. The course of instruction was six years in length. Entrance into the school was by examination only, requiring a good educational background that emphasized mathematics and the sciences.

Della Voss and his associates were committed to the belief that well-prepared technicians and engineers should have practical hands-on experience as well as technical knowledge. To gain practical training experience, he required students to first work in the large mechanical shops that were part of his institute where they were instructed by technologists or specialists in their technical areas. Students received valuable hands-on instruction in these shops, but Della Voss believed that students should be prepared in an intermediate type of instruction before entering the production-oriented shop. In 1868, he established separate school instructional shops for each technical area of study offered in the institute.

This new type of workshop instructional setting required a new method of teaching the mechanical arts. Della Voss set four requirements for instructional methods: (1) competency had to be attained in the least amount of time, (2) supervision of student work had to be improved, taking into account the gradual advancement of student achievement, (3) the study of practical work must provide for sound, systematic acquisition of knowledge, and (4) the method of instruction used must facilitate the demonstration of student progress. Instructional methods were developed for the technical areas of turning, carpentry, fitting, and forging.

A new system of instruction was developed to teach the fundamentals of the mechanical arts in the following manner: (1) in the least possible time, (2) in a way that would allow giving instruction to a large group of students at one time, (3) by a method that would integrate general education subjects with vocational content, and (4) in a way that enabled teachers to determine the progress of any student on demand. The course content was derived from a thorough analysis of each mechanical art taught and a series of graded exercises ranging from simple to complex. Unlike sloyd, that emphasized constructing useful objects that students could take home, the exercise or work sample in the Russian system was not necessarily a complete or useful object and was usually discarded when completed by the student.

Principles of the Russian System

The basic principles of the Russian System of instruction were:

1. Each mechanical area of work (joinery, woodturning, blacksmithing, locksmithing, etc.) was taught in a separate shop.
2. Each shop was equipped with as many workplaces and sets of tools as there were student slots so that all students could receive instruction at the same time.
3. The courses of models were arranged according to increasing difficulty of the exercises involved and were delivered by the instructor in sequence.
4. All models were made from drawings and each student was provided with one mounted on cardboard and varnished to keep them clean.
5. Drawings were made by students in the class, for elementary drawing under the direction of a drawing teacher who received details for the drawing from the shop instructor.
6. Students must complete the model according to an established skill standard before beginning another one.

7. Early exercises were accepted partially correct but later exercises had to be to exact dimension, therefore the same marks given to students at different periods of the course are relative to the instructional sequence and rigor of the work.
8. Every teacher must be more knowledgeable of his specialty than is necessary to merely perform the exercises in the form of demonstrations; and teachers must keep in constant practice so they serve as examples of perfection to students.

Courses of Instruction

Each course was divided into three successive periods. In the first period, students were given the names of tools, told how to care for them, and shown how to use them. They were also taught the important properties of the materials to be used and given fundamental methods of holding and using tools. In the second period, students were taught to combine the exercises of the first period to make a variety of joints or perform a variety of basic operations involving tool usage in the mechanical art field. In the third period, students made the entire sub-assembly of some machine or object and acquired an extended practical knowledge of materials. During the course, students were taught how to care for their tools and as much useful knowledge as possible that they would need later on when employed.

Victor Della Voss developed an instructional methodology that could be used to teach a number of individuals the knowledge and skills required to enter mechanical trades. His system of instruction would become the answer to instructional methodology for manual training in the United States and other countries. It would have a profound impact on vocational education continuing even to today.

INDUSTRIAL CIVILIZATION

As the 17th century ended, Europe became the provincial capital of the world. The New World had been explored and commerce with the East grew increasingly profitable. European cultural life flourished as a result of the printed word and the widening interest in technology and invention. Iron production was rapidly increasing, requiring new and deeper mines to obtain ore and wood was in great demand for ship building and a fuel source for making iron. The demands for wood was deforesting Europe, and deep mines had problems with ground water. In 1709, ironmaster Abraham Darvy succeeded in making iron in a blast furnace using coal and later coke made from coal. Thomas Newcomen invented the steam engine, to drive the pumps to control ground water in the minds. These two inventions, the making of iron from coke and the steam engine spurred other industrial development and Europe was well on its way to the industrial revolution (*Academic American Encyclopedia*, 1994).

In the 1760s, James Watt made major improvements to Newcomen's steam engine which made it safer and more efficient. John Wilkinson designed a boring machine to make better steam engines. Improvements were made in spinning and weaving machinery that expanded the textile industry. New methods of farming and the mechanization of farm tools changed the farming industry. Iron began to be used more in buildings and bridges that were previously built out of stone. Steam-powered boats and steam locomotives solved the problems of transporting goods to and from manufacturing centers (*Academic American Encyclopedia*, 1994).

Power Age

The 1800s marked the beginning of the power age of machine tools. The basic machine tools invented in the 1800s were capable of producing the parts from which other machines and tools could be made. These machines included the screw cutting lathe (1800), planer (1817), milling machine (1818), drill press (1840), band saw (1853), grinder (1880), and first micrometer and master gage blocks (1877). Highly-skilled workers produced machines that could be operated by skilled and semi-skilled workers to produce products needed by a rapidly growing industrial society. A quote from Henry Ward Beecher clarified the importance of tools and machines. "A tool is but the extension of man's hand and a machine is but a complex tool. And he that invents a machine augments the power of a man and the well-being of mankind." Tools combined with natural resources and human energy are the common elements of all production. Armed with tools and machines, one individual after another began to invent new machines and products that ushered in the industrial civilization and has led to the technological world we live in today (Wilkie, 1977).

The industrial revolution which began in Great Britain spread to the rest of Western Europe and North America, and everywhere created the need for skilled workers to produce the goods required of a growing world population. The age old apprenticeship method, now under government control, could not meet the demand for trained workers and industrial and government leaders began to look to schools for preparing entry level workers.

This limited overview of formal education in Europe was presented to inform the reader that the foundations of the American educational system were built on the type of education that had evolved in Europe. This is particularly true for education of a practical nature which reflected educational ideas like apprenticeship, manual labor, arts and crafts, sloyd and the Russian system of manual training. Components of these different types of work training are found in our modern work-preparation programs. Some of the reasons that European educational reformers advocated the inclusion of practical subjects into schools included: (a) a meaningful form of exercise, (b) a method of enhancing instruction in other subjects, (c) a means of financing educational effort through the labor of students, (d) a means of keeping youth busy so they would not be mischievous, and (e) a means of developing the mind through applications of the hand. The Russian system of manual training was the only European educational system designed to produce a skilled worker.

SELF ASSESSMENT

1. What was the earliest form of education?
2. What is indentured apprenticeship and what functions did it serve?
3. What was education for work like in the early paleolithic and neolithic periods of history?
4. How did work change in the period called the agricultural civilization?
5. How did work and preparation for work change during the Bronze Age?
6. What was education like during the Iron Age and the great Greek Civilization?
7. How were Roman youth educated and what was the educational system for the common person?
8. During the Middle Ages, how did the monks preserve education for work?
9. What type of apprenticeship was established by guilds and why were they formed?
10. Why did masters adopt apprentices?
11. What was the Renaissance and Reformation?
12. What type of education did Martin Luther favor?
13. What type of education did Rabelias favor?
14. What practical arts subject was introduced by Richard Mulcaster?
15. What was the realism philosophy of Francis Bacon?
16. What were the major educational goals and tenets of John Comenius?
17. What types of educational system did Comenius propose?
18. What were the two major ideas proposed by Samuel Hartlib that contributed to education for work?

continued . . .

. . . continued

19. How did the Royal Society of London contribute to the manual arts?

20. What was John Locke's ideas regarding education for work?

21. What type of education did August Francke advocate for German youth?

22. What type of school did Johann Hecker establish in Berlin?

23. What method of education did Jean Rousseau favor?

24. What were some of the educational principles and methods of instruction of Johann Pestallozi?

25. What type of education did Freidrich Froebel favor and what type of education did he establish which continues today?

26. What was the Swedish sloyd system of education championed by Otto Salomon?

27. What were the general instructional principles of sloyd?

28. What was the Russian system of manual training created by Victor Della Voss?

29. What were the principles of the Russian system and how did these principles affect manual training in America?

30. How did the industrial civilization affect work and preparation for work?

31. What advancements occurred in the Power Age that changed our industrial and technological world forever?

ASSOCIATED ACTIVITIES

1. Assist in organizing a collection of historical publications regarding vocational education that can be placed in the school library or learning resource center so vocational students and faculty can discover the rich history of vocational education.

2. Involve the vocational student organization in your occupational area in preparing a brief historical paper on their program area as part of National Vocational Education Week which occurs in February of each year.

3. Encourage students to make reports on articles dealing with vocational and technical education that are contained in the *Vocational Education Journal* and a number of other publications.

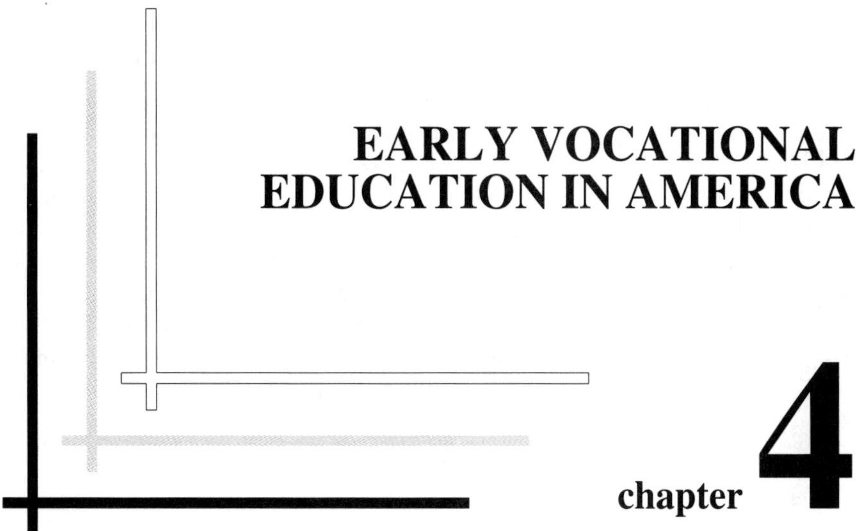

EARLY VOCATIONAL EDUCATION IN AMERICA

chapter 4

INTRODUCTION

The foundations of the American educational system were built on the types of education that had evolved in Europe. In colonial America the responsibility of providing education, both basic and vocational, fell on the extended family with some instruction in reading and writing provided by the church. For over 150 years colonial America used an American version of apprenticeship as the chief source of education and training for the masses, but as the factory system of production developed, the interest in apprenticeship declined. New systems of education and training were surfacing in a progressive America that relegated apprenticeship to serving a small number of people in specific occupational areas. Some of these new educational thrusts included the beginnings of Universal Education, Educational efforts for adults – Mechanics Institute Movement and American Lyceum Movement, Manual Labor Movement, Trade School Movement, Corporate Schools, Educational Reforms in the Common School, Manual Training Movement, Beginnings of the Comprehensive High School, American Sloyd, Arts and Craft Movement, Correspondence Schools, Manual Arts, and Industrial Arts. At the turn of the century, the impact of industrialism was being felt in every phase of life. America had become the world's industrial giant and even though many skilled workers were coming to America through immigration, American industry needed additional skilled workers. These industrial leaders became politically active to pressure state and federal leaders to consider some additional form of work preparation programs besides the fundamental contributions made by practical arts programs in some American schools. Two significant events, the findings of the Douglas Commission released in 1906 and the formation and work of the National Society for the Promotion of Industrial Education, paved the way for the passage of the Smith-Hughes Act of 1917 which provided federal funds for vocational education and established the federal-state-local cooperative effort of providing vocational education in the public schools of America. The educational philosophies of John Dewey and Charles Prosser provided the foundations for the Smith-Hughes Act of 1917. Both philosophies promoted the view that education should become more democratic and practical, but they differed on how to accomplish these outcomes. The contributions of these two leaders were infused into early vocational education legislation and practice and continue to shape vocational and applied technology education today.

OBJECTIVES

After completing this chapter the reader should be able to:

1. Describe education in colonial America.
2. Describe American apprenticeship.
3. Discuss the beginnings of universal education in America.
4. Describe the early educational efforts of adults including the mechanics' institute, American Lyceum, and manual labor movements.
5. Describe early American technical schools, trade schools, and corporate schools.
6. Identify and describe the three major educational reform movements in the common school.
7. Discuss the manual training movement in America.
8. Discuss the American Sloyd System of Education.
9. Discuss the arts and crafts movement in America and the concept of manual arts.
10. Discuss the development of industrial arts and how this program operates.
11. Describe the status of agriculture, home economics, and business education prior to 1917.
12. Discuss the status of practical arts programs in 1900.

13. Discuss the impact of the Douglas Commission on the vocational education movement.

14. Discuss the impact of the National Society for the Promotion of Industrial Education and the Commission for National Aid to Vocational Education on passage of the Smith-Hughes Act.

15. Compare and contrast the educational philosophies of John Dewey and Charles Prosser.

EARLY VOCATIONAL EDUCATION IN AMERICA

Education in the colonies fell chiefly to the church and family, which shouldered the responsibility of teaching children how to read and participate in church services. In addition, families served as the center for apprenticeship training. Most families were engaged in agriculture or in trades such as blacksmithing, carpenter, leather tanning, spinning, etc., and imparted their skills through the father-son, mother-daughter informal apprenticeship system. Wealthy families established private schools for their children or hired tutors, and some even sent their children to Europe for formal schooling. Churches provided elementary education in reading and writing along with church doctrine so that they could read and understand the Bible and church theology. But for many youth, the amount of elementary education they received from their parents was limited because many parents were illiterate and therefore could only provide training in the things required to provide sustenance for the family. From the beginning, colonists supported the idea of literacy for their children, first as a means of purifying the soul, and later to promote social equality through the belief that literacy was the right of all people (Barlow, 1976).

American Apprenticeship

The early colonists imported the concept of apprenticeship to America and adjusted the concept to meet their needs. Two forms of apprenticeship emerged, voluntary and involuntary or compulsory. Voluntary apprenticeship was the practice of an individual binding one's self to a master to learn a trade or craft of one's own free will. Involuntary or compulsory apprenticeship provided a means of taking care of poor children and orphans where a master became responsible for meeting their personal and occupation needs. In general, apprenticeship in colonial America followed the traditions of Europe but town governments controlled apprenticeship through laws governing apprenticeship to insure that childrens' need for education and preparation for productive work would be met instead of apprenticeship being controlled by guilds and later the state in England. It was only natural that town governments would regulate apprenticeship because all decisions regarding the town, e.g. political, educational, economic, and social, were made at the town meetings where people were invited and encouraged to attend and participate.

Apprenticeship agreements provided for room and board; clothing; religious training; general education; knowledge, understanding and experience in the trade skills; and finally instruction in the "mysteries" of the trade or practices that had an elementary scientific basis. Both boys and girls were apprenticed beginning at age eight or nine for varying periods of time with the norm being from five to ten years. Girls usually served until the age of eighteen or until they were married.

Apprenticeship declined in importance in the colonial period and was dealt the heaviest blow by the factory system in the nineteenth century. There were a number of reasons for its decline including: (1) the abundance of land for young men and women to establish their own life, (2) the long periods of apprenticeship (up to ten years) in which marriage was forbidden, (3) the confusion of apprenticeship with indentured servants (individuals who were sold into binding work agreements to pay their way to America), (4) the mobility and freedom of the people, (5) the willingness of the frontier people to make do with handmade furniture and implements, (6) the immigration of mechanics and craftworkers from Europe, and (7) the division of labor in household factories that no longer required workers to make complete products from scratch.

Apprenticeship served as the chief source of education and training for the masses for over 150 years. New systems of education and training were beginning to surface in a progressive America that would relegate apprenticeship to serve only a small number of people. While a small number of workers continued to be thoroughly trained through apprenticeship, most workers learned job skills from their parents or through on-the-job training–learning job skills through observation and imitation.

Beginnings of Universal Education

Apprenticeship in America was considered an educational institution and not solely a means to prepare skilled craftworkers. Very early on, however, colonial town leaders recognized that many masters could not read and write well enough to provide adequate instruction in these subjects which lead to the development of schools to meet this educational need. In 1647, the general court of Massachusetts ordered towns of more than 50 households to employ a teacher to provide basic instruction in reading, writing, and arithmetic. Other colonies began to recognize the importance of elementary education to survival and progress in a free society. In 1685, Thomas Budd developed an educational plan calling for seven years of compulsory education in Pennsylvania and New Jersey which was to be funded by rent from 1,000 acres of land donated to the community to support a school. The proposed curriculum was to have a common core of reading, writing, arithmetic, and specialty areas for girls (spinning, weaving, sewing) and boys (joinery, turning, shoemaking). His proposal for education was not well accepted, but years later in 1747 the Moravian Brethren established a public school based on Budd's plan in Bethlehem, Pennsylvania (Walter, 1993).

Ben Franklin was concerned with broadening educational opportunities for common people and expanding the curriculum beyond the "classics" and religion to include instruction in the common trades in the same school. The Franklin Academy of Philadelphia opened its doors in 1751 but this new educational experiment was short lived, and in 1775 the school changed direction toward serving the elite. This academy later became the University of Pennsylvania (Barlow, 1976).

Franklin's experiment in combining academic and subjects of a practical nature in the academy spread to other parts of the country and have continued to today. A take off on the concept of an academy is the career academies that are currently operating in some states. Career academies are programs designed to integrate academic and vocational and applied technology curricula organized around a theme (occupation areas such as health, aerospace, etc.) that are taught as a "school within a school" where students take a sequence of courses together. Career academy programs encompass a set of jobs ranging from those that require no postsecondary education to those requiring an advanced degree.

Following the Revolutionary War, the need for education emerged as an essential element of a democratic society. Formal education was chiefly supported and conducted by the church or through special schools established for poor and orphaned children by wealthy individuals or societies–organizations formed to provide social and educational services–but a change process was underway resulting from a variety of forces (philanthropic, political, economic, social) to move control of education from churches to the state. The new American constitution did not address education directly, therefore it was considered a state responsibility. In time, education in America came to be viewed as a "concern of the federal government, a function of the state, and a responsibility of the local government" (Barlow, 1976).

Thomas Jefferson furthered the ideas and concepts proposed earlier by Benjamin Franklin that education should prepare a person for life in the business and social world. His plan for a universal, secular, public education system was proposed in

1779 in a bill to the Virginia Legislature entitled "A Bill for the More General Infusion of Knowledge." He believed in educational equality, secularization of school curriculum, separation of church and state, state systems of education, local educational initiative, and academic freedom. His bill, finally passed in 1796, was never implemented by the Virginia Government. Terms used by Jefferson of "public school" and "universal education" had different meaning to the thirteen early states and these two educational concepts received much discussion among educational philosophers and statesmen. While the idea of universal education and public expense continued to be debated, the movement to meet basic educational needs of poor children through private or philanthropic efforts and apprenticeship continued (Martin, 1981).

According to Edwards and Richey (1963), three important occurrences that were landmarks in the movement to establish universal public education at public expense were: (1) a system of public primary schools in Boston in 1818, (2) the establishment of a public high school in Boston in 1821, and (3) the passage in 1827 of a law in Massachusetts requiring the establishment of high schools in cities, towns, and districts of 500 families or more. These three events coupled with the semi-private academies initiated by Benjamin Franklin which featured diversified and flexible curriculum including English, classical, and practical studies, paved the way for a universal, public-supported educational system at the elementary and high school levels. Academies attracted all types of students but they charged tuition which made it impossible for many working class families to afford the kind of education they wanted for their children. What was needed for most American youth was a system of free public elementary and secondary education (Martin, 1981).

From the early 1800s until the passage of the famous Kalamazoo Case in 1872, which paved the way for the right of states to collect taxes to support education, the movement to establish universal elementary and secondary education at public expense gained momentum under untiring efforts of educational leaders like Horace Mann from Massachusetts. Mann was a firm believer in public support and control of education and felt that only through free, public, popular education could the excesses of a capitalistic democracy be eliminated. He believed strongly that education should be equally available to all classes and be delivered through non-authoritarian and non-sectarian means. He further believed that the emphasis of school studies should be on the practical needs of the individual and that the individual should be actively involved in the learning process. Beginning in 1851 with Massachusetts, state after state began to pass legislation requiring the attendance of youth in state-supported schools until the eighth grade. By 1875, the nation's educational system became firmly established and attention began to be focused on the high school curriculum which was viewed by many to be too narrow and traditional. The high school was viewed as the "peoples" school and the belief was that courses should be offered that meet the needs of all students. Some educational reformers were advocating expanding the curriculum to include the introduction of many new practical subjects like those offered in the early academies. It was through this reform movement, many years later, that vocational education had its beginning in the public schools of our nation (Martin, 1981).

Early Educational Efforts for Adults

While many children were receiving elementary education through church schools, the secular sunday school which served all classes of students, private academies, philanthropic institutions, apprenticeships, and eventually state supported schools, older youth and adults also needed access to education to learn the basics and to improve their knowledge of democracy, citizenship, and work. The American labor force strongly supported the concept of free, public-supported schools for their children and the development of schools that could provide the educational advantages offered through apprenticeship. They also recognized the need to develop educational opportunities for employed workers.

Mechanics Institute Movement

In the early 1800s in large towns and cities, a number of societies for mechanics and tradesworkers came into existence to meet the vocational education needs of their members. These were patterned after the mechanics institutes which originated in England. Another adult educational opportunity developed to serve the widely separated small towns of our country in the form of the American Lyceum (Martin, 1981).

The mechanics institute movement in Europe and America arose as part of an effort to improve the economic and social conditions of industrial and agricultural workers and to provide a pool of educated and efficient workers for the merchant and manufacturing ruling class. The first mechanics institute in America was introduced in 1820 when the General Society of Mechanics and Tradesmen of the City of New York opened a library for apprentices and established a mechanics school. The second and most famous of the mechanics institutes in America was the Franklin Institute of Philadelphia opened in 1824. In 1825, a mechanics institute began in Baltimore, and in 1827 a mechanics institute was organized in Boston. These institutes were designed to provide adult workers with an education which contained technical and industrial instruction. The Franklin Institute included the following purposes which were copied by succeeding institutes throughout the country: (1) present lectures on the arts and the application of science to them, (2) hold exhibitions of American manufacturers and award medals to worthy workers, and (3) establish schools to teach architecture and mechanical drawing and chemistry applied to the arts and mechanics (Martin, 1981).

The mechanics institutes were short lived with a few of them developing into technical or trade schools, and the vast majority of them dying as a result of ineffective teaching and the formation of the Land Grant Colleges, American high schools, and private trade schools. These institutes conducted classes in the evening for workers and played a significant role in the establishment of evening programs for adults in community colleges and technical schools of today (Martin, 1981).

American Lyceum Movement

The American Lyceum, created to serve towns of the country, was the counterpart of the mechanics institutes which served cities and large towns. It was based on the concept that "men may improve themselves through sharing their knowledge and expertise." The lyceum was an organization in the towns of America where speeches were given to increase the knowledge of the common person. From this humble beginning a local, state, and national federation was established called the American Lyceum. The format of the lyceum was simple–to gather the inhabitants of a town, village, or district together and call upon members of the audience to contribute something from their own stores of experience for the benefit of all. Presenters could deliver a lecture, essay, or conduct a debate. Topics varied widely and included education, common schools, political and domestic economy, morals, public improvements, agriculture, geology, chemistry, manufacturing, mechanic arts, trade, architecture, geology, meteorology, geography, and mathematics. The lyceum movement, like the mechanics institute movement, was short lived but it served to popularize education for all and placed an emphasis on acquiring useful information. It perpetuated the idea that education was a community affair and responsibility, ideas that were critical to establishing public supported elementary and secondary schools (Martin, 1981).

Manual Labor Movement

Another American educational experiment which took place between 1830 to 1845 that was designed to impart information about manual activity and work was the manual labor movement. Like the mechanics institute movement, manual labor education was widely practiced in Europe before the idea came to America. In Europe, manual labor was combined with subject instruction in schools with expectations that combining the two would influence health of mind and body and that students would be better prepared for the larger social interests of life, politics, economics, and religion. In America, the manual labor movement was first introduced to integrate regular school subjects with agriculture training. Later manual labor was used as a means of providing physical activity, a way to reduce the cost of education by selling student labor or the products of their labor, to promote a respect for all kinds of honest work, to build individual character, to promote originality, to stimulate intellectual development, and to increase the wealth of the country. One of the early manual labor schools was organized by the Methodist Church at Cokesbury College in Maryland in 1787 and featured manual labor in gardening and carpentry taught by experienced persons. Manual labor gained acceptance in a number of literary institutions (higher education) such as Oneida Institute in Whitesboro, New York, and in manual labor schools like those established in New Harmony, Indiana. The manual labor movement lasted for about 15 years and then began to decline rapidly for a variety of reasons including insufficient financial support from the institution or philanthropic society, manual work not made educative, and manual work consisting of odd jobs not related to the student's interest or later calling in life (Martin, 1981; Walter, 1993).

Early American Technical Schools

The most popular subject for courses and lectures in the evening school programs of mechanics institutes and American lyceums were those dealing with science and mathematics and their applications to agriculture and mechanical and manufacturing processes. As the teaching of science became more popular, a new type of full-time institution emerged providing a curriculum to prepare individuals with advanced scientific knowledge in agriculture, the mechanic arts, and engineering. These schools were the early technical schools of our country and many of them later became engineering schools. One of the first of these schools was the Gardiner Lyceum in Maine in 1823 which was a full-time scientific and technical school at the college level. The focus of this school and other technical schools was on the application of mathematics and science to agriculture and the arts. The Gardiner Lyceum lasted for about 10 years and was closed because of lack of financial support from the legislature of Maine (Bennett, 1926).

The second and most famous of the early technical schools was the Rensselaer School established in 1824 at Troy, New York. It was established to give instruction in the application of science to the common purposes of life. It was organized to benefit the sons and daughter of farmers and mechanics in the application of experimental chemistry, philosophy, and natural history to agriculture, domestic economy, the arts and manufacturing. A number of well-cultivated farms and quality workshops in the vicinity of the school were used as work sites for students to experience the practical applications of scientific principles. The technical school attracted many college graduates because of its research and development activity and was recognized as the first graduate school in America. Today, it is Rensselaer Polytechnic Institute, one of the premier engineering schools in America (Bennett, 1926).

Still another school that was organized in 1868 which emphasized practical training and the application of scientific principles was the Worchester County Free

Institute of Industrial Science in Massachusetts. It was organized to train engineers, designers of machinery, factory managers, and other masters of both scientific principles and practical details. One of the departments of the institute was a commercial machine shop which produced articles to be sold from student learning. Students did not receive pay for their work, therefore shop training had a wholly educative purpose. Shopwork was to be essentially on the same educational plane as laboratory science. The school claimed that combining shopwork and science was advantageous to both. Soon after the news spread about the success of the Worchester school, other engineering schools began to introduce shopwork into their programs (Barlow, 1776).

The Land Grant Act of 1862 was one of the most important pieces of legislation for vocational education and for higher education ever passed by congress. It had its beginning in the realization that the best way to promote agricultural education and agricultural innovation was to bring together the professors of science in higher education institutions and the practicing farmer who learned from daily labor how to improve agricultural production. Jonathan Baldwin Turner conceived the idea of a state industrial university which would educate for all agricultural and industrial occupations in the state. He made many presentations at various professional meetings promoting his scheme for establishing these state universities through funds provided by grants of state land that could be used to raise revenue to pay for establishing and maintaining one university in each state of the country. Professor Turner teamed up with Senator Justin Morrill of Vermont to introduce a land grant bill to congress which passed and was signed into law by President Abraham Lincoln in 1862. Thus, the nation received its most important legislative enactment supporting higher education that would prepare teachers and trained leaders for agriculture and the mechanical arts. Out of this act with amendments came the present day state colleges of agriculture and many of the state universities (Bennett, 1926). Examples of schools which started as Agricultural and Mechanical schools include University of Georgia, Mississippi State University, University of Illinois, and The Ohio State University.

Trade School Movement

After the Civil War, the idea of "educated labor" as opposed to just "skilled labor" gained wider acceptance. The public schools of that day resisted the inclusion of practical subjects, especially those that would prepare people for work. But the necessity of providing an education for the vast number of workers could not be overlooked. For over fifty years, private academies had included some practical subjects in the areas of business, domestic science (home economics), agriculture, and mechanical arts. Evening schools had been established as a result of the mechanics institute and lyceum movements to provide related academic instruction to interested adult workers. Agricultural was promoted through a number of societies and departments of agriculture were established in academies, colleges, and universities The land grant colleges and universities were established by the provisions of the Morrill Act of 1862 to provide instruction in agriculture, mechanical arts, and domestic science for higher education students. The manual labor movement resulted in a number of institutions that attempted to meet the needs of the farmer and mechanic. One of the most famous of these manual labor schools was Rensselaer Institute established in Troy, New York in 1824. Some female seminaries were organized as manual labor schools where young women experienced academic instruction combined with several hours of domestic work each day in order to reduce the operating expenses of the institution (Barlow, 1776).

Private schools for business (business colleges) had developed after 1850, and enrollment in these schools increased greatly after the typewriter was invented in 1873. Some high schools included business education as part of the curriculum in the late 1800s. Other high schools had included drawing as part of their curriculum after 1870, but not to prepare people for employment as drafters.

The reconstruction period following the Civil War demanded a new type of school that could prepare people for employment in the rapidly expanding industrial economy. The trade school movement emerged to provide a workable system of industrial education for all American regardless of the color of their skin. One of the first trade schools was Hampton Institute in Virginia, established in 1868 to provide both liberal education and trade training to African-Americans to improve character and social status. Students devoted eight hours each day to the study of a trade in organized courses lasting for a three-year period along with academic courses that required four years. If students completed the entire four-year educational experience they could earn a diploma. Booker T. Washington was one of Hampton Institute's most famous graduates, who later became principal at Tuskegee Institute in Alabama and had a distinguished educational career until his death in 1915 (Barlow, 1976).

The trade school was designed to provide specific trade training supplemented with directly related academic subjects. While the evening schools had attempted such training, they emphasized "book learning" and did not solve the need for an understanding of basic trade skills. Some trade schools were private tuition schools, some where free, and others were operated by manufacturing companies to train their employees. The first trade school to offer specific trade training with supplementary studies directly related to each trade for pre-employment purposes as well as for employed workers was the New York Trade School established in 1881. This school was founded by a wealthy industrialist and was supported through contributions as well as tuition. It was operated by a board of trustees composed of influential educators and business leaders, and was guided by a counsel of trade advisory committees–one of the early references to the use of vocational advisory committees (Barlow, 1976).

Two other early trade schools were the Hebrew Technical Institute organized in New York City in 1883 to serve the large number of Jewish immigrants and the William Free School of Mechanical Trades organized in 1891 in Philadelphia by a wealthy philanthropist. The Hebrew Technical Institute was more of a technical school than a trade school because it offered a wider range of subjects of a general nature. It was organized to combine trade training with general education subject matter. The Williamson School was dedicated to producing graduates who were as good as or better than journeymen who had just completed high quality apprenticeships. The school was very selective in admissions, but was entirely free to those youth who could meet admission requirements. The Williamson School started with a program of manual training for students, added some general education, and finally provided specific, intensive trade training. These three different types of trade schools gave birth to a number of trade schools throughout the country in the late 1800s (Barlow, 1976).

Corporate Schools

Another type of trade school was established by large manufacturing companies in an attempt to revise the old apprenticeship method of training high quality employees. It was believed that an apprenticeship program alone could not solve social and trade problems as well as a good trade school that incorporated academic instruction. One of the first corporate trade schools was established in 1872 by R. Hoe and Company–manufacturers of printing presses. The company needed a more intelligent class of workers to produce improved machinery and responded to this need by establishing a school which met two evenings each week. The school was free to employees, voluntary not compulsory, but advancement opportunities were tied to participation. Subjects studied in this school were those directly related to work requirements and included English, mechanical drawing, arithmetic, geometry, and algebra. The school proved to be very satisfactory and produced a superior class of worker (Barlow, 1976).

In 1902, the General Electric Company established an apprenticeship system which combined the activities of shop and classroom instruction. Academic content was selected which would help apprentices develop a better understanding of machines and machine parts. Included in the studies were courses in interpretation of mechanical drawings (print reading), sketching, and design of auxiliary tools required for modern manufacture.

The plan to provide instruction in industrial science with apprenticeship learning proved to be highly successful and was copied widely by other companies. Modern companies are still using corporation schools to train workers (Barlow, 1981).

In 1901, the Baldwin Locomotive Works of Philadelphia established a corporation school that served three classes of workers: (1) a school for those who had completed elementary school but had not reached 16 years of age which met three evenings each week for three years and provided instruction in geometry, arithmetic, mechanical drawing and shop practice, (2) a school for those over 18 years of age who had completed a more advanced education which met two evenings each week for two years and provided studies in chemistry, advanced mathematics, and mechanical drawing, and (3) an educational program for graduates of colleges and other advanced institutions which did not meet in classes but used reading and reports of technical journals as the teaching medium. The view of this company, and many others, was that public school education could prepare people better for apprenticeships but evening schools would be necessary to supplement daily learning on the job in a company (Barlow, 1976).

Educational Reforms in the Common School

There were a number of other educational experiments launched by educational reformers to introduce manual activity based on the teaching of European educators like Pestalozzi and Froebel into the common schools or America which overly emphasized abstract learning of subject matter. One of these was the Oswego movement which began in Oswego State Normal School in 1861. President Edward Sheldon adopted some of the teaching methods of Pestalozzi to train teachers to change their teaching methods from: (1) memory to reasoning and individual judgment, (2) from book centered to object centered, (3) from over dependence on words in text to oral instruction using objects, (4) from teachers keeping school to teachers teaching with skill, (5) from textbook lessons to oral language lessons, (6) from text dictated lessons to teacher planned lessons, and (7) from reciting what was read to expressing ideas (Wright, 1981).

A second educational reform for the common school was popularly known as the Quincy Plan developed by Francis Parker in 1875 in Quincy, Massachusetts which re-oriented the school system to an activity-oriented curriculum based on the needs and interest of children. He was able to "Americanize" Pestalozzian ideas to develop a model of a truly child-centered curriculum which changed the teaching methods and curriculum of elementary education in this country forever (Wright, 1981).

A third reform period of elementary education was the development of the American kindergarten which was and remains the best example of a truly child-centered school. The kindergartens of America were based on the work of Freidrick Froebel and emphasized natural but directed self-activity, focused upon educational, social, and moral ends. The kindergarten was to be a miniature ideal society–a place where people were courteous and helpful and involved in cooperative activity. It emphasized doing, self-activity, individual expression, directed play, song, color, the story, nature study, gardening, and motor activity. Passive lessons were replaced with object lessons stressing the use of concrete objects that were real to the students. The kindergartens had individual development as their primary aim, motor expression as the teaching method, and social cooperation as its means (Wright, 1981).

The three educational movements just presented have reshaped the elementary schools of America. The academies that once included practical subjects had all but eliminated them with exception of some business subjects and had become primarily academic. In 1890, high schools were highly selective with programs mostly for young people preparing for the professions–ministers, lawyers, doctors, teachers, engineers. With the passage of compulsory school laws, the high schools of America had a much larger and diverse student population to serve. Students came to the high school with different social and cultural backgrounds, with low to high abilities, and with a wide variety of future job interests. The high school was no longer a transition school for those planning to enter college, it became a terminal school for the masses. Many high schools began to offer a two-tract curriculum, a practical one for terminal students and a classical one for college bound youth. The comprehensive high school which offered two parallel curriculums became the common high school model. There were, however, some special purpose high schools such as the manual training high schools and later special high schools for commercial and agricultural pursuits (Smith, 1981).

The industrial revolution had created a large working class that demanded new educational opportunities for their children. Industrialization was more than the growth of factories, labor-saving machinery, and the growth of urban areas; it changed the whole structure of society. It had created two classes of people: a working class and a non-working class. And as time passed, the gap between these two classes continued to widen. Many of the children of the working class worked beside their parents in dangerous factories instead of attending school. The illiteracy rate of the working class soon became a problem. Parents who were illiterate and had limited practical skills could not pass on much of an education to their children. Crime was the second major problem plaguing society in the 1800s. It was out of these undesirable conditions of ignorance, delinquency, and human suffering that the drive to create a system of universal, free public schools was initiated. The working class wanted schools that would provide the basic academic skills for their children but also include instruction in practical subjects that would prepare them for better jobs than the ones they presently endured.

Drawing–initiated by Richard Mulcaster in England a hundred years earlier–had already been included in a number of high schools (required subject in Boston High Schools in 1836) but there was growing public sentiment for inclusion of other types of practical subjects. Elementary schools had included more doing activity into their curriculum. Some high schools had established programs in agriculture, general business and domestic science (home economics) and more were being added as a result of land grant universities. Technical schools at the college level had already experimented with combining shopwork with academic subjects in science and mathematics and found this curriculum to vastly improve the preparation of their engineering graduates. America was moving from an agricultural to an industrial society and business and industry advocated the inclusion of subjects that would give students the underlying principles and practices of industrial occupations as part of their general education so they would be better prepared to live in the new industrial society.

A great debate arose among educational leaders of the late 1800s over the inclusion of more practical subjects into the curriculum of the public high schools of America. Proponents argued that the lack of practical education in the public schools represented a deficiency in the school system and a lack of commitment to serving the majority of the students. Opponents claimed that introduction of practical subjects would interfere with the intellectual culture and schools were not the place to prepare people for business and industry. From 1875 to 1900, the pages of educational literature covered the debate over what should be taught in the public schools, subjects preparing people for culture entirely or a mix of courses preparing people for both work and life. At the center of the debate was the new manual training movement championed by two engineering professors, Calvin Woodward, and John D. Runkle (Barlow, 1976).

Manual Training Movement

The manual training movement in America began at Washington University in St. Louis, Missouri and at the Massachusetts Institute of Technology (MIT). In 1878, Professor Calvin Woodward, Dean of the Washington University Polytechnic faculty had implemented a program of shopwork for engineering students so they would be more versed in the application of engineering principles through the use of tools and machines. He became convinced that secondary students should have access to shop courses and that a combination of academics and shopwork would increase student interest in school and provide a means of supplementing the mostly liberal education of the day. In 1880, with the philanthropic support of several prominent business leaders, the first manual training high school in America was established in St. Louis, Missouri. The new school was a four-year institution which provided instruction in mathematics, science, drawing, language, and literature, as well as practice in the use of tools. Students attended class six periods each day, one period for academic subjects and a double period for shopwork. The desired end of manual instruction was that of acquiring skills in the use of tools and materials and not in the production of specific articles or direct preparation for trades. The laboratory method of instruction was used, consisting of graded lessons in the use of ordinary tools demonstrated by the instructor with opportunities for students to ask question and take notes, followed by students proceeding with their work (Roberts, 1971).

In 1876, John Runkle, president of MIT, took a large party of students and faculty to the Centennial Exposition in Philadelphia where he saw the solution to one of his most pressing problems, which was the methodology of providing practical training to his engineering students. He and his students were fascinated with the Russian Exhibit of the Imperial Technical School of Moscow under the direction of Victor Della Voss. Four of the many instructional tenets of the Russian system that impressed them most was: (1) separate instruction shops from construction shops, (2) provide only one kind of work in each shop, (3) provide as many work stations and tools for each station as a teacher can reasonably handle in one instructional period, and (4) graduate the instruction in each shop according to the difficulty and complexity of the operation. Upon Runkle's return from the exposition, he formulated and received approval from MIT to establish an American version of the Russian manual training system for his engineering students at MIT. In addition, he established the School of Mechanic Arts which was open to qualified grammar school students (Barlow, 1976).

Woodward and Runkle soon became advocates for introducing manual training into the public school of America. They proposed its inclusion because training in the manual arts was desirable and advantageous for all students, regardless of their educational goals. They felt strongly that the education of the schools had been dealing too exclusively with the abstract and the remote and not enough with the concrete and the near at hand. They saw manual training as a way to improve the basic education of all youth. Woodward listed the following outcomes of manual training when combined with academic and moral training:

1. Boys will stay in school longer.
2. Better intellectual development.
3. More wholesome moral education.
4. Sounder judgment of men and things.
5. Better choice of occupations.
6. Material success for the individual and the community.
7. Elevation of manual occupations from the perception of brute, unintelligent labor to work requiring and rewarding knowledge and skill.
8. Basis for an individual career in the mechanical arts.

9. First step in the solution of labor problems.
10. Provide the basis for higher education.

Woodward truly believed in manual activity as a way to enhance general education. He recognized that the overwhelming sentiment of educators was that vocational education had no place in the schools but should be the province of business and industry. He also recognized that business and industry wanted manual training to serve more of a vocational education purpose but organized labor opposed manual training for fear it would flood the market with poorly trained workers who would be inferior to those produced through apprentice programs. He was keenly aware of the many critics that believed that anything manual could ever be elevated to the same plane as the classics and made a part of the public school curriculum. Some educators supported the concept of manual training as long as it was conducted in a separate school (Wright, 1981).

The success of the manual training school in St. Louis led to the establishment of manual training high schools in other cities and towns. Like the pioneer manual training school, most were established as separate and apart from the academic high school and supported as part of a higher education institution or through donations and tuition. One of the earliest separate manual training schools was the Baltimore Manual Training High School, founded in 1884 as part of the regular public school system supported at public expense. The second manual training school, which was part of the public supported school system, was the Philadelphia Manual Training School established in 1885 (Roberts, 1971).

Special Manual Training Schools Become Technical Schools

As manual training high schools grew in popularity, their curriculum included a broader range of courses and elective opportunities. This expansion of programs and curriculum in manual training high schools later led to the formation of the combined cosmopolitan high school (comprehensive high school) and the technical school. Some manual training schools in larger cities placed more emphasis on shopwork, drawing, and science and changed their name to technical schools. Among the first of these schools was the Technical School of Springfield, Massachusetts established in 1898. This school provided instruction in the usual high school subjects together with the fundamentals of drawing, design, and hand and machine tools. Soon other technical school were established in New York City, Detroit, and Chicago (Barlow, 1976).

Beginning of the Comprehensive High School

The comprehensive high school plan occurred in large cities at the beginning of the 20th century. This plan brought together the courses and equipment of general, commercial, and manual training education into one school with courses classified as either academic or technical–a practice carried over to today. The academic program of these early comprehensive high schools included general subjects, classical subjects, domestic science, and manual training. The technical program consisted of commercial subjects, technical cooperative subjects, art and music. The comprehensive high school offered a wider choice of curriculums and courses which reflected the growing concern that students receive preparation for more than college; that they receive preparation for career options not requiring a college education (Roberts, 1971).

Between 1880 to 1920 in America, a number of educational movements emerged to affect the infusion of practical subjects into the high schools. These movements were manual training, American sloyd, arts and crafts, manual arts, industrial arts, and vocational education. The manual training movement as envisioned by Runkle and Woodward did not last many years for a variety of reasons, one of which was the wide variety of programs that sprang up under the name of manual training. Another reason was that manual training exercises that did not result in useful products did little to capture the interest of American youth. Then, there was the ever present push to make manual training more vocational to prepare youth for industrial jobs.

American Sloyd

Woodward's manual training system, adapted from the Russian system, was one method of hand tool instruction that entered public schools. Another one was a form of manual training in Sweden which was called sloyd. In 1888, Gustaf Larson, a teacher of sloyd in Sweden, came to America and established sloyd instruction in Boston. Very early, Larson had to make changes in traditional sloyd methodology to make it work in America. Several of these changes were: (1) Swedish models that were first used had no appeal to American youth and had to be replaced with models of interest to students, (2) traditional sloyd emphasized working from models, but American industry developed products from drawings and drawing was already a school subject of importance in general education. The practice of students working from models was replaced with students working from teacher-prepared drawings and later from student-developed drawings, and (3) the mostly individualized method of instruction was broadened to include more group instruction which had become successful in American schools. These adaptations of Swedish sloyd led to the term "American sloyd" (Smith, 1981).

The major difference between manual training and American sloyd was based on the focus sloyd had on the development of the learner rather than the development of skill in the use of hand tools, and the use of trained teachers rather than the use of skilled craftworkers to teach tool skills. Manual training focused on teaching the use of specific tools by completing exercises or making incomplete objects without sufficient attention directed to the individual needs and capacities of youth. Sloyd, on the other hand, placed careful attention on developing capacities of the individual in the selection of graded models and projects, which were interesting to youth and on the sequence of instructional tasks based on the capacity of each youth leading to the completion of useful objects. Other advantages of sloyd over the Russian system of manual training were: (1) prominence of form study of the object, (2) greater variety of tasks, (3) importance of using completed models, and (4) importance of the teacher being a trained educator. The sloyd movement lasted only a few years but it did change the way practical art subjects were taught and encouraged the use of trained teachers (Smith, 1981).

Arts and Crafts Movement

The arts and craft movement which began in England as a "backlash" against the poor crafts quality of manufactured products came to America after 1880 when Charles Leland introduced the plan in the schools of Philadelphia. The arts and craft movement emphasized the importance of artistic design, practical skill development for a vocational as well as future work applications, revival of artistic pursuits all but eliminated by industrial machinery, and the teaching of decorative arts to the abilities and interest of youngsters. School subject matter included in the arts and crafts included drawing, wood carving, clay modeling, mosaic work, leather carving, metal embossing, embroidery, carpentry, wood turning, wood inlaying, and ornamental wood sawing. Students were given considerable freedom in the selection and designing of projects. The arts and crafts movement had little effect on manual training in America except to broaden the materials and tasks used to train student in tool usage and to emphasize the important of artistic design in the construction of useful projects. While the arts and crafts movement lasted into the early twentieth century primarily through the efforts of various arts and craft societies, its application in schools declined as the public became more concerned with industrial skill development training (Smith, 1981).

Correspondence Schools

Toward the end of the 19th century, the population in America was increasing rapidly due to immigration (primarily from Europe) and the need for large families to perform the many tasks of life in a primarily rural society. Correspondence schools were established to bring education and training to those who (a) did not live near enough to a school to attend classes, (b) could not attend classes because of their rigorous work schedules, (c) wished to receive additional training beyond what they had received in public schools, and (d) did not have a wide selection of courses in their local schools. Many of these correspondence schools offered courses in vocational areas as well as academic areas. One of these early schools was the American School of Correspondence.

The American School of Correspondence was founded in 1895 by R. T. Miller, Jr. in Boston, Massachusetts based on the belief that all Americans should have an opportunity to receive a high school diploma and learn the job skills required to prepare them for the working world. In 1898, Mr. Miller founded American Technical Society (now American Technical Publishers, Inc.) to publish the books and guides for his correspondence school. Typical trade subjects offered by the American School of Correspondence included mechanical drawing, millwright, carpentry, and electrical trades. Mr. Miller moved these companies to the University of Chicago campus in the early 1900s to take advantage of central mailing and to utilize personnel from the University to grade correspondence papers. Both of these companies continue to meet their original founding purposes today.

Manual Arts

Manual arts was primarily a name given to a revised form of manual training which placed greater emphasis on applied design and constructive and decorative arts. Charles Bennett was considered the "father of manual arts" for he spoke out about the neglect of the aesthetic principle in manual training and advocated free as well as mechanical drawings be encouraged, as well as the production of beautiful and useful objects as an outcome of the learning process. He advocated combining creative design with the teaching of tool usage resulting in beautiful projects that would be expressions of art produced by youth. In 1909, Bennett outlined a classification system for elementary school manual arts which included the five area of graphic arts, mechanic arts, plastic arts, textile arts, and book-making arts. The impact of the manual arts movement was chiefly changing the name of manual training and combining drawing and design with construction activities in mechanic arts (Smith, 1981).

Industrial Arts

In 1904 Charles Richards, editor of *Manual Training Magazine*, suggested in his editorial that it was time to change the name of manual training and manual arts to industrial art. He concluded that manual training was nothing less than a subject field of study that taught the elements of industries that had become fundamental to modern civilization. He spoke of the content of industrial arts being drawn from industry (Smith, 1981).

Dean James Russell of Teachers College, Columbia University expanded the idea of industrial arts in 1909. He suggested that the elementary schools (grades 1-8) of the nation had become to "bookish" and recommended that economics and scientific studies be included in the general education curriculum of the elementary school. He described economics as "the study of industries for the sake of a better perspective on man's achievements in controlling the production, distribution, and consumptions of the things which constitute man's natural wealth." He stated that "the chief consideration of content for courses of study should be on the ordering of the industrial processes by which raw materials are transformed into things of greater value for the satisfaction of human needs." Russell, following the philosophy of John Dewey, believed that industrial arts could be the basis for the elementary school program. He advocated that manual training, fine arts, domestic art, and domestic science be dropped from the elementary school curriculum (an unpopular idea) in favor of the elements of industry, or industrial arts (Smith, 1981).

As industrial arts programs replaced manual training in the elementary school, the terms manual training and manual arts gave way to the term industrial arts and the focus of manual training programs slowly evolved toward the study of occupations by which changes are made in the forms of materials to increase their value for human usage and of the problems of life related to these changes as proposed by Gorgon Bonser in 1923. Industrial arts was to be a study of manufacturing industries as the curriculum base with the goal being to develop an understanding of the functioning of our industrial society. Russell and Bonser advocated industrial arts at the elementary school level and vocational education at the secondary school level, but the concept of industrial arts began to replace the name of manual arts and manual training in secondary schools over a period of years (Smith, 1981).

Like manual training and manual arts, industrial arts was to be a component of general education and not vocational education. It was a subject field that all students should take in order to understand the industrial society in which they lived. Manual arts and manual training programs had made significant changes in instructional practices prior to the advent of industrial arts. They had incorporated drawing and design as an integral part of the curriculum; incorporated the making of useful articles to increase the interest of youth; used field trips to expose students to industry and industrial processes; introduced flexibility into the rigid instructional methodology, allowing students to experiment and engage in problem-solving activities with a variety of tools and processes; and incorporated more individualized instruction and the assignment of work to students on the basis of their abilities and interests.

At the same time that the industrial arts movement was beginning, a strong vocational education movement was taking shape. As America became the world's foremost industrial power, competition in world trade accelerated and business and industrial leaders were in desperate need for more skilled workers. A growing number of influential leaders began a crusade to introduce some form of vocational education into the secondary schools of America. Manual training programs came under attack by vocational education proponents as being inadequate to meet the educational needs of 90% of the people that would be involved in industrial pursuits. The constant public pressure placed on manual training programs caused some to introduce more of a vocational flavor to their instructional programs which led to "vocationalizing" some manual training programs. Some manual training teachers actually organized their programs like a commercial factory in which students did production work for schools and community organizations. Instructional emphasis was placed on duplicating industrial operations and processes and developing skills that would later lead students into jobs in industry and the trades. Some proponents argued that manual training should be eliminated entirely and replaced with vocational education programs. Others recommended that manual training programs continue but serve a prevocational purpose–serve as a feeder for vocational programs at the secondary level (Barella, 1981).

The growing public sentiment for vocational education programs at the secondary level made it difficult for industrial arts programs, designed to be part of general education to grow and reach their full potential as an important part of the education of all students. With the passage of Federal legislation establishing vocational education programs in secondary schools, the attacks on manual training, manual arts, and industrial arts subsided and the field was free to find its niche in the American educational system. Influenced by the progressive education movement of John Dewey, William Warner refined the ideas of earlier leaders in industrial arts in 1947 by identifying major areas or courses of study for industrial arts which were management, communications, power, transportation, and manufacturing. Out of Warner's work emerged two theories for the field of industrial arts. One suggested that the domain of industrial arts education is industry–its products, processes, materials, management, organization, and occupations–and the impact of industry. The second theory for industrial arts reflected the changes that occurred in society as a result of technology and recommended that the curriculum of industrial arts programs should be on the study of technology–its evolution, utilization, and significance. As industrial arts programs matured and developed a more consistent identity, they became an important component of practical arts education at the elementary and secondary school level until they were slowly converted into technology education program in the late 1980s (Wright & Barella, 1981).

Agriculture Education Prior to 1917

Prior to the Civil War, agriculture was conducted using age-old techniques and crude implements. Very little scientific knowledge was applied to raising crops and animals. Following the Civil War, tremendous progress was made in mechanizing agriculture production. Many new field machines were developed such as improved tractors, binders, planters, and harvesters. Transportation with refrigeration capacity made it possible to move produce quickly over long distances. The amount of food produced through mechanized farming exceeded the demand even in a rapidly growing America and the prices of food fell sharply, forcing many small farms out of business and causing a flood of rural people to move to urban centers for their livelihood. The education of youth and adults engaged in agriculture was provided through agricultural societies, lyceums, some academies, and a few private agricultural schools, manual labor schools, and public schools (Barlow, 1776).

As agriculture became more scientific, individuals engaged in this occupation needed formal education beyond what they could learn through apprenticeship on the farm and through efforts of societies and lyceums. Some early school efforts used the work-study method to offer elementary courses in agriculture as well as a means of acquiring a general knowledge. Some academies which served students who completed the grammar school offered courses in agriculture. A few high schools offered courses in agriculture which consisted mostly of textbook study and instructor lectures. Some special agricultural schools were established to provide scientific information related to agriculture. Courses in agriculture were offered in some manual training high schools. The Country Life Movement beginning in 1890, stimulated the development of general agriculture in elementary schools and by 1910, seventeen states had passed laws requiring courses in elementary agriculture (Barlow, 1776).

It was out of the concern that neither the efforts of private and public schools, agricultural societies, nor mechanics institutes were effecting needed changes in their respective occupational areas that led to the passage of the Morrill Land Grant College Act of 1862, which established colleges and universities to provide programs combining the practical applications of agriculture and industry with scientific knowledge to improve both agriculture and industrial practices. At first, the Land Grant Act dealt a tremendous blow to existing agricultural programs in high schools because it was assumed that colleges and universities would meet the educational needs of agriculture. However, it soon became apparent that farmers were either unwilling or could not afford to send their sons to universities. Agricultural societies began to advocate the inclusion of agriculture as a subject area in high schools. In 1881, the Storrs Agricultural school was established in Mansfield, Connecticut which combined practical farm studies and related academic instruction. In 1888, a secondary school of agriculture was organized as part of the department of agriculture of the University of Minnesota. In 1889, the state of Alabama passed legislation establishing secondary agricultural schools (Barlow, 1976).

These special agricultural schools required many students to travel long distances from the farm and to reside at the school for two or more years which made them too expensive for the farmer's children and made it impossible for them to be utilized on the farm. The solution which gained increasing support was to establish courses in agriculture in numerous schools, supported with public funds, within a reasonable distance from the farm for youth who finished the common school to further their education (Barlow, 1976).

Congress recognized the need to provide additional support for agricultural education than was being provided through existing institutions. In 1887, agricultural experiment stations were created by the Hatch Act providing for the scientific study of agriculture in addition to the study being provided at land grant institutions. In 1890, the second Morrill Bill provided more money to land grant institutions. In 1914, Congress passed the Smith-Lever Cooperative Extension Act to increase the extension work of land grant colleges and universities. This act provided for instruction and practical demonstrations in agriculture and home economics to be delivered to persons not attending land grant colleges through field demonstrations and publications. It incorporated the county agent system of agriculture with instructional centers in each county supported with federal and county funds (Barlow, 1976).

Home Economics Education Prior to 1917

The establishment and growth of home economics was made unnecessarily difficult because of prejudice against the education of women. There was a general feeling in Colonial America that women had little need for education for their place was in the home. Education beyond simple reading and writing was geared to producing ministers and leaders of the state, and since women were deemed ineligible for these positions, their education was of little concern. During the colonial period, girls as well as boys were taught how to read and write at home if their parents were literate, by their church, by a literate apprenticeship master if they were lucky, and by a school teacher after the Massachusetts law was passed requiring towns to establish schools for their inhabitants. Industrial schools for orphans, poor children, and the delinquent often included instruction for girls in household labor and sewing. Academies, like the Franklin Academy founded in 1751, were open to both girls and boys and other academies and private schools copied the curriculum which included both academic and practical subjects. Girls attending the Boston public schools were taught needlework along with academic subjects. Girls and young women of the affluent often attended private venture schools where they were taught academic subjects and leisure activities like needlework, dancing, drawing, and vocal and instrumental music. For the vast majority of girls and young women who lived in rural America in farms and the frontier, education beyond reading and writing was very limited until after the Revolutionary War (Roberts, 1971).

Following the Revolutionary War, special schools for women began to appear founded by those concerned with extending educational opportunity for women beyond the common school. Female seminaries emerged along the Atlantic seaboard with one of the earliest established in Troy, New York in 1821–Emma Willard's Troy Female Seminary. Female seminaries taught domestic or household duties combined with intellectual subjects. In 1820, girls were taught sewing in the primary grades of Boston schools, and in 1835 the practice was extended into the grammar schools. Girls were taught domestic responsibilities through direct application in the private manual labor schools that emerged in the first half of the nineteenth century. The first girls' high school was opened in Worchester, Massachusetts in 1824 followed by one in Boston and New York two years later. Oberlin College in Ohio, founded in 1833, was one of the earliest co-educational institutions of higher learning. In 1837, Mary Lyon founded Mount Holyoke Female Seminary in Massachusetts which was a college-level institution that provided elementary instruction in cooperative living for women, requiring them to engage in domestic work two hours each day to help reduce operating expenses of the institution. In 1842, the New England Female Medical College was founded, and in 1855 Elmira College in New York opened its doors, which was the first women's college to grant degrees. This college required its young women to take work in domestic science and general household affairs (Barlow, 1776).

The Morrill Act of 1862 resulted in colleges and universities establishing departments of domestic science to provide leadership for establishing homemaking in the public schools of America. Iowa State College started formal instruction in home economics in 1872, which began with instruction in housekeeping and over a period of years included the areas of cooking, house furnishing, care of children, care of the sick, management of help, dress-making, physiology, domestic chemistry, laundry work, and sewing. These institutions were the forerunners of the movement to establish educational programs for women which paved the way for homemaking programs in the public schools after 1880 (Barlow, 1976; Roberts, 1971).

Two important women stimulated the development of home economics in the middle of the nineteenth century. Catherine Beecher published her *Treatise on Domestic Economy for the Use of Young Ladies at Home* in 1841. This scholarly work covered nearly every phase of homemaking and was adopted widely by public and private schools setting the pattern for homemaking education. The acknowledged leader of the home economics movement, however, was Ellen Richards, a graduate of the Massachusetts Institute of Technology in the field of chemistry. She used her knowledge of chemistry for the improvement of living conditions in the home, particularly in sanitation. It was her work in the study of the family and the problems of homemaking that made her the leader of the home economics movement. She was instrumental in establishing a series of ten annual conferences to address issues related to the content and training methods of home economics in manual training schools and was a key leader in establishing the American Home Economics Association in which she served as its first president (Barlow, 1976).

After 1880, when the manual training school movement began, domestic science courses were included among the practical arts. These programs were sometimes called household science, domestic science, domestic art, and home economics. In 1872, Massachusetts authorized schools to offer courses in sewing and other industrial education subjects. The Kitchen Garden Movement, which began in 1877, utilized small toys, games, and songs to teach household arts to children. The Kitchen Garden Association, which became the Industrial Education Association in 1884, affirmed that domestic science was an important program of manual training and began to develop subject matter and methods of instruction for home economic subjects. The Philadelphia High School for Girls offered a course in sewing in 1880 and extended this course into the elementary school in 1885. Domestic science courses began to appear in manual training schools and many public schools throughout the country at the close of the century (Roberts, 1971).

The period between 1899 to 1908 was significant for the home economics movement for it was at this time that a series of ten annual conferences led by Ellen Richards were held at Lake Placid and Chautauqua, New York with one conducted in Boston. These conferences addressed a broad range of topics concerning economics and social aspects of the home including training teachers, courses of study, evening schools, extension teaching, rural school work, home economics in women's clubs, and manual training and education for citizenship. The fourth conference produced an early definition of home economics as "the study of laws, conditions, principles, and ideals which are concerned on the one hand with man's immediate physical environment and on the other hand with his nature as a social being, and is the study especially of the relation between these two factors." In addition, the issues regarding terminology for the field were discussed resulting in the conclusion that the term domestic science was not adequate to describe the various homemaking programs. The sixth conference brought closure to the terminology discussion with "handwork" chosen as the elementary school term, "domestic science" in the secondary school, "home economics" in normal and professional schools, and "euthenics" in colleges and universities.

In 1913, the American Home Economics association, founded in 1909, developed a *Syllabus of Home Economics* which offered a new definition for home economics and described what topics could properly be included under the term home economics. Home economics was defined as "the study of the economic, sanitary, and aesthetic aspects of food, clothing, and shelter, as connected with their selection, preparation and use by the family in the home or by other groups of people." Courses in home economics could be offered as cultural, technical, or vocational in nature and could be offered in the primary and secondary school or in college. The major divisions of the subject matter were food, clothing, shelter, and household and institution management (Roberts, 1771).

Under the leadership provided by the American Home Economics Association and state and local educators, every state had some type of home economics in one or more schools prior to 1917. It was offered as part of general education in most schools with two periods per week as the typical delivery system. For the most part, home economics programs emphasized cooking and sewing with few programs offering a comprehensive program needed for the preparation of homemakers. Such programs would be established a few years later after passage of the Smith Hughes Act of 1917 (Roberts, 1971).

General Business Education Prior to 1917

Historical records indicate that the English grammar schools and semi-private academies offered courses in arithmetic, handwriting, and bookkeeping in the eighteenth and nineteenth centuries for purposes of preparation for life as well as for college entrance.

Bookkeeping was included in the curriculum of the English High School of Boston in 1823. Under an 1827 Massachusetts law, bookkeeping along with other subjects was specified for certain schools of the state. Some high school of the nineteenth century offered commercial courses for general education as well as for practical application. In the nineteenth century, a number of private business colleges emerged to prepare individuals for business and commerce which reduced the emphasis on establishing business education programs at the secondary school level (Roberts, 1971).

At the beginning of the twentieth century, a renewed interest developed in providing business education as part of the manual training high school curriculum for purposes of mental discipline, general education, and vocational usage. It was at this time that business education was introduced into the junior high school curriculum for purposes of general knowledge, exploration for careers, and to reduce the drop-out rate. Business education remained an important part of the practical arts until federal legislation cleared the way for vocational business education programs many years later (Roberts, 1971).

Status of Practical Arts Programs in 1900

In the early years of the twentieth century, the programs of agriculture education, business education, home economics education, industrial education, and industrial arts had been established in manual training schools, public elementary and secondary schools, and public and private colleges and universities. For the most part, these programs were viewed as having a cultural, social, and general education purpose with vocational usage being an unplanned natural outcome. Special schools had been created to offer instruction in these occupational areas for vocational purposes including public and private trade schools, technical schools, evening schools, colleges of engineering and technology, and corporation schools.

Practical subjects were added to school curricula to supplement the purely academic content of most schools with hopes that these subjects would hold the interests of students and help them better understand academic content through practical application, thereby reducing the dropout rate which was estimated to be about 50% by the eighth grade. In addition, these subjects were believed to be important for preparation for life in an industrial economy (Barella, 1981).

The impact of industrialism was being felt in every phase of human life. Technological innovations created new industries and expanded existing ones, causing a tremendous need for skilled workers. The prevailing view of the day regarding business was that individuals had the right to regulate their economic affairs without government interference. This philosophy caused government to side with big business and adopt a hands-off policy concerning regulation of business and industry which allowed big business to exploit their workers. At this time in American history, the process of creating wealth seemed to be more important for most people than religion, education, and politics. Increasing production, employment, and income became the measurers of community success, and personal riches the result of hard work. Labor formed unions to protect themselves against the exploitation of workers and bitter battles occurred between management and labor over the employment of poorly trained workers, working conditions, and pay (Barella, 1981).

America had become the industrial giant of the world and the demand for goods internally and across the seas spurred increased production and industrial activity. Even though many skilled workers were coming to this country from Europe as a result of relaxed immigration laws, American industry needed additional skilled workers and they became very vocal about the need to better prepare workers in the public schools of this country. No longer could educators ignore the issue of preparing students for industrial occupations. Some form of vocational education was inevitable. What was needed was a thorough study of the interest in and need for more specific vocational training than was being offered through existing practical arts programs. This study came in the form of the Douglas commission report of Massachusetts in 1906, and the research of the National Association for the Promotion of Industrial Education and the Commission of National Aid to Vocational Education (Barella, 1981).

Douglas Commission of Massachusetts

Massachusetts had led the way for universal public education thanks to the leadership of educators like Horace Mann. Massachusetts had been one of the first to introduce practical subjects into the public school. They were among the leaders in the manual training movement, and they had passed legislation opening the way for the establishment of industrial schools in 1872. Industrial progress and the education of their citizens was important to the leaders of Massachusetts as evidenced by the re-evaluation of their education system in 1905 to see what needed to be done to better meet the needs of expanding industry. Governor Douglas, responding to a legislative mandate, appointed a Commission on Industrial and Technical Education composed of nine representatives from manufacturing, agriculture, education and labor, to investigate the need for industrial education (the term used then for vocational education), to determine the extent that existing programs were meeting this need, and to make recommendations regarding how to modify existing programs to serve a vocational purpose (Barlow, 1776).

The commission released its report in 1906 which contained the following findings:

1. There was widespread interest in the general subject of industrial education or special training for vocations.
2. There was a practical and specific interest among manufacturers and wage earners because of personal need. Industry wanted workers with more than skill in manual operations; they wanted workers with "industrial intelligence."
3. There was a growing feeling of the inadequacy of the existing public school system to meet fully the needs of modern industrial and social conditions. Schools were found to be too exclusively literary in their spirit, scope, and methods.
4. Their was no evidence that the people interested in industrial education had any concrete ideas as to its scope and method.
5. Their investigation had aroused the suspicion and hostility of many of the labor unions of the state.
6. There was little opposition to technical schools but significant opposition to trade schools.
7. There was general agreement that the financial support for technical education should be born wholly or in part by the state (Barlow, 1776).

The Douglas Commission Report concluded that lack of industrial training for workers increased the cost of production. They stated that workers with general intelligence, technical knowledge, and skill would command the world market. They emphasized that the foundation for technical success required a wider diffusion of industrial intelligence and that this foundation could only be acquired in connection with the general system of education in which it would be a integral part of the curriculum from the beginning (Barlow, 1976).

The Douglas Commission Report generated considerable interest. It brought to the nation's attention the urgent need to introduce programs of vocational education into the nation's secondary schools to prepare workers for America's growing industries. The report was instrumental in starting the definite movement for vocational education in secondary schools which would come some eleven years later with the passage of the Smith-Hughes Act of 1917.

National Society for the Promotion of Industrial Education

The widespread interest in industrial education discovered by the Douglas Commission prompted a group of 13 influential men to gather at a meeting of the Engineer's Club in New York City in 1906 to discuss the formation of a society to further the promotion of industrial education. Two leaders of manual training, James P. Haney and Professor Charles R. Richards, were responsible for arranging the meeting. Prior to adjournment, these men agreed on the need to establish an organization and appointed an ad hoc committee to plan a Fall meeting in which organizational details would be discussed and a large group of industrialists and educators would be invited to hear their views on industrial education. At the Fall meeting, the National Society for Promotion of Industrial Education (NSPIE) was formed with the mission of promoting industrial education through an effort to focus public attention on the value of an educational system which would prepare young men and women to enter industrial pursuits. More specifically, the Society wanted to unite all the forces of industrial education by providing them with opportunities for the study and discussion of mutual problems and to make them aware of experience in industrial education both in this country and abroad. (Barlow, 1976).

One of the first accomplishments of the society was to define the term industrial education. It was determined that industrial education referred to "that area of education between manual training and college engineering." Industrial education was intended to apply to vocational training of direct value to the industrial worker. While the focus of the society was originally on the development of education for trade and industrial workers, it broadened its scope to include other areas of vocational training (Barlow, 1976).

In 1908, the National Society for the Promotion of Industrial Education (NSPIE) formed state societies to carry on the work of informing the citizens of their state about industrial education, realizing each state had different educational, industrial, and social conditions that would alter their views toward industrial education. These societies were most influential in the passage of state legislation favoring industrial education prior to the Smith-Hughes Act (Barlow, 1976).

The National Society for the Promotion of Industrial Education included some of the most informed and dynamic leaders in manufacturing, labor, education, business, and government. Included in these leaders was James P. Haney, Charles Richards, David Sneeden, and the foremost leader in the development and promotion of vocational education in America, Charles Prosser. Prosser served as executive secretary of NSPIE and was the person most influential in securing passage of the Smith-Hughes Act of 1917, which established the principle of Federal support for vocational education in America. With passage of the Smith-Hughes Act of 1917, NSPIE changed its name to the National Society for Vocational Education, and in 1925 it combined with the Vocational Association of the Middle West to form the American Vocational Association, which continues to this day to meet the needs of vocational educators (Barlow, 1976).

Commission on National Aid to Vocational Education

In 1914, President Wilson responded to a joint resolution of Congress and appointed a special nine-member commission to study the issue of federal aid to vocational education. Senator Hoke Smith of Georgia was named as chairman, and Charles Prosser, executive director of NSPIE was one of the members. Hearings, conferences, and reports were used to gather information to determine: (1) the need for vocational education, (2) the need for federal grants, (3) the kinds of vocational education for which grants should be made, (4) the extent and conditions under which aid should be granted, and (5) the proposed legislation. Six months after its creation, the Commission issued its report recommending grants for vocational education in agriculture and the trades. The report included the following important recommendations which were included in the Smith-Hughes Act of 1917:

1. Grants should be used for training vocational teachers, paying part of teachers' salaries, and making studies and investigations which are helpful to vocational education.
2. Federal aid should be given to schools under public supervision and control, and of less than college grade.
3. Instruction was to be limited to youths over age 14 and be designed for profitable employment in agriculture and the trades.
4. Three types of classes should be developed, day school, part-time, and evening classes to provide vocational education.
5. A federal board should be established to oversee federal grants.
6. State boards should be created to administer the grants and states should develop a state plan for administering vocational education programs.

The Commission included a draft bill which was brought before Congress in 1914, but was not acted upon until President Wilson urged its passage in 1916. Representative Dudley Hughes of Georgia introduced an important revision to the original bill to include home economics as a vocational program eligible for federal grants. With the help of NSPIE, the American Federation of Labor (AFL), The National Association of Manufacturers (NAM), the National Education Association (NEA), the Chamber of Commerce of the United States, the Commission on Aid to Vocational Education, the Vocational Education Association of the Middle West, and the general will of the people, federal aid to vocational education became law in the form of the Smith-Hughes Act of 1917 (Barlow, 1776).

EDUCATIONAL PHILOSOPHIES OF JOHN DEWEY AND CHARLES PROSSER

In the late 1800s, industrialization had changed nearly every aspect of society and educational thought was being challenged by emerging social and economic issues. America was a democracy that required every citizen to be literate and to be able to contribute toward the good of society. Industrialization had created great wealth for a few but for many living and working conditions were deplorable. The gap between the wealthy and working class was widening and education was viewed then, as it is today, as the solution to economic and social problems.

Universal educational opportunities were available for most Americans up to at least the eighth grade, which was the elementary and high school of the late nineteenth century. Maximizing each individual's chances for lifelong learning and assisting individuals to obtain the "good life" was the ultimate goal of the educational system. The school curriculum of the late 1800s, however, was focused on preparing students for higher education in colleges and universities despite the fact that only a few students would complete formal schooling and enter higher education institutions.

For most Americans, what was needed was a more practical curriculum that would prepare them for work. Manual training was introduced into schools as a form of general education with a hidden objective of elementary preparation for work. Leaders in education and in business and industry began to realize that the diverse student population enrolled in schools was not receiving the type of education they needed to prepare for life and work. Many who lead the fight for the introduction of vocational education into the public schools did so because of a strong belief that schools needed to provide equality of educational opportunity. They felt that the schools' almost exclusive concentration on academics required for a few students to enter college was undemocratic and unfair to the majority of students, most of whom did not finish high school. They were also concerned with social issues of the working class and believed that individuals who were trained for a job and became wage earners would be more likely to become contributing members of their communities and to society in general. Finally, they recognized that people who work for wages and salaries buy goods and services produced or delivered by others which strengthens the economy and contributes to the wealth of the country. The vocational education movement which became a reality with the passage of the Smith-Hughes Act was based on economic, social, and philosophical factors (Calhoun & Finch, 1982).

As America entered the twentieth century, drastic changes were being made in educational practice and thought. The century old faculty psychology which held that the mind is made up of separate, independent entities or faculties such as memory, imagination, reason, observation, taste, etc. was giving way to American Herbartian psychology which emphasized the interest of the child and de-emphasized memorizing and the textbook method of learning. This psychology lead to the development and presentation of carefully sequenced lessons which were of interest to the child and within the capacity of the child to understand. The focus on teaching methodology did much to open the curriculum to the inclusion of practical subjects (Smith, 1981).

An equally important change that was occurring was a gradual switch from the philosophy of idealism, which had been the prevailing philosophy though most of the nineteenth century, toward pragmatism, instrumentalism, or experimentalism. Pragmatism emphasized the concrete over the more abstract problems of life. It emphasized an understanding of social institutions and the evolutionary character of societies and their ideologies. The role of education was not to train the mind like it was a muscle under the mindset of faculty psychology, but to awaken and broaden the interest of the child. Children and youth should be trained in productive thought and ethical action and be given opportunities to test their ideas whenever possible. Education should be viewed more as a science and use scientific methodology and scientific assumptions. Teachers should use the problem-solving method which involves students in identifying a need or problem, analyzing the problem, experimenting with various solutions, developing workable theories, selecting the most appropriate solution, and testing the chosen solution through concrete application. Under this philosophy, teachers were free to engage students more directly in concrete applications of what they were learning. Two influential psychologists-philosophers that promoted pragmatism were William James and John Dewey (Calhoun & Finch, 1982).

John Dewey was a strong advocate for vocational education. He was critical of the existing traditional liberal education of the time and felt that it did not provide the skills and attitudes that individuals needed to live in an age of science. He believed that children were inherently active beings who want to communicate with others, to construct things, to investigate and create. He advocated accommodating these natural traits in schools through activities such as language, manual and household arts, nature study, dramatics, art, and music. He believed that the curriculum should include a series of situations in which students are involved in solving problems of interest to them such as the "project method" being employed in some manual training schools that would engage students in activities that require thinking as well as doing. In his book published in 1916, *Democracy and Education*, Dewey expressed the view that education must have a practical outcome to be meaningful. Dewey was the undisputed leader of the progressive education movement which is still affecting education today (Smith, 1981).

At about the same time Dewey was promoting his views that education should become more democratic, another educator-philosopher was advocating the same outcome but with a different view on how to accomplish it. Charles Prosser had become an influential leader in the vocational education movement and his aggressive leadership had earned him the position of executive secretary of the National Society for the Promotion of Industrial Education in 1912. He was appointed by President Wilson to the Commission on National Aid to Vocational Education and was instrumental in developing the draft bills for federal aid to vocational education that were passed in 1917 as the Smith-Hughes Act. Undoubtedly, the leaders who were involved in the passage of the Smith Hughes legislation were aware of the progressive education philosophy advocated by John Dewey, which centered around meeting the needs of individuals, but it was Prosser's philosophy of essentialism–a vocational education philosophy grounded in meeting the needs of industry–that permeated the vocational education act. These two philosophies continue to affect vocational education today and should be understood by teachers and leaders of vocational education (Griffin, 1994).

Griffin (1994) studied the educational philosophies of John Dewey and Charles Prosser in her dissertation and compared and contrasted the important tenets of each philosophy. Both men wanted to make education more democratic and more practical. Both supported vocational education and favored programs that mirror real-life situations and make use of on-the-job training. But the manner in which vocational education programs should be infused into the curriculum differed significantly between these two men. See Figure 4-1.

Charles Prosser contended that the purpose of public education in a democracy is not for individual fulfillment but to prepare its citizens to serve the society. He expressed the idea that the interests, needs, and aptitudes of individuals should be served in order to perpetuate the society. Conversely, John Dewey's idea of the purpose of education in a democracy was to equalize individual differences for the improvement of society. Dewey recognized the rapid change that was occurring in society and maintained that individuals needed to be educated to personal initiative and adaptability so they would be better prepared to cope with the changes affecting life in the family, community and workplace (Griffin, 1994).

DIFFERENCES IN EDUCATIONAL PHILOSOPHIES: JOHN DEWEY AND CHARLES PROSSER		
PHILOSOPHICAL CRITERIA	**PROSSER**	**DEWEY**
Teaching Styles and Methodologies	Sequential, begins with basic facts. Instructors have strong industrial experience.	Begins with problem solving–results in knowledge base. Instructors have strong educational experience.
Administrative Structure	Seeks advice from industrial leaders, planner, implementer, cost-effective.	Facilitator of personal choices, advisor.
Personal/School Philosophies	Accents the needs of industry.	Accents the needs of individuals.
Benefits of the Program	Students gain marketable skills to become productive society members.	Students gain life skills and adapt-ability skills.
PROSSER-DEWEY DICHOTOMY		
Transferability of Skills	Transfer occurs naturally between similar tasks. Transfer is not a focus.	Transfer is the focus of a broad education.
Training to Work Transition	Facilitated through current equipment and instructors with industrial background.	Facilitated through focus on transfer.
Development of Problem-Solving Skills	Acquiring a base of knowledge precedes problem-solving skills.	Instruction begins with problem solving skills.
CONTINUATION OF PROSSER PHILOSOPHY		
Major Goal of the School	To meet the needs of industry and prepare people for work.	To meet the needs of individuals and prepare people for life.
Influencing Factors on School Success	Follow Prosser's Sixteen Theorems.	Follow guidelines in *Dewey's Democracy and Education.*

continued . . .

. . . continued

PHILOSOPHICAL CRITERIA	PROSSER	DEWEY
SOCIAL AND ECONOMIC FACTORS		
School Climate	Individualized differences are recognized, and all people and types of work are seen as having value.	Individual differences are equalized.
Adequate Supplies, Space, and Equipment	Schools must have adequate supplies, space, and equipment.	Schools need to have adequate supplies, space, and equipment, but students may use transfer skills to cover deficiencies.
Personal Motivations	Vocational education should be reserved for those who are motivated and can benefit.	Vocational education is for everyone, and everyone can benefit.

Source: Griffin, D. (1994). *North Carolina's first post-secondary technical institution: Past, present, and future.* Unpublished doctoral dissertation, University of Georgia.

Figure 4-1. A comparison of the educational philosophies of John Dewey and Charles Prosser as they relate to vocational and applied technology education.

The philosophy of Charles Prosser emerged in the Smith-Hughes Act and remained the dominant educational psychology guiding vocational education until the passage of the Vocational Act of 1963 and subsequent amendments. Prosser established sixteen theorems based on his philosophy, which were instrumental in the formation of vocational education programs and practiced for over 50 years. The impacts of these theorems are still felt somewhat today. Prosser's theorems, reworded, are as follows:

1. Vocational education should occur in the most realistic setting possible that replicates the actual work environment.
2. Vocational education should only be given where the training jobs are carried on in the same way with the same operations, the same tools, and the same machines that are used in specific occupations.
3. Vocational education should provide students with thinking habits–technical knowledge and scientific problem-solving skills–and the manipulative skills required in the occupation itself.

4. Vocational education should be planned and delivered in a manner that capitalizes on the student's interest, aptitudes, and intrinsic intelligence.
5. Vocational education is not for everyone, but for those individuals who need it, want it, and are able to profit from it.
6. Vocational education should provide opportunities for students to repeat operations of thinking and manipulative skills until habits are formed characteristic of those required for productive employment.
7. Vocational education should be taught by instructors who have successful experience in the applications of skills and knowledge required of competent workers.
8. Vocational education should be comprehensive and of sufficient duration that students can master competencies required to obtain and retain employment in a chosen occupational area.
9. Vocational education should prepare individuals for the occupations as they currently exist in the work force and for future labor markets as a secondary concern.
10. Vocational education should provide opportunities for students to perform operations on actual jobs when possible and not just simulated work tasks.
11. Vocational education curriculum should be based on the actual work tasks performed by experienced, competent workers and verified and updated frequently.
12. Vocational education curriculum should include the directly related body of content that is unique to occupational areas and emphasize the application of mathematics and scientific principles to problems of the occupation.
13. Vocational education should meet the needs of individuals when it is needed and in such a way as they can benefit from it.
14. Vocational education is more effective when its methods of instruction are best suited to each individual's interest, aptitudes, and abilities.
15. Vocational education should be implemented in a flexible manner but should be grounded on sound standards and evaluated continuously in order to make adjustments in light of changing employment requirements.
16. Vocational education requires more funds to operate than general education and the educational cost per student is higher because of the lower number of students that can be served in vocational classes. If sufficient funds are not available, vocational programs should not be attempted (Prosser & Allen, 1925).

Most vocational educators acknowledge that the prevailing philosophy today guiding vocational education is the philosophy of John Dewey. Today, vocational education is faced with many challenges in helping students become productive, contributing members of a rapidly changing society. Many of the lower level skilled jobs have been eliminated by advancing technology and jobs of today require individuals who have a wide range of knowledge and skills so they can function in a variety of positions within their field. Jobs of today require skills in thinking and problem-solving, which is one of the major tenets of Dewey's philosophy. Dewey believed that individuals are capable of adapting and solving problems. The social and cultural problems facing educators today calls for emphasis on human development in order to stabilize and improve American society–one of Dewey's principles. One of the goals of modern vocational education is to assist individuals to become more adaptable and self-sufficient, which will render them capable of pursuing a number of career options–another Dewey principle (Griffin, 1994).

SELF ASSESSMENT

1. What type of education was provided to youth in colonial America?
2. What functions did American Apprenticeship serve in colonial America?
3. What were some events that led to establishing a system of universal education in colonial America?
4. What were the views of Ben Franklin and Thomas Jefferson regarding preparing people for practical life?
5. What were the three landmark movements that promoted universal education in America?
6. What type of educational opportunities were provided for adults in the late 1700s and early 1800s?
7. What was the mechanics' institute movement?
8. What was the American Lyceum Movement?
9. What was the manual labor movement?
10. What were early American technical schools and what type of instruction did they offer?
11. What was the trade school movement?
12. How did corporate schools operate?
13. What were three early attempts to reform the common school to include manual activity into the curriculum?
14. What were some of the arguments for and against including practical subjects into the elementary and secondary schools of America?
15. Who were the leaders of the manual train movement and what was manual training?
16. What were the stated outcomes of manual training?
17. How did the comprehensive high school become the most universally accepted type of high school?

continued . . .

. . . continued

18. How did American sloyd differ from Swedish sloyd?

19. How did sloyd instruction differ from manual training?

20. What was the arts and crafts movement in America and how did it affect manual training?

21. How did manual arts affect manual training?

22. What is industrial arts and how did this practical arts field come into existence?

23. What was the status of agricultural education prior to 1917?

24. What was the status of home economics prior to 1917?

25. What was the status of business education prior to 1917?

26. What was the status of practical arts prior to 1900?

27. What conclusions did the Douglas Commission reach regarding the need for vocational education in the public schools of Massachusetts?

28. How did the National Society for the Promotion of Industrial Education affect the movement toward including vocational education into the nations schools at public expense?

29. What were the recommendations of the Commission of National Aid to Vocational Education which were later included in the Smith-Hughes Act?

30. How were the educational philosophies of John Dewey and Charles Prosser alike and different?

31. What were Charles Prosser's sixteen theorems of vocational education?

ASSOCIATED ACTIVITIES

1. Assist in organizing a collection of historical publications regarding vocational education that can be placed in the school library or learning resource center so vocational students and faculty can discover the rich history of vocational education.

2. Involve the vocational student organization in your occupational area in preparing a brief historical paper on their program area as part of National Vocational Education Week which occurs in February of each year.

3. Encourage students to make reports on articles dealing with vocational and technical education that are contained in the *Vocational Education Journal* and a number of other publications.

FEDERAL VOCATIONAL LEGISLATION

chapter 5

INTRODUCTION

The Smith-Hughes Act of 1917 initiated the concern of Congress that the security and welfare of the nation is dependent upon the ability of the American people to govern themselves and to educate its citizenry for productive work and meaningful living. Federal legislation has always been enacted to help solve major problems facing the nation as a whole or to address a cultural need such as ensuring the constitutional rights of all Americans. As skills needed for work and living became more complex – a trend that continues today – the training of skilled workers became a continuous identified need. Congress responded to the need to provide support for vocational education beginning with the passage of the Morril Act of 1862, which supported college and university programs of vocational education and continue that support today with current vocational legislation.

Congress continues to affirm its belief that federal support for vocational education is an investment in the future of the nation's workforce. A highly skilled workforce is viewed as essential to maintaining the nation's standard of living, defense preparedness, economic strength, and to maintaining a leadership position in the free world.

As the nation changed from a predominantly agrarian society in its early years to a highly industrialized, technological society, vast social, religious, philosophical, psychological, educational, and cultural changes took place requiring congressional action to address the nation's needs. These changes were addressed in educational legislation over the years. The development of vocational and applied technology education has been influenced greatly by many federal enactments since the Smith-Hughes Act of 1917. A review of these enactments aids in understanding our present form of vocational and applied technology education and the need to continue some form of federal support in partnership with states and local communities.

OBJECTIVES

After completing this chapter the reader should be able to:

1. Describe the relationship between the federal and state governments and local educational agencies with respect to vocational education.

2. Describe the major provisions of legislation involving vocational education from the passage of the Morrill Act of 1862 to the passage of the School-to-Work Opportunities Act of 1994.

FEDERAL VOCATIONAL LEGISLATION

Federal legislation was enacted to help solve major problems facing the nation as a whole or to address a cultural need such as the pressing need for skilled people in agriculture and the mechanic arts at the turn of the century. This recognized need required action for the good of the nation. Leaders of the federal government realized that the security and welfare of the nation as a whole lay in the ability of the American people to govern themselves and to educate its citizenry for productive work and meaningful living. As skills needed for work and living became more complex–a trend that continues today – the training of skilled workers in agriculture and the mechanic arts became a continuous identified need. Congress has been engaged in passing legislation for the support of vocational education ever since the Morrill Act of 1862.

The information which follows in this section is a brief review of federal acts that shaped vocational education for over 130 years based in part on the scholarly work of Nystrom and Bayne (1979), and the statutes themselves as listed in *The United States Statutes at Large*. Most vocational educators associate the beginning of federal support for vocational education with direct federal funding to vocational programs first provided by the Smith-Hughes Act of 1917, but federal support for vocational education began with the passage of the Morrill Act of 1862, which authorized land grants for the establishment of educational institutions which were to include programs for agriculture and the mechanic arts.

Ever since passage of the Smith-Hughes Act of 1917, which established the federal-state-local cooperative effort of providing vocational education, the federal government has maintained an active interest in vocational education. Federal policy from 1917 to passage of the Vocational Act of 1963 focused on expanding and improving vocational education programs and building vocational education capacity to serve the corporate needs of business and industry. From 1963 to the present, federal policy has continued its focus on improving and expanding programs to prepare people for work but it added a focus on meeting the human needs of persons by increasing assess to high-quality vocational education for all students, especially those from special populations.

From the Smith-Hughes Act of 1917 to the current legislation, Congress has reaffirmed its belief that federal support for vocational education is an investment in the future of the nation's workforce. A high-skilled workforce is viewed as essential to maintaining the nation's standard of living, defense preparedness, economic strength, and leadership position in the free world.

As the nation changed from a predominantly agrarian to a highly industrialized, technological society, vast social, religious, philosophical, psychological, educational, and cultural changes took place. These changes were reflected in educational legislation over the years.

In addition, many factors over the 78 year period since Smith-Hughes affected legislative priorities including : several wars, a major depression, labor-management strife, the space race, continuous technological advancements, changes in population demographics, increased standards of living and economic security, increased numbers of individuals in school and increased level of education for the populations as a whole, social unrest and increasing incidents of crime, high youth unemployment, high periods of unemployment and underemployment, desegregation, widespread discrimination, sex-bias and sex-role stereotyping, increasing number of women entering the labor force, multi-cultural diversity, changes in educational psychology, unacceptable levels of school dropouts, and the widening skill gap and shortage of highly-skilled workers (American Home Economics Association, 1991).

The reader should note the progressive evolution and expansion of vocational education legislation which included new areas of study resulting from technological change. In addition the reader should note the change form specific occupational programs designed to meet the needs of business and industry to programs designed to meet the needs of people. Finally, the increasing interest of Congress on meeting the needs of special populations through vocational programs should be noted.

The following information is provided to assist the reader interested in further information about the enactments presented in this chapter. Federal enactments are first assigned a public law (PL) number consisting of a multi-digit code number with the first two or three digits standing for the session of congress and the remaining numbers following a hyphen a chronical listing of the bills in that particular session of Congress. For Example, PL 85-864, the National Defense Education Act of 1958, is a law passed during the 85th session of Congress and was assigned the number 864 indicating its sequence in the 85th session of Congress. Once bills become law, they are assigned a volume number and a statute number for inclusion in the multi-volume *United States Statutes at Large* resource. PL 85-864 was assigned the code of 72 Stat. 1580 which means it is in the 72nd volume of the *United States Statutes at Large* under law numbered 1580. Specific legislation can also be located in the Statutes at Large publications with only the public law number. Identify the volume(s) labeled as the 85th Congress and sequentially locate the 864th order of legislation. The reader can obtain the Public law number and the U.S. code number for federal and state laws in a multi-volume publication entitled *Shepard's Federal and State Act and Cases by Popular Names* published by McGraw-Hill, Inc. available in college and university libraries. A Listing of the acts contained in this chapter with reference information is contained in Appendix A.

Morrill Act of 1862 (PL None)

Federal legislation for vocational education at the college level began with the 1862 Morrill Act known as the Land Grant Act in which states were given land that could be either sold or leased to raise money for establishing at least one college in the state. In this college, liberal and practical education studies were to be combined into a curriculum that was vocational without being viewed as being inferior to a purely academic curriculum. The land grant colleges and universities established by this act opened the doors to higher educational opportunities to a far wider range of students and paved the way toward acceptance of vocational education in institutions of higher education and later in the high schools of America. The intent of congress was to call importance to the mechanical arts and agriculture in this country and to ensure that this form of education was accepted as vital to the national welfare and a necessary incentive to spur economic growth.

Hatch Act of 1887 (PL None)

The Hatch Act was also known as the Experimental Stations Act in that it provided funds for each state to establish an agricultural experiment station in which agricultural research could be conducted and the results written in the form of useful information that could be used to inform people in the application of agricultural science.

Morrill Act of 1890 (PL None)

The second Morrill Act was known as the Maintenance Act. It authorized additional funds from the sale or lease of public lands to more fully support and maintain the agriculture and mechanical arts programs established in the original Morrill Act.

Adams Act of 1906 (PL 47)

The Adams Act increased the appropriations of funds provided to states for the operation of experiment stations provided by the Hatch Act.

Nelson Amendments to Morrill Act of 1907 (PL 242)

The Nelson Amendments increased the amount of funds used to support land-grant colleges and designated that a portion of the monies should be spent in the preparation of instructors for teaching agriculture and the mechanical arts.

Smith-Lever Act of 1914 (PL 95)

The Smith-Lever Act, known as the Agriculture Extension Act, provided for a program of cooperative extension work in agriculture and home economics in which instruction and practical demonstrations in agriculture and home economics was to be given to persons not attending or resident in college. This act was a significant piece of legislation in that it provided American farmers and homemakers needed training in demonstrations and project work at the farm and in the home as vocational education of less than college grade. The practice of 50-50 matching began with this act, for the state was required to finance half of the cost of the extension programs and the federal government the other half.

Smith-Hughes Act of 1917 (PL 347)

The Smith-Hughes Act, known as the Vocational Act of 1917, started the federal-state-local agency partnership for establishing and operating vocational education programs in public institutions of less than baccalaureate level. This act was the most specific and exacting of all enactments in its requirement upon states in the use of federal money which was provided in perpetuity for public schools. It represented national endorsement of vocational education in the public school system, a dream of many educational reformers and business and industry leaders for many years. The Smith-Hughes Act contained the following provisions which shaped the form of vocational education for many years:

1. Created a Federal Board for Vocational Education.

2. Provided categorical aid only within narrowly defined limits, thereby giving the Federal Board control over state programs.
3. Provided for a designated amount of funds to be given to states annually until $7,000,000 was reached to promote vocational education programs in the areas of agriculture, trades and industry, and home economics.
4. Provided annual appropriations for the following: (a) salaries of teachers, supervisors, and directors of vocational education areas–States paid half of salaries and federal government the other, (b) teacher preparation in the areas of agriculture, home economics, and trade and industrial subjects, and (c) support for the activities of the Federal Board for Vocational Education.
5. Mandated the creation of state boards to govern vocational education in cooperation with the Federal Board.
6. Required the development of state plans describing the kinds of vocational education to be offered by the state.
7. Required development of an annual report on the state vocational education system to be submitted to the Federal Board.
8. Required states to bear half the cost of salaries for vocational education personnel and to cooperate with local schools to provide funds to support high quality instruction in vocational programs–facilities, equipment, and materials.
9. Required that federal funds had to be under public supervision and control.
10. Required that vocational training be provided to individuals who: (a) have selected a vocational area and desire preparation in it, (b) have already been employed and seek greater efficiency in that employment, and (c) have accepted employment and wish to advance to positions of responsibility. Vocational education was to be less than college grade, for persons over 14 years of age who desire day time training, and for persons over 16 years of age who seek evening class training.

Smith-Sears Act of 1918 (PL 178)

The Smith-Sears Act authorized funds for establishing retraining programs for returning disabled servicemen from World War I. Many of these veterans enrolled in vocational programs.

Smith-Bankhead Act of 1920 (PL 236)

The Smith-Bankhead Act, known as the Federal Rehabilitation Act, provided for the establishment of programs for the rehabilitation of non-military disabled person into civilian employment. This act created state rehabilitation boards and an assistant director for vocational rehabilitation at the federal level. Many rehabilitation students enrolled in vocational programs to prepare for new jobs.

Smith-Fess Act of 1920 (PL 236)

The Smith-Fess Act, known as the Industrial Rehabilitation Act, provided federal aid for the vocational rehabilitation of industry-disabled persons. This act only lasted for four years, but established a precedent that would lead to other vocational rehabilitation acts years later.

George-Reed Act of 1929 (PL 702)

The George-Reed Act was a supplemental authorization enactment which provided additional funds beside those provided through previous legislation for home economics and agricultural education with no additional funds authorized for trade and industrial education. This was not a popular law for industrial education leaders.

George-Ellzey Act of 1934 (PL 245)

The George-Ellzey Act increased the supplemental funds for agriculture and home economics and reinstated support for trade and industrial education that had ended with the termination of the George-Reed Act, which lasted only three years.

George-Deen Act of 1936 (PL 673)

The George-Deen Act was another supplemental authorization enactment for increasing funding to agriculture, home economics, and trade and industrial education. In addition, it responded to a societal need to provide vocational education for individuals engaged in distributive occupations. Money was also authorized for teacher education programs. This act began to broaden the scope of vocational education–a trend that would continue for many years.

Vocational Education for National Defense (1940 to 1946)

A series of ten legislative acts were passed as war emergency majors that utilized the framework of vocational education for preparing people for the war effort. Vocational programs that were converted for national defense purposes were entirely funded by the federal government. The success of vocational education in preparing people for war industries firmly established vocational education as an important component of national defense.

Servicemen's Readjustment Act of 1944 (PL 78-346)

The Servicemen's Readjustment Act, known as the GI Bill of Rights, was passed to assist World War II veterans in making the adjustment to civilian life. One of the important stipulations of this act was that returning GIs had to declare a vocational objective in order to receive financial support to cover the cost of their education. This act encouraged inclusion of occupationally oriented programs into higher education institutions of America. It also encouraged enrollment of veterans in adult vocational education programs which helped to develop a network of post-secondary vocational-technical schools in every state. The GI Bill subsidized the cost of education and included subsistence for thousands of World War II veterans, and with subsequent legislation, provided the same services to veterans of the Korean and Vietnam Wars.

George-Barden Act of 1946 (PL 79-586)

The George-Barden Act, known as the Vocational Act of 1946, was another supplemental authorization bill that increased funding for existing vocational programs including agriculture, home economics, trade and industrial education, and distributive education. Like the George-Deen Act, it added areas that could receive funds, such as allocations for the Office of Vocational Education in Washington and authorization to include vocational education for the fishery trades. This act relaxed tight federal control over how the money provided by the act could be spent, giving more decision making control to the state and local education agencies–a trend that continues even to today.

Health Amendments Act of 1956 (PL 84-911)

The Health Amendments authorized funds to address the need to provide more nurses for a growing health care system and added practical nursing as one of the vocational areas that could be supported with federal funds.

Fishery Amendment, George-Barden Act of 1956 (PL 84-911)

An amendment to the George-Barden Act was enacted to further promote the fishing industry and to include the distribution aspects of that industry. The way money was to flow to support vocational education for fishery trades was changed to a system based on the size of each states's fishing industry, and was to be regulated by the U.S. Commissioner of Education and the Secretary of the Interior.

National Defense Education Act (NDEA) of 1958 (PL 85-864)

The National Defense Education Act is an excellent example of Congress responding to a critical need in society and enacting legislation to address this need. The launching of the Russian Satellite, Sputnik I, raised great concern about the standing of America in technical and scientific areas. A quick review of our space program revealed huge manpower shortages in electronics, aerospace engineering, mathematics, foreign languages, and other highly technical occupations. Congress acted quickly by passing the comprehensive National Defense Education Act (NDEA) of 1958. The NDEA Act was the first act to stress the importance of science, mathematics, foreign language, and technical competencies but subsequent legislation would continue this focus as occupations became more complex, requiring higher levels of applied academics and technical skills.

The population primarily served by this legislation, unlike most previous legislation which supported vocational education programs for secondary students, was on postsecondary training.

Title VIII of the act created the area school concept and provided funds for the operation of these postsecondary area schools in each state. The intent of Congress was to extend vocational education to residents of areas inadequately served and to encourage the development of postsecondary vocational programs that emphasized a combination of manipulative skills and related technical knowledge including mathematics, science, and applied technology that would enable graduates to work effectively as technicians–aids to engineers and scientists. The focus of this act was on providing vocational and related training for youths, adults, and older persons, including related instruction for apprentices, designed to fit them for employment as technicians or skilled workers in scientific or technical fields.

This act impacted both traditional as well as vocational education and aroused public interest in all students going to college. The NDEA included ten titles, with nine of them outlining and authorizing funds for different programs to receive federal aid. The subject of these titles were as follows:

1. Loans to qualified students in institutions of higher learning that were intended to encourage them to prepare for teaching in elementary and secondary schools or to prepare as specialists in science, mathematics, engineering, and foreign languages. Graduates who entered elementary of secondary teaching were eligible to have one-half of their loans forgiven. Many capable students were given an opportunity to complete a higher education degree that would not otherwise because of the high cost of a college education.

2. Strengthened instruction and promoted enrollments in America's secondary schools in the areas of science, mathematics, and modern foreign languages by providing for the purchase of equipment, the remodeling of buildings, and the employment of qualified state supervisors.

3. Provided for fellowships to be awarded through institutions of higher learning to promote research, the extension of knowledge, and the training of college teachers.

4. Provided funds for state departments of education to aid in testing, counseling and guidance in elementary and secondary schools, and funds for counselor training through regular courses and short-term institutes in colleges and universities.

5. Provided for federal aid for research and instruction in modern foreign languages through research studies and language institutes for teachers.

6. Provided funds for research and experimentation on the more effective utilization of television, radio, motion pictures, and related media for instructional purposes.

7. Provided funds for a science information service administered by the National Science Foundation.

8. Provided funds to assist state educational agencies for statistical services to improve their educational records and reports.

9. Provided funds to establish and maintain vocational schools on an area-wide basis to serve individuals, geographic regions, and occupations not being adequately served by existing vocational education programs.

Captioned Films for the Deaf Act (PL 85-905)

The Captioned Films for the Deaf Act authorized a loan service of captioned films for the deaf.

Education of Mentally Retarded Children Act of 1958 (PL 85-926)

The Education of Mentally Retarded Children Act authorized federal assistance for training teachers of the handicapped.

Manpower Legislation

The 1960s were years of social unrest and instability for our country. The Vietnam War had caused internal social problems and the rapid march of technology was displacing unskilled workers, causing widespread unemployment and underemployment. A growing number of people who had no skills and had lost their self-respect, plagued the nation's inner cities and countryside. Ironically, at the same time, there were high periods of unemployment and industry was in need of skilled workers. The number of economically depressed areas was beginning to rise. There was growing public sentiment that government needed to act to solve problems of unemployment, the rising cost of living, the rights of minority groups, and the shortage of skilled workers for business and industry. The federal government took action by implementing a number of acts directed toward retraining underemployed or unemployed adults through the Department of Labor. These acts created a number of programs that have been collectively called manpower programs. The current manpower act is the Jobs Partnership and Training Act as Amended in 1992.

Area Redevelopment Act of 1961 (PL 87-27)

The Area Redevelopment Act (ARA) was directed at providing retraining opportunities to individuals in economically depressed areas of the United States. Subsistence payments were given to trainees which served to encourage them to enroll and stay in training programs. A large sum of money ($4,500,000) was allocated to support vocational training, and existing vocational education programs provided training for some of the participants.

Manpower Development and Training Act (MDTA) of 1962 (PL 87-415)

The Manpower Development and Training Act provided training opportunities for underemployed and unemployed individuals based on training needs as determined by the Department of Labor and local employment services agencies. Like ARA, a large sum of money ($370,000,000) was authorized to be spent over a three year period. A number of training programs were administered through existing state agencies for vocational education. Many MDTA trainees were enrolled in area vocational schools in day and evening programs.

Health Professions Educational Assistance Act of 1963 (PL 88-129)

The Health Professions Education Assistance Act provided federal funds to expand teaching facilities for health programs and for loans to students in the health professions.

Higher Education Facilities Act (HEFA) of 1963 (PL 88-204)

The Higher Education Facilities Act authorized a five year program of federal grants and loans to colleges and universities for the expansion and development of physical facilities. In the early 1960s, college enrollment had reached an all time high due, in part, to the influence of the National Defense Education Act, resulting in a critical need for the Federal government to assist institutions of higher learning to provide housing for these students. The HEFA provided money to public institutions on a 40% federal to 60% state matching ratio and to private institutions on a 33.3% federal matching basis. This act provided much-needed assistance to junior colleges, undergraduate programs, and graduate programs involved in training skilled technicians and many of the existing occupational programs in various community colleges owe a large part of their physical facilities to this legislation.

Vocational Education Act of 1963 (PL 88-210)

As stated earlier, the early 1960s was a stressful period in our history characterized by a dramatic increase in youth unemployment and underemployment, a critical shortage of technicians and skilled workers, a constant need to retrain workers displaced by automation, and a growing need to provide new educational opportunities at the secondary and postsecondary levels. Congress had already enacted manpower legislation through the Department of Labor to deal with the problems of adults who were underemployed and unemployed, but something needed to be done to reduce the pool of people exiting from the high schools without the skills needed to find employment.

President Kennedy, in his message to Congress in 1961 on American education, called for an examination of existing vocational education legislation with a view toward modernizing the acts currently in force. He appointed an advisory board, known as the Panel of Consultants, to conduct a study of the current national vocational acts and to make recommendations for improving and redirecting vocational education programs. The Panel released it report entitled *Education for a Changing World of Work* in November of 1962. The report contained a number of findings and recommendations including the need to drastically increase the amount of federal money allocated to support vocational education programs and the need to eliminate funding by occupational categories in favor of a more flexible organizational structure that would better serve the needs of people.

The Perkins-Morse Bill, known better as the Vocational Act of 1963, was signed into law by President Johnson, marking a new era for vocational education. It affirmed the Federal Governments' commitment to vocational education as an essential program for the common welfare and national defense of the country. The central theme of this enactment was to broaden the conceptions of education for work to better meet the needs of different groups of people. The purpose of this act was to "authorize Federal grants to states to assist them to maintain, extend, and improve existing programs of vocational education, to develop new programs for vocational education, and to provide part-time employment for youths who need the earning from such employment to continue their vocational training on a full-time basis, so that persons of all ages in all communities of the State–those in high school, those who have completed or discontinued their formal education and are preparing to enter the labor market but need to upgrade their skills or learn new ones, and those with special education handicaps–will have access to vocational training or retraining which is of high quality, which is realistic in the light of actual or anticipated opportunities for gainful employment, and which is suited to their needs, interests, and ability to benefit from training."

Under the Vocational Act of 1963, 90% of the funds were allocated on the basis of a state's population, and these funds were to be spent for the following purposes:

1. Vocational education for high school students.
2. Vocational education for individuals who have completed or discontinued their high school education but are available for full-time study to prepare for employment.
3. Vocational education for persons who are already employed and need training or retraining to achieve employment stability or advancement in employment.
4. Vocational education for persons who have academic, socioeconomic, or other handicaps that prevent them from succeeding in the regular vocational education program. Ten percent of the funds provided by this act were to be spent on research and development of experimental programs to better serve the needs of handicapped individuals who could not succeed in regular vocational education programs.
5. Construction of area vocational schools.
6. Ancillary services–teacher training, vocational guidance, job placement, curriculum development, state leadership, etc.–and activities to assure quality in all vocational education programs.

The Vocational Education Act of 1963 included a number of important provisions which affected vocational education. These are as follows:

1. An Advisory Committee on Vocational Education was established in the Office of Education for the purpose of advising the Commissioner of Education on the national administration of vocational education program with respect to actual training requirements.
2. For the first time in federal vocational education legislation, states were permitted to transfer or combine categorical training allotments to meet their unique needs, thus ending specific categorical funding to most programs.
3. An Advisory Council was to be appointed in 1966 for the purpose of reviewing the progress of vocational education programs and making recommendations for improvement. This council was to reconvene periodically, with intervals of no less

than five years, and prepare reports on the state of vocational education in the nation. These Advisory Council Reports have significantly influenced other federal vocational legislation.

4. Work Study programs for vocational students were created by this act to allow students with financial need to become employed in order to begin or continue their vocational education.

Finally, the Vocational Act of 1963 broadened the definition of vocational education and defined the different types of area vocational schools. Vocational education meant "vocational or technical training or retraining which is given in schools or classes under public supervision and control, or under contract with a State board or local educational agency, and is conducted as a part of a program designed to fit individuals for gainful employment as semi-skilled or skilled workers or technicians in recognized occupations. This includes, in addition to the programs under the Vocational Act of 1946, as amended, any program designed to fit individuals for gainful employment in business and office occupations."

The definition of area vocational education schools of this act was instrumental in developing the delivery system of vocational education used today. Area vocational education schools meant (a) a specialized high school used exclusively or principally for the provision of vocational education to persons who are available for full-time study in preparation for entering the labor market; or (b) the department of a high school exclusively or principally used for providing vocational education in no less than five different occupational fields to persons who are available for full-time study in preparation for entering the labor market; or (c) a technical or vocational school used exclusively or principally for the provision of vocational education to persons who have completed or left high school and who are available for full-time study in preparation for entering the labor market; or (d) The department or division of a junior college or community college or university which provides vocational education in no less than five different occupational field under the supervision of the state board for vocational education leading to immediate employment, but not leading to a baccalaureate degree.

Civil Rights Act of 1964 (PL 88-352)

The Civil Rights Act of 1964 dealt with basic human rights and responsibilities in the workplace. Its major purpose was to insure that individuals, regardless of race, gender, national origin, or handicap would receive equal treatment and that selection for employment, education, apprenticeship or membership in a labor organization would be based solely on qualifications. Issues addressed by this act included equal employment opportunities, voting rights, equal education, fair housing, and public accommodation. Provisions of this act regarding handicapped individuals were to be revisited later in the Americans with Disabilities Act of 1990.

The Civil Rights Act provided federal grants to institutions of higher education to conduct special institutes for training elementary and secondary teachers to deal more effectively with special education problems resulting from desegregation and grants to local school boards to conduct inservice training for instructional staff to deal with problem evolving from desegregation. School boards could also apply for technical assistance to comply with desegregation mandates of this act.

Economic Opportunity Act of 1964 (PL 88-452)

The Economic Opportunity Act, another manpower legislative enactment, was established to strengthen and supplement existing legislation in order to increase the opportunity for everyone to receive education and training for work and to live with dignity. This act included provision that impacted vocational education including the establishment of:

1. Job Corps which are programs that prepare young men and women between sixteen and twenty years of age for the responsibilities of citizenship and to prepare them for employment through residential training centers. This program is still in operation today under the JTPA Act.
2. Work Training Programs which provided young people between ages sixteen and twenty-one, useful work experiences in public and other types of State and local work-study programs.
3. Work-Study Programs for youth from low-income families who were enrolled in higher education were provided with part-time employment so they could continue their education.
4. Work Experience Programs designed to provide and expand opportunities for work experience and other types of training to individuals in need but were unable to support or care for themselves or their families.

Elementary and Secondary Education Act (ESEA) of 1965 (PL 89-10)

The Elementary and Secondary Act was designed to provide sound educational opportunities to children and youth between the ages of five and seventeen with a particular emphasis on the education of students from low-income families. This enactment was in response to an alarming degree of illiteracy that existed in urban and rural area of the country. It was also deemed necessary to supplement the educational effort of states and local communities to improve the quality of elementary and secondary education nationwide. Title I of ESEA was to strengthen local educational agencies and to provide additional assistance to areas serving low-income and educationally deprived youngsters. Title II provided resources in the areas of school libraries, textbooks, and other instructional materials. Title III provided financial assistance to agencies developing exemplary programs and projects that would serve as models for regular school programs.

This idea of funding exemplary programs as models to be incorporated in regular school programs was incorporated into the Vocational Act of 1963, a practice that would appear again and again in subsequent federal vocational legislation. In ESEA, Congress had established a precedent of letting state and local school educational leaders make decisions regarding which programs to offer and discontinued their practice of mandating specific programs in federal legislation.

National Technical Institute for the Deaf Act of 1965 (PL 89-36)

The National Institute for the Deaf Act provided for the establishment and operation of residential schools for postsecondary education and training for the deaf.

Higher Education Act of 1965 (PL 89-329)

The Higher Education Act was a companion bill to ESEA, with the same focus to assist local agencies to solve local educational problems. Previous legislation such as NDEA placed emphasis on national control of education which led to placing less priority on solving local educational problems. This neglect at the local level contributed to the unrest, turmoil, and rioting that existed in many communities of the country. What was needed was a partnership between federal, state, and local educational agencies to address specific local problems.

The Higher Education Act provided assistance to colleges and universities in solving local problems. Among its important provisions were: (a) establishment of community service and continuing education programs that would serve the needs of the community, (b) educational opportunity grants and subsidized low-interest, insured-loan payments to assist student without adequate financial support to enroll and continue their education, and (c) establishment of the National Teacher Corps to assure an adequate source of qualified teaching personnel.

Adult Education Act of 1966 (PL 89-750)

The Adult Education Act authorized grants to states to encourage expansion of educational programs for adults, including training of teachers of adults and demonstrations in adult education.

Elementary and Secondary Education Amendments (ESEA) of 1966 (PL 89-750)

The ESEA Amendments modified existing elementary and secondary programs and provided for state grants to initiate, expand, and improve programs and projects for the education of handicapped children at the preschool, elementary, and secondary school levels.

Education Professions Development Act (EPDA) of 1967 (PL 90-35)

The Education Professions Development Act was created when the Higher Education Act of 1965 was amended and was intended to combine all the elements of previous legislation regarding teacher education together into one act. This act was instrumental in providing a vital source of college and university vocational teacher educators. Title V included five personnel-preparation programs which were:

1. National Teacher Corps.
2. Teachers in area of critical shortage.
3. Fellowships for teachers and other educational professionals.
4. Improved opportunities for training for personnel serving in areas other than higher education.
5. Training programs for higher education personnel and, after the passage of the Vocational Amendments of 1968, training for vocational education personnel.

Elementary and Secondary Education Amendments of 1967 (PL 90-247)

The ESEA amendments authorized support of regional centers for education of handicapped children, model centers and services for deaf-blind children, recruitment of personnel and dissemination of information on the education of the handicapped, technical assistance for education in rural areas, support for dropout prevention programs, and support for bilingual education programs.

Vocational Education Amendments of 1968 (PL 90-576)

The Vocational Amendments of 1968 was a significant piece of legislation in that it virtually canceled all previous vocational legislation except the Smith-Hughes Act, which was retained because it was the first federal legislation for vocational education at the secondary level. Congress recognized the need to consolidate vocational legislation to eliminate duplication of effort and to improve administrative efficiency. This act was essentially a rewrite of the Vocational Act of 1963.

The overriding purpose of these amendments was to provide access for all citizens to appropriate training and retraining which was nearly the same purpose as the Vocational Education Act of 1963. The major differences were that the Amendments emphasized vocational education in postsecondary schools and broadened the definition of vocational education to bring it closer to general education. This act authorized the appropriation of millions of dollars for vocational education in an attempt to find solutions to the nation's social and economic problems.

Under the Amendments, federal funds could be used for:

1. High school and postsecondary students.
2. Those who have completed or left high school.
3. Those in the labor market in need of retraining.
4. Those who have academic, socioeconomic, or other handicaps.
5. Those who are mentally retarded, deaf, or otherwise handicapped.
6. Construction of area vocational school facilities.
7. Vocational guidance for all persons mentioned.
8. Training in private schools under contract with public schools.
9. Ancillary services (preparation of state plans, administration, evaluation of programs, teacher education, etc.).

Special provisions of the Vocational Amendments of 1968 included the following:

1. Created a 21-member National Advisory Council with members to be appointed by the President. This council has been very influential in subsequent federal legislation.
2. Created state and local advisory councils to be involved in state and local plan development and in giving guidance to vocational education at the state and local school levels.
3. Required much more detailed state plans giving more control over local plans.
4. Earmarked funds for new exemplary programs and projects that were aimed at finding new ways to bridge the gap between school and work–a current focus of the School-to-Work Opportunities Act of 1994.
5. Provided funds for state-based research.
6. Provided funds for programs and projects designed to broaden or improve vocational education curriculums.
7. Provided funds for vocational education leadership and professional development for experienced vocational educators who wanted to engage in full-time study for a period not to exceed three years.
8. Provided funds to support a teacher/industry worker exchange program to update the occupational competencies of vocational teachers.
9. Earmarked funds for the support of cooperative vocational education programs

to cover the additional cost that it takes to operate these program. Cooperative education programs have been an important part of the vocational education delivery system for many years and are viewed as essential in today's diverse labor market.

10. Provided funds for consumer and homemaking education.
11. Provided funds to support work-study programs for needy vocational students.

Nurse Training Act of 1971 (PL 92-158)

The Nurse Training Act was an amendment to the Public Health Services Act, which provided funds for increasing and expanding provisions for nurse training facilities.

Education Amendments of 1972 (PL 92-318)

The passage of the omnibus bill, the Education Amendments of 1972, reflected the attempt by Congress to further consolidate previously enacted legislation. This act amended the Higher Education Act of 1965, the Elementary and Secondary Education Act of 1965, the Vocational Act of 1963, and several other enactments. It extended portions of the Vocational Act of 1963 and its amendments of 1968 till fiscal year 1975 and made a number of adjustments to assist vocational education to better serve the needs of all people who needed training and retraining for productive employment.

The Education Amendments of 1972 continued support of programs begun in the Vocational Act of 1963 including exemplary programs and projects, residential vocational schools, consumer homemaking education, cooperative vocational education, curriculum development, work-study programs, and the National Advisory Council of Vocational Education that continued monitoring the status of vocational education and issuing reports that identified issues which needed addressing in new legislation. In addition, this act introduced some new provisions important to vocational education, such as special programs for the disadvantaged and a new definition of vocational education that allowed federal funds to be spent for industrial arts programs and for training volunteer firefighters.

There were two other portions of this act that were significant for vocational education, Title III which established the National Institute of Education (NIE), and Title X which expanded community colleges and occupational education at the postsecondary level. The NIE was created to conduct educational research that would improve the quality of education for every American regardless of race, color, religion, gender, national origin, or social class. Title X provided funds for community colleges and the expansion of occupational education offerings at the postsecondary and adult levels. States were required to complete a comprehensive plan for the establishment and operation of occupational programs at the postsecondary level. To provide leadership to the expansion of postsecondary and adult occupational education, a Bureau of Occupational and Adult Education was established in the U.S. Office of Education.

Rehabilitation Act of 1973 (PL 93-112)

The Rehabilitation Act of 1973, Sections 503 and 504, affirmed the rights of handicapped persons in the workplace. There were no funds provided in this act for its mandates so this enactment is viewed more as a civil rights act which extended the Civil Rights Act of 1964. Section 503 required employers with federal contracts of more than $2500.00 to initiate affirmative action to hire handicapped individuals. Employers were to make reasonable accommodations for all handicapped persons interested in employment.

Section 504 prohibited discrimination on the basis of handicap in any private or public program or activity receiving federal funds and was designed to provide opportunities for handicapped persons to enter the mainstream of American life. Under this section, agencies receiving federal funds were required to: (1) provide opportunities, benefits, aids, or services for handicapped persons equal to those provided for the non-handicapped, (2) provide aids, benefits, and services for the handicapped in the same setting as the non-handicapped except in cases were effectiveness would be compromised, (3) provide barrier-free environments to insure facility and program accessibility, and (4) provide equal treatment and services in recruitment, training, promotion, and compensation for the handicapped.

Comprehensive Employment and Training Act of 1973 (PL 93-203)

The Comprehensive Employment and Training Act was a consolidation of earlier manpower legislation that began in the early 1960s, which marked the beginning of the federal government's involvement in establishing training programs for the unemployed and underemployed. The purpose of this new law was to decentralize and streamline manpower programs, to make them more administratively efficient, and to make them more responsive to local employment and manpower needs. This act nearly eliminated the practice of categorical manpower programs and introduced the concept of prime sponsors who, after careful planning, would receive block grants to operate training programs to meet local labor market needs. These prime sponsors often turned to established vocational education programs to provide training for their constituents.

Education Amendments of 1974 (PL 93-380)

The Educational Amendments of 1974 were primarily adjustments made to the Elementary and Secondary Education Act of 1965. This act, however, included some important provision that impacted vocational education. One of these provisions was encouragement in the development of a written Individualized Education Plan (IEP) for each child participating in Title I of the 1965 Act, which were children with special needs. This provision encouraged the involvement of parents and guardians, as well as vocational teachers, in the development of the IEP for handicapped students enrolled in vocational classes.

One of the provisions of the 1974 Amendments, Title IV, was the Women's Educational Equality Act of 1974. Congress found that educational programs in the U.S. were inequitable as they relate to women, and frequently limited full participation of all citizens. This act provided the financial incentive for states to develop programs specified in the act to bring about educational equity for women.

Another provision of Title IV of the 1974 Amendments was support for career education. Sidney Marland Jr., U.S. Commissioner of Education, introduced the concept of career education to express a major reform needed in secondary education and promoted this concept through the funds he had available in his discretionary grants. In a short period of time, this concept became a major education movement in the country and attracted the attention of the educational world and Congress. This concept of career education was viewed not as another program but as a continuum that begins with early childhood and extends to old age and that its' mission is primarily job or work related. Vocational educators were quick to recognize the potential of career education in the early years in helping youngsters select occupations and eventually vocational programs that would prepare them for their chosen careers. Congress added its' sanction of career education by establishing an Office of Career Education to carry out provisions relating to the definition and assist in the implementation of career education programs in the nation's schools. Career education was defined in the 1974 Amendments as an educational process designed to:

1. Increase relationship between schools and society.
2. Provide opportunities for counseling, guidance, and career development for all children.
3. Relate the subject matter of the curricula of schools to the needs of persons to function in society.
4. Extend the concept of the educational process beyond the school into the area of employment and the community.
5. Foster flexibility in attitudes, skills, and knowledge in order to enable persons to cope with accelerating change and obsolescence.

6. Make education more relevant to employment and to the need to function in society.
7. Eliminate any distinction between education for vocational purposes and general or academic education.

The career education movement was actually receiving federal support before the 1974 Amendments through exemplary programs and projects of previous legislation. Congress had simply recognized its importance and provided separate funding for expansion of the movement. With federal support, career education was the "hot topic" of the 1970s, but by 1981 had all but disappeared. The need to provide students with awareness and orientation to careers has not diminished, however, and is an important part of the School-to-Work movement of the 1990s.

The Amendments established a National Center for Educational Statistics (NCES) in the Office of the Assistant Secretary for Education and charged it with the responsibility for the collection and diffusion of educational statistics.

One other provision of the 1974 Amendments mentioned here is the provision to conduct research into the problems of providing bilingual vocational education. Congress discovered that many youth and adults could not profit completely from vocational education programs because of their limited ability to deal with the English language. These persons were then unable to fill the need for more and better trained personnel in critical occupational areas.

Education for All Handicapped Children Act of 1975 (PL 94-142)

The Education for All Handicapped Children Act of 1975 marked the beginning of a national effort to provide free and appropriate education for all handicapped children ages 3-21. In this act, Congress was affirming the belief that if adequate funds were provided to state and local agencies, they could provide the services required to meet the needs of handicapped children. This act specified a number of assurances or protective measures for handicapped learners and their parents in making public education free and appropriate for all youngsters. These assurances included:

1. A complete due process procedure.
2. Written, Individualized Education Plans would be developed and maintained for each handicapped student.
3. Handicapped students would be placed in the least restrictive environment and whenever possible, they should be educated with non-handicapped students–marking the beginning of the mainstreaming concept.
4. Bias free testing and evaluation procedures would be used in assessing handicapped students for placement purposes.

5. Policies and procedures would be developed and implemented to protect the confidentiality of student records.

This act replaced Title IV of the Elementary and Secondary Education Act and provided grant programs to states to help educate disabled students, and added new programs and funding areas including research, early intervention, and personnel training. These state grants were to assist in providing special education services to all disabled individuals from age 3-21. Grants were also awarded to public agencies and nonprofit organizations for preschool and early intervention demonstration programs which were to: (a) facilitate the intellectual, emotional, physical, mental, social, speech, and language development of disabled children; (b) encourage parent or guardian participation; (c) inform the community about disabled preschool children; and (d) offer training about model programs to state and local personnel who provide services for disabled children to age eight (*Education of the Handicapped*, 1991).

Other provisions of this act included:

1. Defined handicapped individuals to include mentally retarded, hard of hearing, deaf, speech impaired, visually impaired, seriously emotionally disturbed, orthopedically impaired, and other health impaired or learning disabled.
2. Defined special education as "specially designed instruction provided in classrooms, in physical education, at home and in hospitals."
3. Defined related service as "transportation and other support services, including speech pathology, psychological services, physical and occupational therapy, recreation and medical services needed for a disabled child to benefit from special education."
4. Defined an individual education program (IEP) as "a written statement drawn up by the teacher, parent, and a school representative that must include: the child's present educational level; annual goals, including short-term instructional objectives; the specific educational services to be provided and the extent to which the child will participate in regular education programs; initiation date and length of services; and evaluation procedures."
5. Authorized the establishment of six regional resource centers that were to provide technical and training assistance to state agencies and the establishment of one federal technical assistance center to deal with national priorities.
6. Authorized grants to states and agencies to assist in providing special education, vocational, and transition services to deaf-blind individuals.
7. Authorized grants to public and nonprofit agencies for research, development of new techniques, personnel training, and information dissemination to better meet the needs of severely disabled children.
8. Provided grants to agencies that assist the transition of disabled youth to postsecondary education, vocational training, employment, continuing education of

adult services. These grants were aimed at improving secondary special education programs and the vocational skills of disabled students.

9. Authorized grants to assist universities and nonprofit agencies in training personnel for careers in special education. These grants could be used to provide training as well as fellowships for trainees. In addition, grants could be obtained to conduct special projects and develop new approaches for preservice and inservice training of personnel who serve disabled children.

10. Authorized grants to agencies for improving special education and related services through the development of teaching techniques, effective curricula, technologies, model programs, and instruments for measuring progress.

11. Established a service to loan films and other educational media to deaf students and the establishment of the National Theater of the Deaf, Inc. to provide experiences for deaf individuals.

12. Authorized grants, contracts, and cooperative agreements for local and state agencies and universities to advance the use of instructional technology and mediated materials to teach disabled children.

13. Authorized grants to states for establishing interagency systems to provide early intervention services to all disabled children from birth to age three (*Education of the Handicapped*, 1991).

Education Amendments of 1976 (PL 94-482)

The Education Amendments of 1976 were a continuation on the part of Congress to write omnibus and comprehensive legislation that extended and revised existing legislation. These amendments came out of a desire of congress to redirect American education in an attempt to correct some of the nation's problems and to change the prevailing attitudes regarding the roles of men and women in society. One of its major thrusts was to extend and further revise the Vocational Act of 1963 as amended to meet the following purposes: (a) to extend, improve, and maintain existing programs of vocational education; (b) develop new programs of vocational education; (c) overcome sex discrimination and sex stereotyping; and (d) to provide part-time employment to youths who need earning to continue their vocational training on a full-time basis.

There were a number of new directions for vocational education specified in the Education Amendments, which included the following:

1. Required the development of programs to eliminate sex discrimination and sex stereotyping.

2. Required the development of a five year state plan that involved all agencies dealing in vocational education in its development.

3. Required an annual program plan and accountability report for each fiscal year.

4. Required each state to name a state board or agency to be the state agency responsible for administration of all public vocational programs within the state.
5. Established programs for the handicapped, for disadvantaged individuals, for persons of limited English proficiency, for persons who completed or left high school and who are enrolled in organized programs of study for which credit is given toward an associate or other degree not leading to a baccalaureate or higher degree, and for persons who have already entered the labor market or who are employed. Ten percent of the Act's funds were to be spent for programs for the handicapped.
6. Continued funding for exemplary and innovative programs, particularly those in urban centers with high concentration of economically disadvantaged individuals, unskilled workers, and unemployed workers; those that provided training for persons in sparsely populated rural areas; those that provided training to limited English-speaking persons; those programs designed to awaken occupational aspirations of youth with academic, socioeconomic, or other handicaps; and those programs that focused on discovering new ways to bridge the gap between school and work–a current concern of vocational education.
7. Encouraged improvement in programs of vocational guidance and counseling.
8. Continued support of consumer and homemaking education and placed special emphasis on the changing roles of men and women as workers and homemakers.
9. Required the development of a national vocational education data reporting and accounting system.
10. Extended federal assistance for programs of career education and the National Institute of Education.
11. Required states to develop an evaluation system to determine effectiveness of all vocational programs in the state.
12. Established the National Occupational Information Coordinating Committee (NOICC) and a system of State Occupational Information Coordinating Committees (SOICCs) to improve communication among vocational and manpower administrators, and to develop and implement an occupational information system to meet the common occupational information needs of vocational education and manpower training programs at the national, state, and local levels.
13. Changed the professional development for vocational education personnel to focus on providing opportunities for experienced vocational educators to spend full time in advanced study of vocational education, for certified teachers of other subjects to become vocational teachers if they have work experience in a vocational field, and for persons from industry with experience in a vocational field who wish to become vocational teacher in areas needing additional vocational teachers.
14. Continued the emphasis on improving bilingual vocational education through training programs for teachers and programs for students who have limited ability in use of the English language.

15. Provided emergency assistance for remodeling vocational facilities to comply with the Architectural Barriers Act of 1968 to make educational facilities accessible to handicapped persons.

Youth Employment and Demonstration Projects Act of 1977 (PL 95-93)

The Youth Employment and Demonstration Projects Act established youth employment training programs that promoted education-to-work transition, literacy and bilingual training, attainment of certificates of high school equivalency, job sampling including vocational exploration in the public school sector, and institutional and on-the-job training including development of basic skills and job skills.

Career Education Incentive Act of 1978 (PL 95-207)

The Career Education Incentive Act authorized the establishment of career education programs for elementary and secondary schools.

Comprehensive Employment and Training Act (CETA) Amendments of 1978 (PL 95-524)

The 1978 Amendments to CETA represented a major revision of previous manpower legislation to connect manpower training programs with other related programs involved in preparing people for work. Greater emphasis was to be placed upon utilization of existing services and facilities for manpower training if appropriate. Such services would include state employment services, state and local vocational schools, as well as the services of the state vocational rehabilitation agencies. Greater emphasis was also to be placed on the utilization of public vocational education facilities.

This act provided funds for the following programs: (1) comprehensive employment and training services, (2) youth programs, (3) National Commission on Employment Policy, (4) counter-cyclical public service employment program, (5) private sector opportunities for the economically disadvantaged, and (6) young adult conservation corps.

A significant provision of this act to vocational education was that vocational boards and prime sponsors were required to consult with other agencies such as vocational rehabilitation, Bureau of Education for The Handicapped, State Employment Service and others in formulating the five-year plan for vocational education and training. This requirement resulted in prime sponsors identifying the services to be provided to handicapped individuals in their five-year and annual training plan.

Educational Amendments of 1978 (PL 95-561)

The Educational Amendments established a comprehensive basic skills program aimed at improving student achievement in reading, mathematics, and written and oral communication. This act also established the community schools concept which encouraged the use of public buildings, including schools, to function as community centers for the education of adults.

Department of Education Organization Act of 1979 (PL 96-88)

This act established a Department of Education with responsibilities formerly assigned to the Education Division of the Department of Health, Education, and Welfare.

Job Training Partnership Act of 1982 (PL 97-300)

The Job Training Partnership Act (JPTA) of 1982 was an extension and major revision of the Comprehensive Employment and Training Act as amended in 1978, marking a new era for vocational education and the private sector to collaborate in providing job training and related services. The intent of Congress in this act was to increase the role of private business and industry in the training and employment of unskilled adults and disadvantaged youth and adults. For the first time in manpower training legislation, JPTA gave states and localities substantial choice in the direction of their employment and training policies. Under this act, a working partnership was formed between the public and private sectors with federal funds flowing down to states and on to local or regional service areas (SDAs), each of which had to utilize a private industry council (PIC) to determine what training programs were needed and how these programs would be implemented. The PICS were to be widely representative of individuals knowledgeable about training needs and training programs in the service areas and consist of the following partners: (a) business and industry leaders and officials, and (2) representative from organized labor, rehabilitation, employment services, economic development, and education. The PICs had the responsibility to determine the training agencies most suited to conducting the training and to establish programs to prepare eligible youth and adults for entry into the labor force.

The JPTA was a training enactment with no funds to support employment subsistence programs. Seventy percent of the funds were to be spent on training with 30% to be divided between administrative cost and support services. The training programs were targeted for unskilled youth and adults who are economically disadvantaged or have serious problems in gaining employment. This act also included special provisions for summer youth employment and training programs, dislocated and older workers, native Americans, migrants and seasonable farm workers, and veterans. The act also renewed authorization of the successful Job Corps program–a program directed toward improving the employability prospects of economically disadvantaged youth through residential training centers.

According to Griffin (1983), JPTA provided benefits to vocational education in the form of:

1. Added funds to reach out and serve more disadvantaged individuals and groups
2. Additional services to those disadvantaged individuals currently in the programs including such services as job search assistance, job counseling, remedial education and basic skills training, on-the-job training, vocational exploration, literacy and bilingual training, and follow-up services
3. New programs offered by vocational educators and by professionals not formerly part of the school system
4. More active interest from the private sector in the workings of vocational education
5. More local planning for vocational education that stimulated more local involvement of the community in vocational education.

Education Handicapped Act Amendments of 1983 (PL 98-199)

The Education Handicapped Act Amendments of 1983 included an important section entitled "Secondary Education and Transitional Services for Handicapped Youth" which was designed to support and coordinate educational and service programs to assist handicapped youth in the transition from secondary to postsecondary education, employment, or adult services. The act provided incentives to expand preschool special education programs and early intervention programs. Responsibility for administering and monitoring all Education of the Handicapped Act programs was transferred to the Office of Special Education Programs (OSEP).

The act also provided funds to support the development of demonstration projects for postsecondary educational programs for handicapped persons and the development of cooperative models for planning and development.

Rehabilitation Act Amendments of 1984 (PL 98-221)

The Rehabilitation Act of 1973 was amended to authorize demonstration projects to address the problems encountered by youth with disabilities in making the transition from school-to-work.

Carl D. Perkins Vocational Education Act of 1984 (PL 98-524)

The Carl D. Perkins Vocational Education Act, known as the Perkins Act, continued the affirmation of Congress that effective vocational education programs are essential to the nation's future as a free and democratic society. The act had two interrelated goals, one economic and one social. The economic goal was to improve the skills of the labor force and prepare adults for job opportunities–a long standing goal traceable to the Smith-Hughes Act. The social goal was to provide equal opportunities for adults in vocational education. These two goals are reflected in the nine stated purposes of the act which are as follows:

1. Assist the states to expand, improve, modernize, and develop quality vocational education programs in order to meet the needs of the nation's existing and future work force marketable skills, and to improve productivity and promote economic growth.
2. Assure that individuals who are inadequately served under vocational education programs are assured access to quality vocational education programs, especially individuals who are disadvantaged, who are handicapped, men and women entering nontraditional occupations, adults who are in need of training and retraining, individuals who are single parents or homemakers, individuals with limited English proficiency, and individuals who are incarcerated in correctional institutions.
3. Promote greater cooperation between public agencies and the private sector in preparing individuals for employment, in promoting the quality of vocational education in the states, and in making the system more responsive to the labor market in the states.
4. Improve the academic foundation of vocational students, and to aid in the application of newer technologies (including the use of computers) in terms of employment or occupational goals.
5. Provide vocational education services to train, retrain, and upgrade employed and unemployed workers in new skills for which there is a demand in that state or employment market.
6. Assist the most economically depressed areas of a state to raise employment and occupational competencies of its citizens.
7. Assist the state to utilize a full range of supportive services, special programs, and guidance and placement to achieve the basic purposed of this act.
8. Improve the effectiveness of consumer and homemaking education, and to reduce the limiting effects of sex-role stereotyping on occupations, job skills, levels of competency, and careers.
9. Authorize national programs designed to meet designated vocational education needs, and to strengthen the vocational education research process.

Under the Perkins Act, each state was required to provide educational services and activities designed to meet the special needs of, and to enhance the participation of: (a) handicapped individuals, (b) disadvantaged individuals, (c) adults who are in need of training and retraining, (d) individuals who are single parents or homemakers, (e) individuals who participate in programs designed to eliminate sex bias and stereotyping in vocational education, and (f) criminal offenders who are serving in a correctional institution.

Title II, Part B of the Perkins Act–Vocational Education Program Improvement, Innovation, and Expansion–identified 24 different areas that states could use funds to meet the needs identified in their state plans. This list is to exhaustive to present here, but an example area is the improvement of vocational education programs within the state designed to improve the quality of vocational education, including high-technology programs involving an industry-education partnership, apprenticeship training programs, and the provision of technical assistance.

Of particular interest to readers of this book is the Criteria For Services and Activities for the Handicapped and for the Disadvantaged spelled out in Title II, Part A, Section 204. State boards providing vocational services and activities for handicapped and disadvantaged individuals had to provide the following assurances that:

1. Equal access will be provided to handicapped and disadvantaged individuals in recruitment, enrollment, and placement activities.
2. Equal access will be provided to handicapped and disadvantaged individuals to the full range of vocational programs available, including occupationally specific courses of study, cooperative education, and apprenticeship programs.
3. Vocational education programs and activities for handicapped individuals will be provided in the least restrictive environment, and will, whenever appropriate, be included as a component of the Individualized Education Plan (IEP) cooperatively developed between vocational education and special education personnel.
4. Information will be provided to handicapped and disadvantaged students and parents of such students concerning the opportunities available in vocational education at least one year before the students enter the grade level in which vocational education programs are first generally available in the state, but no later than the beginning of the ninth grade, together with the requirements for eligibility for enrollment in such vocational education programs.
5. Each student who is enrolled in vocational programs shall receive: (a) assessment of their interests, abilities, and special needs with respect to successfully completing the vocational program, (b) special services, including adaptation of curriculum, instruction, equipment, and facilities, designed to meet student needs,

(c) guidance, counseling, and career development activities conducted by professionally trained counselors, and (d) counseling services designed to facilitate the transition from school to post-school employment and career opportunities.

Significant changes in this act from previous vocational education legislation included:

1. Formation of a 13-member State Council on Vocational Education consisting of seven members from the private sector, five of whom are representatives of business, industry and agriculture, two of whom are representatives of labor organizations, and the remaining six members are to be representatives from secondary and postsecondary vocational institutions. The chairperson must be from the private sector. State councils have more responsibilities than the old advisory committees including the development of a report every two years on the effectiveness of the vocational education delivery system funded under the Perkins Act and JPTA.
2. Formation of state technical committees from the private sector to advise the state board and council on the development of model curriculums to address state labor market needs.
3. Provisions that allow states to use funds to strengthen the academic foundations of vocational education through courses or special strategies designed to teach the fundamental principles of mathematics and science through practical applications which are an integral part of the student's occupational program.
4. Specification of certain services to be provided for handicapped and disadvantaged individuals including: (a) information about local vocational education opportunities; (b) assessment of student interests, abilities, and special needs; (c) guidance, counseling, and career development activities; (d) counseling services to facilitate the transition from school to employment; and (e) other special services, such as adaptation of curriculum, instruction, equipment, and facilities.
5. Creation of a full-time state sex equity coordinator to assist in eliminating sex bias and stereotyping in vocational education, and to administer the funds for single parent and homemaker programs and sex equity activities.
6. Elimination of the requirement for states to prepare a separate accountability report. Instead, each state is required to produce an annual progress report based on stated objectives and use this report as a tool in planning and improving programs. Thus the focus of state reports to the federal government has switched from financial "accountability" to "program outcomes."
7. Development of state plans covering a two-year period instead of the annual plan and five-year plan required in previous legislation.
8. Creation of a National Council on Vocational Education consisting of 17 members appointed by the President, nine of whom must be representatives of the private sector.

9. Coordination of the Perkins Act with the Job Training Partnership Act (JPTA) in order to provide programs of assistance for dislocated workers funded under title III of JPTA.
10. Development of measures for the effectiveness of programs under the Perkins Act including such evaluative measures as: the occupations to be trained for–reflecting an assessment of the labor market needs of the state, the levels of skills to be achieved in particular occupations–reflecting the hiring needs of employers, and the basic employment competencies to be used in performance outcomes–reflecting the hiring needs of employers.
11. Specification of a national assessment of vocational education to be conducted by the National Institute of Education and the results reported to Congress in the form of interim reports in January and July of 1988, with the final report submitted by January 1, 1989.

The Card D. Perkins Act reflects the philosophy of Congress that vocational education programs are best administered by local communities who are in the best position to make educational decisions, and that non-governmental alternatives promoting linkages between public school needs and private sector sources of support should be encouraged and implemented to strengthen vocational education and training programs.

Handicapped Children's Protection Act of 1986 (PL 99-372)

The Handicapped Children's Protection Act provided for monetary support for parents and guardians who find themselves in administrative hearings or court with a school system over a dispute concerning their child's right to a free appropriate special education and related services.

Education Handicapped Act Amendments of 1986 (PL 99-457)

The Education Handicapped Act Amendments was amended to continue and expand discretionary programs and transition programs. This act also changed the age of eligibility for special education and services for all children to age 3, and established the Handicapped Infant and Toddler program designed to meet the needs of children from birth to their third birthday who need early intervention services.

Rehabilitation Act Amendments of 1986 (PL 99-506)

The Rehabilitation Act Amendments authorized funding for programs in supported employment services for individuals with disabilities.

Technology-Related Assistance for Individuals with Disabilities Act of 1988 (PL 100-407)

The Technology-Related Assistance Act provided assistance to states in developing needed programs of technology-related assistance to individuals with disabilities and their families. Technology-related assistance was broadly defined in the act, giving states flexibility in providing assistive technology services to meet the unique needs of disabled consumers and their families.

Children with Disabilities Temporary Care Reauthorization Act of 1989 (PL 101-127)

This act authorized funds to provide temporary child care (respite care) for children who have a disability or chronic illness and crisis nurseries for children at risk of abuse and neglect.

Americans with Disabilities Act (ADA) of 1990 (PL 101-336)

The American with Disabilities Act furthered the provisions which began in the Rehabilitation Act of 1973, banning discrimination based on disability and guaranteeing equal opportunities for individuals with disabilities in employment, public accommodation, transportation, state and local government services, and telecommunications. This act was the most comprehensive enactment ever written to identify and protect the civil rights of Americans with disabilities.

The act applies to public and private organizations regardless of whether they receive federal funds, and covers the three areas of services, physical accessibility, and employment. Employers who have 15 or more employees cannot discriminate in hiring and promoting workers with disabilities, and they are required to make reasonable accommodations to enable disabled persons to work for their company. Public accommodations and transportation are also prohibited from discrimination on the basis of disabilities. This mandate requires public and private transportation carriers, and a myriad of public and private entities such as hotels, restaurants, bars, theaters, libraries, parks, and schools, to make reasonable accommodations, remove architectural barriers, and provide auxiliary assistance so that individuals with disabilities can use public accommodations and transportation services.

The essential elements of ADA in the areas of services, physical accessibility, and employment are as follows:

- ADA affects services including: integration, program accessibility, safety, communication, and the provision of aids, services, and preparation of self-evaluations.

- ADA affects physical accessibility including: accessibility audits, removal of barriers both inside and outside a facility, alterations of new construction, and preparation of transition plans.
- ADA affects employment including areas of: posting of job notices, setting of job qualifications, interviewing, testing of applicants, hiring, the provision of reasonable accommodations and training, and other areas of employment.

This act requires public and private schools to: (a) make any program, service, or activity readily accessible to and usable by students with disabilities, (b) provide information so students with disabilities can act on information about a program, service, or activity, (c) ensure that when evaluating disabled students, screening and testing procedures are fair, accurate, and non-discriminatory, and (d) provide an opportunity for disabled students to participate in any activity, service, or program school offered (Morrissey, 1993).

Carl D. Perkins Vocational and Applied Technology Education Act of 1990 (PL 101-392)

The Carl D. Perkins Vocational and Applied Technology Education Act amends and extends the Carl D. Perkins Vocational Act of 1984, authorizing the largest amount of funds ever for vocational education. The act intended to assist states and local schools in teaching the skills and competencies necessary to work in a technologically advanced society for all students. A major goal of this enactment was to provide greater vocational opportunities to disadvantaged persons. Basic state grants were exclusively devoted to special populations. These grants are specifically earmarked for programs that address the vocational needs of poor and handicapped students and those with limited English-language proficiency.

In addition to basic grants primarily devoted to improving programs for special populations, the act included 11 other categories as follows:

1. Tech prep–The Perkins Act of 1990 authorized funds for tech prep programs, which are cooperative arrangements that combine two years of technology-oriented preparatory education in high school with two years of advanced technology studies at a community college or technical institute. Tech prep programs are to integrate academic and vocational education which is a priority of this new act.
2. Supplementary grants for facilities and equipment–States and local districts with the highest concentration of disadvantaged students may obtain funds to improve vocational education facilities and equipment under this provision.

3. Consumer/homemaking education–Congress continued its emphasis on preparing people to live effectively in the family by providing funds for states to develop or improve instruction in nutrition, health, clothing, consumer education, family living and parenthood, child development, housing, and homemaking.
4. Career guidance and counseling–The act, like other legislation of the late eighties and nineties, placed emphasis on helping students make the transition from school to employment. The act provided for career development programs that help people make the transition from school-to- work, maintain current job skills, develop skills needed to move into high-tech careers, develop job search skills, and learn about other job training programs such as JPTA.
5. Community-based organizations–The act provided funding for local non-profit and other community groups to carry on vocational education programs and services to disadvantaged people.
6. Bilingual vocational education–The act authorized funds for programs specifically designed to provide bilingual vocational education and English-language instruction for those persons with limited English language proficiency.
7. Business/labor education partnerships–The act provided funds for support of business/labor/education partnerships that can improve the quality of vocational education and assist in upgrading minimal standards in key occupational areas.
8. Community education and light house schools–The act authorized funds to establish and evaluate model high school community education employment centers in urban and rural areas serving disadvantaged persons, and to establish and evaluate lighthouse schools or model vocational institutions that provide information and technical assistance to the field of vocational education about curriculum, develop linkages with other providers of vocational education and training, and disseminate model approaches to meeting training needs of special populations and for eliminating sex bias.
9. State Councils on vocational education–This act extended support for state councils on vocational education established in the original Perkins Act because of the key role these councils play in advising state agencies that establish vocational education policy.
10. Tribally controlled postsecondary institutions–The act authorizes funds to assist in the operation and improvement of tribally controlled postsecondary vocational institutions.
11. National Council of Vocational Education–The act provided temporary support for the activities of the National Council on Vocational Education created in earlier legislation until September 30, 1992 when the Council was disbanded (Wilcox, 1991).

The Carl D. Perkins Vocational and Applied Technology Act placed strong emphasis on improving vocational programs for the disadvantaged, integration of academic and vocational education, Tech-prep, accountability , and increased flexibility on state and local educational agencies. The act requires each state to create a set of core standards and performance measures that will form a benchmark for Perkins-mandated evaluations. Each state must conduct an initial assessment of its programs, submit a three-year state plan detailing how it plans to administer Perkins funds, and make regular statewide assessments of vocational education programs as part of the accountability process.

The New Perkins Act eliminated set-asides (targeted funds) for support services for special populations in its intent to allow flexibility for state and local agencies to design and deliver services which better meet the needs of special populations. The act continues all the assurances of due process, equal access, least restrictive environment, supplementary services, etc. of previous legislation and adds a new provision requiring local educational agencies to provide appropriate information about vocational programs to special populations prior to entry into eight grade (West, 1992).

Education of the Handicapped Amendments of 1990 (PL 101-476)

This act, which began in 1975 as The Education of All Handicapped Children Act, was revised in 1983 and 1986 as Education Handicapped Act Amendments, and amended again in 1990 when its name was changed to the Individuals with Disabilities Education Act (IDEA). This act, as amended, is the most important piece of legislation passed by Congress for educating disabled children and youth. The IDEA enactment expanded many of the discretionary programs authorized by previous legislation and created a number of new ones. Provisions of IDEA include the following:

1. Required schools to provide assistive devices–any item or piece of equipment or product system that is used to increase, maintain, or improve the functional capabilities of children with disabilities–to students who fall under the 11 categories of disabilities specified in IDEA.
2. Established special programs on transition.
3. Established a new program to improve services for children and youth with serious emotional disturbances.
4. Established a research and dissemination program on attention deficit disorders.
5. Expanded the list of nine conditions which children may have in order to be eligible for special education and related services to 11, adding the conditions of autism and traumatic brain injury.

6. Required that transition services and assistive technology services be made available for disabled children and youth and specified in their IEPs.
7. Expanded the definition of related services to include rehabilitation counseling and social work services.
8. Expanded the definition of special education to include instruction in all settings, including workplace and training sites.
9. Placed emphasis on meeting the needs of traditionally neglected populations to include minority, poor, and limited English proficient individuals with disabilities.
10. Provides a new structure to develop IEPs and ITPs based on multidisciplinary assessments and adds new assurances for each disabled student in the IEP and ITP planning process.

Developmental Disabilities Assistance and Bill of Rights Act of 1990 (PL 101-496)

The Developmental Disabilities Assistance and Bill of Rights Act authorizes grants to support the planning, coordination, and delivery of specialized services to persons with developmental disabilities. The act also provides funds for the operation of state protection and advocacy systems for persons with disabilities.

Job Training Reform Amendments of 1992 (PL 101-367)

The Job Training Reform Amendments revised the JPTA of 1982, changing the focus of JPTA programs toward improving services to those facing serious barriers to employment, enhancing the quality of services provided, improving the accountability of funds and the programs they support, linking services provided to real labor market needs, and facilitating the development of a comprehensive and coherent system of human resources service. Many of the revisions are administrative in nature but there are some provisions that are of importance to vocational educators as follows:

1. New requirements for on-the-job training (OJT) include: (a) development of an OJT contract to specify the type and duration of training to be developed and other services to be provided in order to ensure that proposed costs are reasonable, (b) OJT is to be conducted in the highest skill occupations appropriate for the eligible participant and should not be viewed as subsidized employment for low-skill occupations which need very little training time, and (c) the length of OJT training time supported with JPTA funds is limited to six months.
2. Eligible participants are to undergo an objective assessment which is to be a client-centered, diagnostic approach to evaluation of the needs of the participant without regard to services or training programs already available in the service

delivery area (SDA). This assessment is to be an ongoing process and should be multi-faceted, making use of the full array of options including such items as structured group interviews, paper and pencil tests, performance tests, behavioral observations, interest inventories, career guidance instruments, aptitude tests, and basic skill tests.

3. An individual service strategy (ISS) or an employability development plan is to be developed for each JPTA participant based on an objective assessment. The ISS is to include the appropriate mix and sequence of services with justification for each, indicate any need for supportive services, and to develop the individual continuum of services that will lead to an employment goal.

4. Performance standards must be developed for older worker programs, adult and youth programs, and dislocated workers. These standards may include standards for employment competencies which are to be based on such factors as entry-level skills and other hiring requirements.

5. The Nontraditional Employment for Women (NEW) Act is part of the Amendments of 1992 which has the purpose of providing a wider range of training opportunities for women under existing JPTA programs; to provide incentive for the establishment of programs that train, place, and retain women in nontraditional fields; and to facilitate coordination of JPTA and vocational education resources available for training and placing women in nontraditional employment. Non-traditional employment is defined as occupations or fields or work where women comprise less than 25% of the individuals employed in such occupations or fields of work.

6. A new year-round Youth Program is established consisting of various activities that can be used to address the needs of in-school and out-of-school youth with priority given on youth currently out of any formalized school system, including dropouts.

7. The Amendments emphasize targeting services to the hard to serve, and they recognize the need to provide appropriate supportive services to allow participants to stay in a JPTA program longer. Therefore, the Amendments provide for several types of payments, all of which must be charged to the training-related and supportive services category.

8. The Amendments include new guidelines for the make-up and duties of the private industry councils (PICs). The act requires that no less than 15% of the PIC membership be from organized labor organizations and Community-Based Organizations.

9. The Amendments require that SDA's operating adult programs and year-around youth programs establish appropriate linkages with other federal human resource programs and other agencies providing service to JPTA populations to avoid duplication and to enhance delivery of services.

10. The Youth Fair Chance program was established to provide comprehensive services to youth living in high poverty areas in urban and rural communities. The purpose of this program is to provide all youth living in designated target areas with improved access to the types of services and support necessary to help them acquire the skills and knowledge they need to succeed. Services include employment, training, education, child care, transportation, and social services.

Technology-Related Assistance for Individuals with Disabilities Act Amendments of 1994 (PL 103-218)

The Technology-Related Assistance for Individuals with Disabilities Act Amendments of 1994, known as the Technology-Related Assistance Act or Tech Act, amended the Technology-Related Assistance for Individuals with Disabilities Act of 1988. The purposes of Tech Act amendments included: (a) to provide discretionary grants to states to assist them in developing and implementing a "consumer-responsive, comprehensive, statewide program of technology-related assistance for individuals with disabilities of all ages, (b) to fund programs of national significance related to assistive technology, and (c) to establish and expand alternative financing mechanisms to allow individuals with disabilities to purchase assistive technology devices and services. In passing this act, Congress acknowledged the powerful role that assistive technology can play in maximizing the independence of individuals with disabilities. When fully implemented, this act has the potential to open many new opportunities for individuals with disabilities and their families to receive needed assistive technology services (Learning Disabilities Research and Training Center, 1994).

Goals 2000: Educate America Act of 1994 (PL 103-227)

The Goals 2000: Educate America Act was a blueprint for improving our nation's schools through establishing national goals and standards and assisting state and local agencies in helping every child meet these standards which will ensure that youngsters are learning what they need to learn in order to succeed in today's technological world. The act emphasized high standards for all students, support for comprehensive efforts at all levels to assist every child in reaching high standards, development of a framework for a Goals 2000 plan and development of a process for building a broad partnership (U.S. Department of Education 1994).

Goals 2000 identified eight national education goals, authorized funds for the improvement of schools K-12, established a framework to encourage state and local education agencies to develop comprehensive plans for integration and implementation of federal education programs, and provided for the development of national education performance standards and content standards that states will be encouraged to adopt. The act included the following major titles:

1. Establishment of eight National Education Goals.
2. Creation of the National Education Goals panel to build public support for the goals, report on the nation's progress toward meeting the goals, and review standards submitted to the National Education Standards and Improvement Council created by Goals 2000.
3. Creation of the National Education Standards and Improvement Council to oversee achievement standards in mathematics, science and other academic subjects, and to certify voluntary national standards; state standards for content, student performance, and opportunities to learn; and student assessment systems.
4. Establishment of the State and Local Education Systemic Improvement Program.
5. Creation of a National Skills Standards Board to stimulate the development of a voluntary national system of occupational standards and certification. The Board is to identify clusters of major occupations in the U.S. and encourage development of skill standards in each cluster. Voluntary standards which are submitted to the Board that meet established criteria will be certified (U.S. Department of Education, 1994).

The focus of Goals 2000 was on improving student learning by establishing goals for students and schools, and encouraging states and local school systems to adopt high standards and form partnerships to improve the educational delivery system for all youngsters. The act contained a suggested framework which identified ten elements that a Goals 2000 plan should include (U.S. Department of Education, 1994). These elements are:

1. Teaching and learning, standards, and assessments.
2. Opportunity-to-learn standards or strategies, and program improvement and accountability.
3. Technology.
4. Governance, accountability, and management of schools.
5. Parent and community support and involvement.
6. Making improvements system-wide.
7. Promoting grassroots efforts.
8. Dropout strategies.
9. Creating a coordinated education and training system.
10. Milestones and time lines.

School-to-Work Opportunities Act (STWOA) of 1994 (PL 103-239)

The School-To-Work Opportunities Act was passed to address the national skills shortage by providing a framework to build a high skilled workforce for our nation's economy through partnerships between educators and employers. The STWOA emphasized preparing students with the knowledge, skills, abilities and information about occupations and the labor market that will help them make the transition from school to post-school employment through school-based and work-based instructional components supported by a connecting activities component. Key elements of STWOA included: (a) collaborative partnerships, (b) integrated curriculum, (c) technological advances, (d) adaptable workers, (e) comprehensive career guidance, (f) work-based learning, and (g) step-by-step approach. This act promises to play a key role in the educational reform of our nation's secondary schools and is expected to expand post-secondary programs and services to include a wider audience. It is hoped that the school-to-work transition programs will redirect the focus of high schools toward integration of academic and vocational coursework, teaching all aspects of an industry, integrating school-based and work-based learning, and establishing functioning partnerships among elementary, middle, secondary, and postsecondary schools (Brustein & Mahler, 1994).

The act provided funds to states and local agencies that meet the requirements established by STWOA. Basic program requirements fall under three major components: (a) schools-based learning, (b) work-based learning, and (c) connecting activities. See Figure 5-1.

Improving America's Schools Act of 1994 (PL 103-382)

The Improving America's Schools Act is a reauthorization of the Elementary and Secondary Education Act (ESEA) which placed primary emphasis on serving disadvantaged students. The overriding goal of Title I has been revised to improve the teaching and learning of children in high-poverty schools to enable them to meet challenging academic and performance standards being established by the Goals 2000 Act. The Safe and Drug-Free Schools and Community Act is part of this enactment, which provided funds to school districts and schools in support of a comprehensive effort to combat problems of violence and drug use in schools. The act established a new Dwight D. Eisenhower Professional Development Program, which provides support for school districts and schools to develop plans for improving instruction and gives school personnel opportunities to determine the type of training and retraining they need. The act assisted schools in gaining access to the Information Superhighway and other technological advances to transform classrooms and improve student learning through the application of technology. The act provided an opportunity for states to obtain grants to support the planning and initial implementation of public charter schools.

KEY COMPONENTS AND ELEMENTS OF STWOA

SCHOOL-BASED LEARNING COMPONENT

- Career Counseling
- Selection of a Career Major
- Program of Study (Goals 2000)
- Integration of Academic and Vocational Education
- Evaluation
- Secondary/Postsecondary Articulation

WORK-BASED LEARNING COMPONENT

- Paid or non-paid Work Experience
- Job Training
- Workplace Mentoring
- Instruction in Workplace Competencies
- Instruction in all Aspects of the Industry

CONNECTING ACTIVITIES COMPONENT

- Matching Students With Employers
- Establishing Liaisons Between Education and Work
- Technical Assistance to Schools, Students and Employers
- Assistance to Integrate School-based & Work-Based Learning
- Encourage Participation of Employers
- Job Placement, Continuing Education or Further Training
- Collection & Analysis of Post-Program Outcomes of Participants
- Linkages with Youth Development Activities andIndustry

Source: Bruestein, M. & Mahler, M. (1994). *AVA Guide to the School-to-Work Opportunities Act.* Alexandria, VA: American Vocational Association.

Figure 5-1. Key program components and elements of STWOA identified by Michael Brustein and Marty Mahler in the *AVA Guide to the School-to-Work Opportunities Act*, 1994.

According to the American Vocational Association's *Legislative Update* (1994), the New Improving America's Schools Act increased opportunities for vocational-technical education input into state and local educational plans and strengthened vocational-technical education in the following areas:

1. States must coordinate the activities under the act with school-to-work, vocational education, cooperative education, mentoring, and apprenticeship program involving business, labor, and industry.

2. Targeted Assistance School Programs must include applied learning techniques; college and career awareness and preparation and teaching methods, which may include applied learning and team teaching; and services to prepare students for the transition from school-to-work, including the formation of partnerships and the integration of school-based and work-based learning.

3. Grants for professional development are available for developing curricula and teaching methods that integrate academic and vocational instruction, included applied learning, and team teaching strategies.

4. Education of Migratory Children grants to states must include assurances that, when possible, programs will provide for the transition of secondary students to postsecondary education of employment.

5. Dropout prevention programs must contain descriptions of the program goals, objectives, and performance measures that are to be used to assess the effectiveness of the program in improving vocational skills.

6. Demonstration of Innovative Practices programs can include grants to public or private partnerships involving business that emphasizes the integration of academic and vocational learning and make school relevant to the workplace, through applied and interactive teaching methodologies, team teaching strategies, learning opportunities connecting school, workplace, career exploration awareness, and career guidance opportunities.

7. Funds made available through the Dwight D. Eisenhower Professional Development Program can be used to train teachers in innovative instructional methods, including the integration of academic and vocational learning and applied learning and other teaching strategies that integrate real-world applications into the core academic subjects.

8. National Programs for Technology make funds available to develop demonstration and evaluation programs of applications of existing technology in preschool education, elementary and secondary education, training and life-long learning, and professional development of educational personnel.

9. Funds are made available through the Star Schools Program for activities that provide information about employment opportunities, job training, and professional development for vocational education teachers and staff.
10. The Magnet Schools Assistance provision provides state and local education agencies with assistance in providing instruction within magnet schools that will result in strengthening the vocational skills of students.
11. The Women's Educational Equity program provides funds for leadership training for women and girls to develop professional and marketable skills to compete in the global marketplace, improve self-esteem and benefit from exposure to positive role models; school-to-work transition programs, and programs that increase opportunities for women and girls to enter a technologically demanding workplace and, in particular, to enter high skilled, high paying careers in which women and girls have been under represented; and the development of guidance and counseling activities, including career education programs.
12. Bilingual Education Language Enhancement and Acquisition programs grants now include vocational and applied technology education.
13. The Indian, Native Hawaiian and Alaska Native Education Program provides funds for school-to-work transition activities including tech-prep, mentoring and apprenticeship
14. Urban and Rural Education Assistance grants now include in-school youth employment. vocational education and career education programs that improve the transition from school-to-work.

CURRENT LEGISLATION AFFECTING VOCATIONAL AND APPLIED TECHNOLOGY EDUCATION

There are only a few legislative acts that are currently in force that impact vocational and applied technology education. These include: (a) the original Smith-Hughes Act of 1917 that is a perpetual act which has been in force since 1917, (b) the Education of the Handicapped Amendments of 1990, (c) the Americans with Disabilities Act of 1990, (d) the Developmental Disabilities Assistance and Bill of Rights Act of 1990, (e) the Carl D. Perkins Vocational and Applied Technology Act of 1990, (f) the Job Training Reform Amendments of 1992, (g) the Technology-Related Assistance for Individuals with Disabilities Act Amendments of 1994, (h) the Goals 2000: Educate America Act of 1994, (i) the Improving America's Schools Act of 1994, and (j) the School-To-Work Opportunities Act of 1994.

A limited account of the significant events and legislative enactments which have contributed to the evolution of vocational and applied technology from the dawn of history to the present is contained in Appendix B.

Continuing Federal Support for School-to-Work, Job Training, and Vocational and Applied Technology Education

From the passage of the Smith-Hughes Act of 1917 to the most recent School-to-Work Opportunities Act of 1994, Congress has attempted to solve some of the nation's most pressing social and economic problems by enacting vocational and job training legislation to assist states and local educational and training agencies as they design and implement programs that prepare individuals for meaningful, productive employment. At first federal lesiglation was highly prescriptive, however, since the Vocational Education Act of 1963, most federal legislation has specified basic requirements but has given states and local agencies considerable flexibility on how to meet the legislative mandates. Congress has also attempted to consolidate many separate enactments affecting vocational education into only a few that are active today. There are, however, a large number of separate federal job training programs operating which have become targets for consolidation bills introduced in Congress.

Vocational and applied technology education programs are supported by a combination of federal, state, local, and private funds with most of the funding coming from state and local education budgets. The amount of federal support for vocational education has remained fairly constant for many years at around 10%. It is estimated that funds received through the Carl D. Perkins Vocational and Applied Technology Act constitute about 11% of the total vocational-technical education budget. While the federal share of financing vocational and applied technology education is relatively small, federal support has driven much of the needed change in programs over the years.

Many vocational educators today are concerned about the proposed changes in appropriations for vocational education and proposed changes in vocational and job training legislation. The 1995 Congress, with a Republican majority, is actively engaged in implementing the Contract for America, the Republican plan to reform the way Congress conducts business and reform the federal government itself.

Instead of continuing the authorization of the Carl D. Perkins Vocational and Applied Technology Education Act which is the current vocational education act, Congress has proposed repealing the act along with the newly passed School-to-Work Opportunities Act of 1994 and implementing a new system of block grants to states that give extended power to governors to determine how federal funds are to be spent. Legislative action is presently occurring in the House and Senate on two bills that would consolidate the Carl D. Perkins Vocational and Applied Technology Education Act of 1990 and more than 100 other education and training programs into block grants designed to give governors and local community leaders more say in how federal funds for vocational education and training are spent. The House bill – the Consolidated and Reformed Education, Employment and Rehabilitation Systems Act (CAREERS) – would create four linked, state block grants to deliver youth vocational education and at-risk-youth job training, adult education and family literacy, adult job training and vocational rehabilitation services. The Senate bill – the Workforce Development Act (WDA) – proposes a single block grant divided into percentages for education and economic development activities. Neither of these proposed bills require continuance of individual programs currently enjoying line item status under the Perkins Act such as Tech Prep or consumer-homemaking education. Both bills would require states to establish "One-stop" delivery systems for career counseling, labor market information and guidance on providers of education and training. Both bills give governors increased authority to take the lead in determining workforce needs of their states and in designing statewide educational systems, but differ greatly in their use of state and local education agencies in the decision making process (Dykman, 1995).

The proposed new block grants would replace "categorical funding" – a term for spending money according to specific rules, regulations, and directions for its allocations. The bills would consolidate many other vocational education and job training enactments including the Perkins Act, School-to-Work Opportunities Act, Job Training Partnership Act, Vocational Rehabilitation Act, parts of the Adult Education Act and the Stewart McKinney Homeless Assistance Act, the National Literacy Act, The Library Services and Construction Act and the Technology for Education Act, the Wagner-Peyser Act, Job Corps, and the Self-Sufficiency Assistance Act.

The two proposed bills do not agree on how money flows to states and local school systems but one thing is for certain and that is there will be a reduction in the overall amount of federal funds for vocational-technical education. Block grants, such as the one proposed for vocational education and training, not only cut spending but also change the decision making process and ask for more involvement from business and industry in the design of educational programs which could be determental to long term occupational preparation programs (Dykman, 1995).

It would be wrong to conclude that Congress no longer values vocational education and training because both bills recognize the importance of vocational-technical education to economic development. What Congress seems to be after is a unified, national workforce development system that is more sensible for employers, educators, and new graduates. It would also be incorrect to assume that vocational-technical education is "on the way out" because of reduced federal funding. Vocational-technical education is institutionalized in every public high school and technical school in the country. States and local school systems have developed capacity to offer vocational-technical education and training through a diverse number of programs. Currently there is only about 10% of federal funds in a local school's budget. Most of the state and local money goes for salaries and building and maintenance of facilities. The federal money allows schools to provide special services to better serve the needs of students. It is reasonable to conclude that changing federal funding to block grants may result in reduced federal funds but will not change the state and local school commitment of providing vocational-technical education to prepare individuals for the new workplace.

If both the CAREERS Bill in the House and the WDA Bill of the senate are approved, the pending legislation that is likely to emerge out of the House and Senate conference committee will be a hybrid of both with some new features that will launch a new national philosophy of workforce education. Just prior to the August recess, the Senate leadership moved to attach the WDA Bill to the Welfare Reform Bill scheduled to be voted on for September 5th. At this time it is unclear what will be the outcome of the WDA Bill which has now become title VII to the Welfare Reform Bill (National Tech Prep Network, August 15, 1995).

Federal and State legislation can expand opportunities to improve vocational-technical education or it can severely limit the ability of vocational educators to prepare students for the highly advanced workplace. It is more important now than ever before for vocational-technical educators to become advocates for legislation and to provide input to the political leaders who will make decisions that will affect vocational programs, students and the careers of vocational educators (Dykman, 1995).

It is difficult to predict what changes will be made in federal support for vocational and applied technology education and education in general. It is reasonable to conclude, however, that changes will be made with Congress dedicated to trimming the federal budget, consolidating programs, and maximizing efficiency. Vocational and applied technology educators need to keep informed and express their views to their senators and representatives so that federal support for vocational-technical education and the school-to-work initiatives continue.

SELF ASSESSMENT

1. Why is federal legislation so important to vocational education?
2. How did the Morrill Act contribute to the development of vocational education?
3. What was the major provision of the Hatch Act of 1890?
4. Of what significance were Nelson Amendments?
5. What were the major provisions of the Smith-Lever Act?
6. What were the major provisions of the Smith-Hughes Act?
7. What did the Smith-Sears, Smith-Bankhead, and Fess-Kenyon Acts have in common?
8. What were the major provisions for vocational education of the George-Reed, George-Ellzey, and George-Deen Acts?
9. How did the Servicemen's Readjustment Act help develop vocational education?
10. What were the major provisions of the George-Barden Act and its health and fishery amendments regarding vocational education?
11. How did the National Defense Education Act affect vocational education?
12. What were the condition that led to manpower legislation in the early 1960s?
13. What was the purpose of the Area Redevelopment Act of 1961?
14. How did vocational education profit from the Manpower Development and Training Act?
15. What were the major provision of the Vocational Education Act of 1963?
16. How did the Higher Education Facilities Act affect facilities for vocational education?
17. Of what significance to vocational education was the Civil Rights Act of 1964?
18. What were the four work programs established by the Economic Opportunity Act of 1964?
19. What were the major thrusts of the Elementary and Secondary Act of 1965?
20. What were the major provision of the Higher Education Act of 1965?

continued . . .

. . . continued . . .

21. How were residential schools for postsecondary education and training for the deaf established?

22. What was the focus of the Elementary and Secondary Education Amendments of 1966?

23. What were the main provisions of the Education Professions Development Act of 1967?

24. What were the areas in which federal funds could be spent to support vocational education under the Vocational Amendments of 1968?

25. Of what significance was the Elementary and Secondary Education Amendments of 1967 for disabled individuals?

26. What were the significant contributions to vocational education provided by the Educational Amendments of 1972?

27. Of what significance was the Rehabilitation Act of 1973?

28. How did the Comprehensive Employment and Training Act of 1973 and its Amendments of 1978 differ from previous manpower legislation and how did this act affect vocational education?

29. What were the major provisions of the Educational Amendments of 1974?

30. What were the major provisions of the Education of All Handicapped Children Act of 1975?

31. What were the new directions for vocational education proposed in the Educational Amendments of 1976?

32. Of what significance was the Youth Employment and Demonstration Projects Act of 1977?

33. What type of programs were established nationwide as a result of the Career Education and Incentive Act of 1978?

34. How did the Job Training and Partnership Act of 1982 affect vocational education?

35. What were the major provisions of the Education Handicapped Act Amendments of 1983?

36. What was the focus of the Rehabilitation Act Amendments of 1983?

37. What were the purposes of the Carl D. Perkins Vocational Education Act of 1984?

38. What services and activities were to be provided for handicapped and disadvantaged individuals as part of Title II, Part B of the Perkins Act of 1984?

39. What were the important provisions of the Education Handicapped Act Amendments of 1986?

. . . continued

40. What new support was provided to disabled individuals in the Rehabilitation Act Amendments of 1986?

41. What specialized assistance was provided to disabled individuals and their families through the Technology-Related Assistance for Individuals with Disabilities Act of 1988?

42. What were the major provisions of the Education of the Handicapped Amendments of 1990 or the new Individuals with Disabilities Education Act as it was to be called?

43. What are the major provisions of the Americans with Disabilities Act of 1990?

44. Of what significance was the Developmental Disabilities Assistance and Bill of Rights Act of 1990?

45. What is the major purpose of the Carl D. Perkins Vocational and Applied Technology Education Act of 1990 and what are the eleven categories in which federal funds can be spent to improve vocational and applied technology education?

46. What are the major provisions of the Job Training Reform Amendments of 1992 with respect to vocational education?

47. What are the major provisions of the Technology-Related Assistance for Individuals with Disabilities Act Amendments of 1994?

48. What is the overriding purpose of the Goals 2000: Educate America Act of 1994 and what are the major titles of the Act?

49. How can vocational and applied technology education programs be strengthened through provisions of the Improving America's Schools Act of 1994?

50. What are the major provisions of the School-To-Work Opportunities Act of 1994?

51. What are the elements under the school-based learning, work-based learning, and connecting activities of the School-to-Work Opportunities Act?

ASSOCIATED ACTIVITIES

1. Contact the State Department of Education and obtain copies of current laws governing education.

2. Obtain materials on the current laws affecting vocational education and develop a reading program so you can assist in the implementation of legislative mandates and be well-informed about opportunities to secure grant funds to start innovative programs in your occupational field.

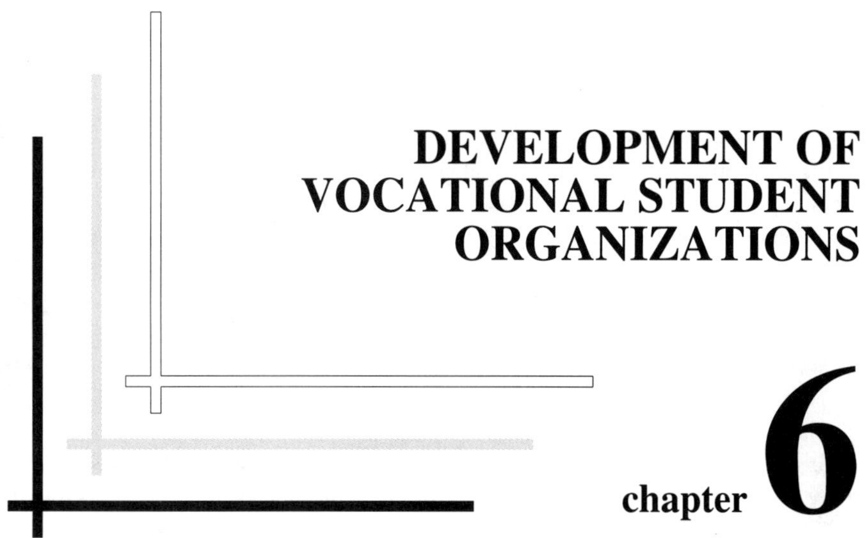

DEVELOPMENT OF VOCATIONAL STUDENT ORGANIZATIONS

chapter 6

INTRODUCTION

Vocational student organizations (VSOs) are essential to quality programs of vocational and applied technology education. Vocational student organizations provide a unique mix of instructional programs and activities which provide middle (junior high), secondary, postsecondary, adult, and collegiate students opportunities for leadership and career development, motivation to learn and achieve, and recognition for effort and progress. The mission of vocational student organizations is to provide the best learning environment and preparation possible so students can enhance their leadership and technical skill development in their chosen occupational areas. Today, ten national vocational student organizations are recognized by the U.S. Department of Education.

Vocational student organizations have been important to vocational programs for over 66 years. Soon after the passage of the Smith-Hughes Act of 1917, which provided federal support for vocational programs, leaders recognized the need to provide some type of organized clubs that would provide vocational students with social and recreational activities, motivation to take full advantage of their instructional programs, and provide them opportunities to showcase their skills. A number of local student organizations developed and as vocational education became more widespread, each major service area of vocational education developed a national vocational student organization. In recent years, some of these organizations have changed their names and all of them have changed their programs and activities to better meet the career and leadership skill needs of all students, including those from special populations.

Students who participate in VSOs are provided with many benefits, including the satisfaction of belonging to an organization with other students along with many other benefits such as opportunities to develop positive self-concepts, social skills, problem-solving skills, communication skills, leadership skills, and occupational skills, all of which are valued universally by employers.

Even though VSO activities are considered an integral part of the regular instructional program, a number of real or perceived barriers inhibit students from active participation. The challenge for making VSO activities attractive and accessible for all students is being accepted by VSO leaders at the national, state, and local school levels.

This chapter presents information about the development, general characteristics, benefits and advantages, programs and activities, and student involvement in VSOs. It presents information that can be used by vocational and applied technology education teachers to encourage students to participate in VSO activities and to assist them in making this participation more complete and successful.

OBJECTIVES

After completing this chapter the reader should be able to:

1. Describe how VSOs were developed, their purposes, and relationships to vocational and applied technology education programs.

2. Identify some of the benefits and advantages that are provided by active VSOs for students, teachers, schools, and communities.

3. Describe the federal legislation that has guaranteed all students the right to participate in VSO activities.

4. Identify some of the real and perceived barriers that students from special populations may experience in becoming involved in VSOs.

5. Identify some of the VSO activities in which students from special populations and other students can participate.

6. Identify some instructional strategies that teachers and VSO support team members can use to increase the participation of students from special populations in VSO activities.

7. Identify some modifications that can be made to regular VSO activities that can increase the participation of students from special populations.

DEVELOPMENT OF VOCATIONAL STUDENT ORGANIZATIONS

Historical Perspectives

Student organizations have been a part of vocational education programs since the passage of the Smith-Hughes Act of 1917 which provided federal support for vocational education programs. Vocational student organizations (VSOs) were not mentioned in the Smith-Hughes Act, but funds were provided for training teachers whose duties would later include advising and supervising vocational student organizations. The George-Barden Act of 1946 was the first to mention a vocational student organization, the vocational agriculture student organization which was founded in 1928. This act stated that funds could be used for vocational agriculture teacher activities related to the VSO. Four years later in 1950, another federal law, commonly known as PL 740, officially chartered the Future Farmers of America (FFA), thus establishing the integral relationship of the vocational student organization to the instruction program and directly involving the U.S. Office of Education in supporting vocational student organizations. This act set the precedent for all vocational student organizations to be recognized as essential components of a quality vocational education program (Vaughn, Vaughn, and Vaughn 1993, p. 4).

Three other federal acts included references to vocational student organizations. The Vocational Education Act of 1963, along with its amendments of 1968 and 1976, broadened vocational education by eliminating specific occupational categories and provided a specific definition of vocational instruction which included activities for VSOs. The amendments of the 1963 Act reaffirmed that VSOs are an essential part of instruction and specified which activities were to be considered integral for which federal funds could be used and which ones were not (Vaughn, Vaughn, and Vaughn 1993, pp. 4–5).

The Carl Perkins Vocational Act of 1984 (PL 98-524) included vocational student organization activities in its definition of vocational education. The definition of vocational education according to the act was: organized educational programs which are directly related to the preparation of individuals for paid or unpaid employment, in such fields as agriculture, business occupations, marketing and distributive occupations, technical and emerging occupations, modern industrial and agriculture arts, and trade and industrial occupations, or for additional preparation for a career in such fields, and in other occupations requiring other than a baccalaureate or advanced degree, and vocational student organization activities as an integral part of the program.

Vocational student organizations, as defined by the Carl Perkins Vocational and Applied Technology Act of 1990, was: those organizations for individuals enrolled in vocational education programs which engage in activities as an integral part of the instructional program. Such organizations may have state and national units which aggregate the work and purposes of instruction in vocational education at the local level (The AVA Guide to the Carl Perkins Vocational and Applied Technology Education Act of 1990, p. 163).

Finally, the School-To-Work Opportunities Act (STWOA) of 1994 continued the recognition of the value of VSOs by including them in the definition of local partnerships. Local partnerships means a local entity that is responsible for local School-to-Work Opportunities programs that consists of employers, representatives of local educational agencies, local postsecondary educational institutions (including representatives of area vocational education schools, where applicable), local educators (such as teachers, counselors, or administrators), representatives of labor organizations or nonmanagerial employee representatives, and students; and may include such entities as vocational student organizations. The act requires states to include in their state plan information on how they will continue to obtain the involvement in the statewide School-to-Work Opportunities system of employers and other interested parties such as locally elected officials . . . vocational student organizations, State or regional cooperative education associations, and human service agencies (STWOA, 1994).

The National Vocational Advisory Council on Vocational Education in its historic 7th Report (1972) acknowledged the work that vocational student organizations had done and made six recommendations to the U.S. Secretary of Health, Education and Welfare for the further development of these organizations. Undoubtedly influenced by the Advisory Committee report, the U.S. Office of Education (now the Department of Education) recognized the vital role that vocational student organizations play in vocational education and developed a policy statement that acknowledged that these organization activities were intracurricula and that federal monies could be used to support certain activities of the organization.

On February 11, 1990 The U.S. Department of Education released a policy statement describing their position on vocational student organizations as being an integral part of vocational-technical education instructional programs. See Figure 6-1.

Policy of the United States
Department of Education
For Vocational Education Student
Organizations

The United States Department of Education maintains a close relationship with ten vocational student organizations and welcomes their cooperation and support in strengthening programs of vocational-technical education. Recognizing that the past performance and future potential of these ten organizations are compatible with the overall purposes and objectives of education today, the United States Department of Education strongly endorses their objectives and seeks to involve their thinking in the improvement of vocational-technical education.

In view of this, these policies represent the position of the United States Department of Education:

1. The United States Department of Education recognizes the educational programs and philosophies embraced by the following vocational student organizations as being an integral part of vocational-technical education instructional programs:

   Business Professionals of America
   Distributive Education Clubs of America
   Future Business Leaders of America—Phi Beta Lambda
   National FFA Organization
   Future Homemakers of America
   Health Occupations Students of America
   National Postsecondary Agriculture Student Organization
   National Young Farmer Education Association
   Technology Student Association
   Vocational Industrial Clubs of America

2. The United States Department of Education recognizes the concept of total student development as being necessary for all vocational-technical education students to assume successful roles in society and to enter the labor market.

3. The United States Department of Education will facilitate technical and supportive services to assist vocational student organizations through State agencies in their efforts to improve the quality and relevance of instruction, develop student leadership, enhance citizenship responsibilities, overcome sex and race discrimination and stereotyping, and serve students of special populations, especially with respect to efforts to increase minority participation in these organizations.

4. The United States Department of Education recognizes the responsibility for vocational-technical instructional programs and related activities, including vocational student organizations, rests with the State and local education agencies.

5. The United States Department of Education approves of Federal and State grant funds for vocational-technical education to be used by the States to give leadership and support to these vocational student organizations and activities directly related to established vocational-technical education instructional programs at all levels under provisions of approved State plans for vocational-technical education.

Efforts on the part of State and local education agencies to recognize and encourage the growth and development of these vocational student organizations are highly important and deserve the support of all leaders in American Education.

Richard W. Riley
Secretary of Education

Augusta Souza Kappner
Assistant Secretary for
Vocational and Adult Education

Source: Policy of the United States Office of Education for Vocational Education Student Organization (1990). Washington, DC: U.S. Office of Education.

Figure 6-1. A policy statement of the United States Department of Education for Vocational Student Organizations (VSOs).

Federal legislation has provided the foundation for vocational education programs and the inclusion of vocational student organizations in legislative acts and the support of the U.S. Department of Education has made it possible for these organization to become a vital part of local vocational education programs. Vocational and applied technology teachers are expected to include information and activities which relate directly to these VSOs in their curriculum.

Over the years each major service area of vocational education, such as vocational agriculture and trade and industrial education, has developed a national student organization to serve students enrolled in their programs.

The vocational agriculture educators were the first to establish a VSO by founding the Future Farmers of America in 1928. By 1988, nine other national VSOs had been formed (Vocational Student Organizations, "A Reference Guide," 1990). Today, VSOs are more than simply an organized activity to provide social and recreational opportunities for students; they are an integral part of every vocational program. Vocational student organizations have become a major instructional tool for teachers to provide the leadership, citizenship, and occupational skills and knowledge required to prepare students for jobs and careers in our fast-changing technological society. They have become the highly visible component of vocational and applied technology education in America, and therefore have provided the vehicle for business, industry, and community involvement in the educational process in our nation's secondary and postsecondary schools.

Purposes of Vocational Student Organizations (VSOs)

Most vocational student organizations have been formed to serve students in a specific vocational service area with the exception of Future Business Leaders of America (FBLA), which originally was open to all business education students at the secondary level. All VSOs carry on activities as an integral part of their respective vocational programs. Vocational student organizations' purposes are similar and focus on the areas of leadership development, student personal growth, exploring careers, improving the home and family, developing citizenship and patriotism, improving scholarship and vocational preparation, improving school and community, developing respect for the dignity of work, developing high ethical and moral standards, participating in cooperative effort, developing creativity, and developing social skills and worthy use of leisure time. Each VSO has a motto and creed that states the basic beliefs which guide their actions. Also, each VSO has an emblem and official colors which are symbolic of their organization and serve to remind members of the purposes of their organization.

One of the basic needs of individuals is a sense of belonging, a feeling of being accepted in something larger than the individual. Vocational student organizations provide the basic vehicle for students to meet this need of belonging and becoming a part of an organized group. Other reasons why students join groups or organizations are recognition, expanded opportunities, helping others, making new friends, security, being involved in a worthwhile cause, developing leadership abilities, and self expression. VSOs provide opportunities for students to meet friends, to work together with students in a specific interest field, to gain individual and group recognition for achievements, and to develop leadership. Students join groups or organizations for recognition, expanded opportunities, helping others, making new friends, security, being involved in a worthwhile cause, developing leadership abilities, and self expression. Vocational student organizations provide opportunities for students to meet friends, to work together with students in a specific interest field, to gain individual and group recognition for achievements, to develop leadership and occupational skills required for entrance into a chosen career, and to render services to school and community to make them better places in which to learn, live, and work.

The Vocational Industrial Clubs of America (VICA) members approved a VICA Bill Of Rights in 1992, which can serve as a compact for quality for all vocational and applied technology students. This Bill of Rights represents an agreement between teachers and students, as they work together in the interest of their schools and communities. VICA's 10 basic rights are:

1. To be respected for our occupational choices
2. To meet occupational standards set by employers and to be proficient in the workplace basics
3. To receive a world-class academic education
4. To earn credentials and degrees which qualify us for further education and work
5. To receive career guidance that fits our interests and aptitudes, and allows for freedom of choice
6. To work in the occupations for which we have trained
7. To study in safe and stimulating schools
8. To serve our communities
9. To learn from competent instructors committed to the success of their students
10. To meet face-to-face with business, industry, and organized labor.

Relationship of VSOs to Vocational Education Programs

Vocational student organizations are not "clubs" or extra curricular organizations to which only a few individuals belong. Rather, a VSO is a powerful instructional tool that works best when integrated into the vocational and applied technology education curriculum and classroom by an instructor who is committed to the total development of students. Vocational and applied technology teachers have long recognized the need to provide students with more than technical knowledge and skills; they recognize the need to provide authentic, interesting activities for students to develop personal-social skills, leadership skills, and employability skills (Vocational Student Organizations, 1990).

While there are still some educators who view VSOs as extra-curricular in nature (activities take place outside of the instructional program), most recognize VSO activities as an integral part of vocational education programs which contribute to the comprehensive learning experiences of students. In actual practice, VSO activities are scheduled along with other classroom and laboratory learning experiences. Vocational student organization activities often complement and reinforce learning experiences for the student, thereby adding another dimension to the instructional program.

Students from special populations, along with other students, can participate and benefit from VSO activities. The overriding purpose of all student organizations is to provide learning experiences, opportunities, and recognition that contribute to maximum development of the individual student. Of no less importance is preparing students for active participation in our democratic and free enterprise society.

There are a number of techniques that VSO advisors can use to integrate the VSO into the regular vocational and applied technology classroom. The following techniques were presented in Vocational Student Organizations, "*A Reference Guide*" (1990) as typical of the role that the VSO can play in the classroom and laboratory:

1. Review professional oaths as well as the oaths of VSOs.
2. Elect chapter officers and use them to call the class to order, take roll call, maintain financial records, monitor class protocol and member behavior, prepare bulletin board and posters, and prepare articles and news releases.
3. Establish committees for VSO and classroom functions and encourage all students to participate in them.
4. Use parliamentary procedure to enable the class to arrive at decisions in an orderly manner.
5. Prepare chapter newsletters that allow students to practice many important communication skills.
6. Emphasize professional dress and grooming as important to personal and career success.
7. Sponsor field trips and involve VSO members in planning for them and coordinating the visit.
8. Encourage members to attend civic, professional, or trade meetings where they will learn the importance of contributing to the community and their profession. Have members share their experiences in class with others students who were unable to attend.

9. Assign VSO members tasks of interviewing selected business and industry leaders and share findings with other students. Students can learn how to develop and use interview questionnaires to gather data in an organized manner.
10. Assign students the task of preparing for and delivering an extemporaneous talk. The VSO contest rating sheets can be used to evaluate and provide feedback to the presenter.
11. Assign students the task of preparing for and presenting a talk to community groups. Most VSOs have a prepared speech contest rating instrument that can be used to prepare students for this talk. Communication skills will help students accelerate their career advancement in the workforce.
12. Arrange for students to participate in mock interviews that enable them to better market themselves in future actual job interviews.
13. Encourage members to participate in VSO team competitions that can build enthusiasm among members and provide opportunities to learn how to let along with other members of a group.
14. Encourage members to get involved in collecting funds for worthwhile organizations (i.e. Muscular Dystrophy, March of Dimes).
15. Encourage members to help prepare for implementing the Special Olympics in their community.
16. Encourage members to adopt a mentally disabled or elderly person and be attentive to their needs.
17. Encourage members to become involved in the many worthwhile school and community projects that provide a variety of learning experience and demonstrate that VSO members support their school and community.

General Characteristics of VSOs

The organizational structure of VSOs is similar with a national organization, state association, and local chapters and/or clubs. Vocational student organizations at the national level are incorporated and listed under the Internal Revenue Service code 501(C)3 for nonprofit organizations. Vocational student organizations are governed by a board of directors and managed by an executive director and staff who execute the policies established by the organization. The student-directed VSO, such as the Distributive Education Clubs of America (DECA), is governed by a set of national officers which form the National Executive Council who receives direction from a delegate assembly which convenes annually at the National Conference. Most VSOs have a third organizational form, a foundation which enables business, industry, organizations, and individuals to cooperate in enhancing and furthering the programs of VSOs.

State VSOs are chartered by the national organization and consist of a set of state officers who form the executive council under the guidance of a state VSO director--usually a member of the State Department of Education in the VSO service area. State associations support the national organization's goals, purposes, policies, and activities and provide leadership to organizational structures below it such as districts, regions, areas, and local chapters/clubs.

Local VSO chapters/clubs are student-directed through a set of elected officers under the guidance of the vocational or applied technology education teacher who serves as VSO advisor. Vocational student organization chapters or clubs plan programs of work which lists the various activities required to accomplish the purposes of the organization and the national program of work.

These activities which make up programs of work are usually selected from the following major categories: professional, leadership, personal growth, civic and community, social, service, safety, public relations, cooperation, financial, and scholastic or educational.

Membership in VSOs is open to all students enrolled in vocational programs or those who have been enrolled during the school year. Most VSOs have several types of membership which include active member, honorary member, alumni member, associate member, professional member, and collegiate member. Active members are those students presently enrolled in vocational programs and those who have been enrolled during the school year.

VSO members have many opportunities available to them to develop the knowledge, skills, and appreciations required to become leaders in their chosen career fields. Leadership, communication, and social skills can be developed through participation in VSO meetings, conferences, special seminars, and a variety of career fields. Leadership, occupational skills, and knowledge can be further developed through participation in individual competitive events, team competition events, and chapter/club events which are offered by most VSOs. Winners in these competitive events are recognized in a variety of ways including receiving trophies, plaques, medals, pins, certificates, newspaper coverage, and recognition at meetings and banquets.

Vocational student organization members can be identified by their official dress which consists of a colored blazer, sweater, or jacket with the emblem of the organization attached to the left breast pocket, white shirts and blouses, appropriately colored tie, slacks, skirts, shoes, and socks.

The national VSO office provides many interesting and informative materials to support local VSO chapter/club activities. All VSOs publish a student magazine such as *Teen Times*, the official magazine of the Future Homemakers of America; *School Scene*, the magazine of the Technology Student Association; and the *VICA Journal*, the official journal of the Vocational Industrial Clubs of America.

National vocational student organizations have additional publications and mediated materials listed in educational materials catalogs such as newspapers, newsletters, brochures, posters, instructional aids, and a wide variety of chapter/club materials such as handbooks, computerized programs, videotapes, competitive events guides, and recognition certificates. National VSOs also work with suppliers such as the VICA supply service, Midwest Trophy Manufacturing Company, Inc., to provide other VSO support materials such as blazers and other clothing, pennants, awards, certificates, pins, and other memorabilia.

BENEFITS AND ADVANTAGES PROVIDED BY VSOs

When VSOs are organized as an integral part of the educational program and are implemented properly, they can be very influential for increasing program enrollment, enhancing program visibility, involving employers and community leaders, securing commitment of important support people and groups, motivating both vocational and applied technology teachers and students to higher levels of individual and groups performance, recognizing effort and achievement, and providing the means by which personal and career goals become reachable for all vocational and applied technology students (Vocational Student Organizations, 1990).

Benefits for Students

Harris and Sweet (1981) and Vaughn, Vaughn, and Vaughn (1993) identified a number of benefits provided through active participation in VSOs. These benefits apply to all learners, including students from special populations. These benefits are as follows:

1. Civic responsibility
2. Interest in vocational education
3. Leadership skills
4. Social skills through committee work and recreational activities
5. Respect for the dignity of work
6. Effective use of free time
7. Understanding of employer/employee relationships
8. Spirit of healthy competition
9. Vocational understanding
10. Recognition and prestige
11. Enthusiasm for learning
12. Firsthand knowledge of the democratic process
13. Home improvement skills
14. Employability skills

15. Sense of independence and accomplishment
16. Opportunity to plan and carry out an idea
17. Opportunity to see adult sponsors as role models
18. Self-improvement and scholarship
19. Occupational competence.

The list of benefits include most of the desirable behaviors needed by all students but several of them reflect critical needs of many students from special populations, notably a sense of independence and accomplishment and enthusiasm for learning.

Sarkees (1983) identified some advantages of participating in VSO activities which are important for learners from special populations. These are building self-confidence, developing interpersonal relationship skills, improving vocational related and employability skills, providing motivation to learn, providing valuable information about citizenship and living independently in our democratic society, developing leadership skills, and providing an opportunity for effective student-teacher interaction.

Vocational student organization activities were developed to improve self-concept, develop respect for work and pride in a chosen occupation, develop high ethical and moral values, create an understanding and appreciation of the work ethic, and develop a sense of cooperation with others to accomplish chapter/club activities and school and work assignments. Active participation in VSO activities help students from special populations develop a strong identity, a feeling of belonging, a sense of independence, and a healthy relationship with fellow students and adults (Sarkees, 1983).

The personal, social, and academic benefits of involvement in VSOs go hand in hand. Learners from special populations get to know other students and their teacher on a personal basis through individual activities and cooperative team work. At the same time they are strengthening their commitment to the goals, objectives, and learning experiences of the vocational and applied technology education program and are becoming motivated to succeed in classroom and laboratory activities (Sarkees, 1981).

Vocational Student Organizations reinforce workplace basics. Vocational Student Organizations "*A Reference Guide*" (1990) provided the following information on how participation in VSO activities helps develop workplace basics:

Knowing how to learn. VSOs encourage student-directed learning and experimentation thereby requiring members to absorb, process, and apply new information quickly and effectively. Employers place great value on people who are capable of learning on their own.

Reading, writing, and computation. VSOs provide a variety of opportunities to apply and refine reading, writing, and computational skills in operating the student-led "chapter" and in participating in the professional development and national competitive events programs.

Communicating effectively. VSOs encourage the application and refinement of speaking, listening, and feedback skills in chapter meetings, committee work, and in preparation for competitive events.

Creative thinking and problem solving. VSO members are provided opportunities to practice and refine their problem-solving skills in groups or committees to conduct chapter management activities. By learning how to work cooperatively as a member of a team, (VSO chapter) members, as employees, will be better prepared to discover new solutions to existing problems that may serve as barriers to improved quality of products, productivity, and competitiveness.

Personal management. VSOs contribute greatly to the improvement of personal management skills, including heightened self-esteem, goal-setting, goal achievement, career direction, education, and training analysis. VSOs provide real situations in which more "authentic skills" that make a productive and competitive workforce can be developed.

Group effectiveness. VSOs are "group-oriented" and chapter activities provide opportunities for members to develop and refine interpersonal, negotiating, and team-building skills. A major objective of VSOs is to help members develop skills and attitudes that can be successfully applied in the workplace to resolve problems and foster innovation. VSO members who have developed these essential team-work skills will achieve the flexibility and adaptability that America's workforce must have to remain competitive in the global economy.

Influencing others. Exhibiting leadership potential is the hallmark of VSOs. A major purpose of all VSOs is the development of leadership and the capability of others to act in a prescribed manner or move in a positive direction. Leadership is a learned skill that must be practiced and refined in real situations. Active involvement in VSO activities provides members with numerous opportunities to develop, practice, and refine their leadership skills. In the workplace of today, leadership skills are among the most important workplace basics.

Benefits to Teachers, Schools, and Communities

In addition to providing many benefits to vocational and applied technology education students, VSOs provide benefits to teachers, school, and community. Benefits to teachers include a valuable teaching tool, opportunities for self-improvement, opportunities to enrich instructional experiences, a means of adding excitement to daily routines, a valuable student recruitment tool, publicity for the vocational and applied technology education program, and opportunities to improve the total program.

Benefits to the school include motivating students to apply themselves more to school and learning, promoting community involvement in school activities, and bringing school and life into closer harmony with one another. The community also receives benefits such as better-prepared citizens, services provided to citizens in need, and a source of young people who have leadership and employment skills. Finally, the United States benefits by having a source of competent workers who can work in team environments to solve problems, introduce innovation, and produce products of high quality in the most efficient and cost-effective manner possible.

BARRIERS TO INVOLVEMENT IN VSOs

With so many benefits and opportunities provided by VSOs, it is hard to imagine why every vocational and applied technology student does not belong to the VSO in their vocational service area. There are many reasons for this finding, including: (1) some vocational students are denied the opportunity to become a member because local school administrators too often consider VSO activities disruptive of more formal and fashionable education and discourage their establishment (National Advisory Council 7th Report, 1972) and (2) vocational teachers often ignore the vast potential of an active VSO as an integral part of their instructional program. Vocational and applied technology teachers give the following reasons for not starting a VSO in their classes:

1. Dues are too high for students to pay.
2. School activity periods are not provided.
3. Transportation is not available for after school activities.
4. VSO activities take up too much of after school and weekend time.
5. Students are not interested in VSO activities.
6. Parents are not supportive.
7. Students are less likely to take vocational courses the entire year.
8. Teachers are more accountable for student success in meeting curriculum objectives and they have less time for VSOs.
9. Difficult to obtain school funds to support VSOs as an integral part of instruction.
10. Difficult to obtain approval for VSO fundraising events.

11. Lack of preparation to become an effective VSO advisor.
12. Lack of State Department of Education support for VSOs.

There is another major barrier which limits student participation in VSOs and that is the negative attitudes and myths that some students, vocational and applied technology educators, and administrators have toward active participation of learners from special populations in VSO activities. Traditionally, learners from special populations have avoided pursuing membership in VSOs because they lack motivation and self confidence and feel inadequate to compete with other students in VSO activities such as competitive events. Other perceived factors which discourage students from special populations from becoming involved in VSOs were identified by Birchenall and Wanat (1981) and are as follows:

1. A tendency toward selective and elitist membership in VSOs.
2. Negative attitudes of administrators and supervisors concerning the integration and preparation of students from special populations in VSOs.
3. Emphasis on competition and winning instead of student development.
4. Insufficient or inappropriate activities for students from special populations.
5. Lack of recruitment and public relations activities to encourage students from special populations to join VSOs.
6. Insufficient support services to accommodate the special needs of students with disabilities.
7. Attempt to create separate student organizations for students from special populations.

Of all the barriers mentioned, probably the major one is the unwillingness of some teachers to implement a VSO in their classrooms even though it is considered an integral part of a quality vocational and applied technology education program. There are challenges which confront teachers who are considering establishing a VSO such as learning how to get a club or chapter started and reviewing all of the materials available from the VSO national office about the VSO in their vocational area. There are challenges in learning how to become a VSO advisor and how to truly integrate VSO activities into the vocational program. There are challenges of how to modify VSO activities to allow participation of students from special populations. But then, there are challenges associated with any endeavor that is worthwhile. One teacher addressed the problems associated with VSOs this way: "Teachers who feel that a VSO is a pain in the neck are shortchanging their students and denying them the opportunity to gain the qualities necessary for success that are often impossible to develop in the regular classroom alone. You ask if the benefits are worth the problems? You bet they are" (Butler, 1981).

FEDERAL LEGISLATION

Federal legislation enacted in the past twenty years supports the rights of disabled individuals to become regular participants in VSOs. Section 504 of the Rehabilitation Act of 1973 (PL 93-112) mandated that no otherwise qualified handicapped individual shall be excluded from participation in programs or activities supported with federal funds. Since vocational education programs are partially supported with federal funds and VSOs are integrated into vocational programs, this legislation applies (Sarkees, 1983).

The Education of All Handicapped Children Act (PL 94-142) specified that states shall use the mandated set-aside funds to assist handicapped students to participate in regular vocational education programs. This legislation also contains the concept of least restrictive environment. Many learners with disabilities are capable of succeeding in regular vocational programs given appropriate support and are capable of participating in VSO activities (Sarkees, 1983).

Part B of the Individuals with Disabilities Education Act of 1975 required that every disabled child between 3 and 21 be provided with a free public education. It is very prescriptive and includes integration of disabled students and the provision of assistive devices and services to help these students succeed in regular programs which include VSOs (The Educator's Guide to the Americans With Disabilities Act, 1993).

The Vocational Amendments of 1976 (PL 94-482) stated that VSOs must be listed in state annual and five-year vocational education plans and that these organizations should be an integral part of vocational education supervised by qualified educational personnel. The amendments state that participation in VSOs should be available to all students in the instructional program without regard to membership in any student organization (Federal Register, 1977).

The Carl D. Perkins Vocational and Applied Technology Act of 1990 required a focus on serving the needs of special populations, including disabled students. While much of the text of the Perkins Act addresses how funds are to be spent, it requires states to provide for "full participation" by members of special populations, including disabled students in vocational and applied technology education programs, including VSOs.

The Americans with Disabilities Act (ADA) of 1990, which took effect in 1992, is the most comprehensive enactment barring discrimination against disabled individuals. The ADA is based on five key principles that include a focus on the individual, integration, equal opportunity, physical accessibility, and the provision of reasonable accommodation and auxiliary aids and services (The Educators Guide to the Americans with Disabilities Act, 1993).

Clearly, students from special populations are guaranteed the right to participate in VSO activities if they are available in their vocational and applied technology education programs in local schools.

SELF ASSESSMENT

1. When and how did VSOs develop?
2. What is a nationally recognized VSO?
3. What are some of the benefits and advantages VSOs provide to students, teachers, schools, and communities?
4. Why should business and industry be invited to actively participate in VSO activities?
5. What is the mission or purpose of VSOs?

ASSOCIATED ACTIVITIES

1. Write to the national headquarters of VSOs and obtain copies of appropriate materials to increase your knowledge and to help you support their operation.
2. Attend VSO leadership workshops and conferences which may be offered locally, regionally, or at the state and national levels.
3. Visit a school with vocational and applied technology education programs and observe how VSO activities are incorporated as an integral part of the curriculum.
4. Volunteer your services to a vocational teacher/advisor to support VSO activities and events.
5. Attend and/or actively participate in the VSO competitive events held at your school, area, district, region, and state.

TEN NATIONAL STUDENT ORGANIZATIONS

chapter 7

INTRODUCTION

The United States Department of Education recognizes ten national vocational student organizations and considers them to be an integral part of vocational education instructional programs. These vocational student organizations include (1) National FFA Organization (FFA), (2) National Young Farmers Education Association (NYFEA), (3) National FHA Organization (FHA), (4) Future Business Leaders of America (FBLA), (5) Distributive Education Clubs of America (DECA), (6) Vocational Industrial Clubs of America (VICA), (7) Technology Student Association (TSA), (8) Business Professionals of America (BPA), (9) Health Occupations Students of America (HOSA), and (10) National Postsecondary Agriculture Student Organization (NPASO or PAS).

These vocational student organizations share many common goals such as leadership, cooperation, and citizenship.

They are organized in a similar manner with a national executive director and staff, state director, and local vocational student organization chapters or clubs guided by advisors. These organizations are for the vocational students and are governed by students using a democratic process. All of these students organizations have unique activities and instructional materials that can enhance vocational education instructional programs at the local level.

OBJECTIVES

After completing this chapter the reader should be able to:

1. Describe the ten U.S. Department of Education recognized VSOs and the general characteristics common to all of them.

TEN NATIONAL VOCATIONAL STUDENT ORGANIZATIONS

The United States Department of Education issued a policy statement on vocational student organizations in 1990 in which ten vocational student organizations were recognized as being an integral part of vocational education instructional programs. These ten VSOs include:

1. National FFA Organization (FFA) – formally Future Farmers of America (FFA)
2. National Young Farmers Education Association (NYFEA)
3. National FHA Organization (FHA) Future Homemakers of America (FHA) – Home Economics Related Occupations (HERO)
4. Future Business Leaders of America (FBLA) – Phi Beta Lambda (PBL)
5. Distributive Education Clubs of America (DECA) – Delta Epsilon Chi (DEC)
6. Vocational Industrial Clubs of America (VICA)
7. Technology Student Association (TSA)
8. Business Professionals of America (BPA)
9. Health Occupations Students of America (HOSA)
10. National Postsecondary Agriculture Student Organization (NPASO) or (PAS)

The Future Farmers of America (FFA)

The Future Farmers of America was founded in 1928 to serve high school vocational agriculture students preparing for careers in agricultural production, processing, supply and service, mechanics, horticulture, forestry, and national resources. Today, members are preparing for more than 200 careers in agriculture including the major career areas of agriscience and engineering; agricultural marketing, merchandising and sales; management and finance; social science professionals; production agriculture; education and communications; horticulture; forestry; natural resources; agricultural mechanics; and agriculture processing.

The primary goal of the FFA is to develop agricultural leadership, cooperation, and citizenship. The vocational agriculture/FFA program has three major components: (1) the course of study for students preparing for careers in agriculture and agribusiness, (2) the supervised occupational experience program in which each student participates, and (3) the incentives and awards programs to encourage students to excel, in both vocational agriculture and the FFA. Through participation in FFA activities, students learn how to conduct and take part in meetings, handle financial matters, speak in public, solve their own problems, develop leadership skills, compete in contests, and assume civic responsibility (FFA Student Handbook, 1991). Contact:

The National FFA Organization
National FFA Center
PO Box 15160
5632 Mt Vernon Memorial Highway
Alexandria VA 22309-0160

Phone 1-703-360-3600 Fax 1-703-360-5524

The Future Homemakers of America (FHA)

The Future Homemakers of America (FHA) was founded in 1945 to help students prepare for their future multiple role as homemaker, wage earner, and community leader. FHA expanded its organization in 1971 to include a division of Home Economics Related Occupations (HERO) for students studying occupational home economics.

FHA and HERO chapters are interrelated because they share a common focus on home economics subject matter, knowledge, and skills. They both claim the same mission of promoting personal growth and leadership development through home economics education. Members focus on the multiple roles of family member, wage earner, and community leader and develop skills for life through character development, creative and critical thinking, interpersonal communication, practical knowledge, and vocational preparation. Chapter members create and become involved in projects that address concerns like: community service, self-esteem, family relations, peer pressure, career exploration and training, teen pregnancy and parenthood, managing finances, fitness and nutrition, alcohol and drug abuse, the environment, and care of children and the elderly.

FHA chapters emphasize consumer homemaking education involving instructional experiences with areas of child development and family relations, food and nutrition, clothing and textiles, home furnishings, and consumer education and home management. Special emphasis is placed on strengthening the family, developing life skills, and leadership skills and on exploring home economics related careers and jobs. HERO chapters emphasize preparation for jobs and careers in home economics related occupations in such areas as child care, food service, clothing, home furnishings and equipment, and institutional and home management. In addition, HERO chapters place special focus on developing personal growth, leadership development, and community involvement (FFA/HERO Chapter Handbook, 1991). Contact:

National FHA Organization
1910 Association Drive
Reston VA 22091

Phone 1-703-476-4900 Fax 1-703-860-2713

Future Business Leaders of America (FBLA)
Phi Beta Lambda (PBL)

The Future Business Leaders of America (FBLA) was founded in 1940 as a sponsored student organization by the National Council for Business Education. FBLA is the vocational student organization which is open to secondary students enrolled in business and office education. Its purpose is to bridge the gap between the classroom and office world by giving students a chance to learn firsthand about the business community.

Phi Beta Lambda (PBL) was created in 1958 to serve the many business education students enrolled in postsecondary education institutions and is open to postsecondary students participating in business, office, and business teacher education. FBLA- PBL's mission is to bring business and education together in a positive working relationship through innovative leadership development programs. The purpose of FBLA-PBL is to provide as an integral part of the instructional program additional opportunities for students in business and office education to develop vocational and career supportive competencies, and to promote civic and personal responsibilities.

To accomplish the purpose of the organizations, both FBLA and PBL provide its members a wide range of exciting customized conferences, awards, publications, scholarship, and partnership opportunities in addition to regular membership services. Contact:

FBLA/PBL Inc
1912 Association Drive
Reston VA 22091

Phone 1-703-860-3334 Fax 1-703-758-0749

Distributive Education Clubs of America (DECA)
Delta Epsilon Chi (DEC)

The Distributive Education Clubs of America (DECA) was founded in 1947 to serve students enrolled in secondary school programs of marketing, distribution, merchandising, and management. A postsecondary division of DECA – Delta Epsilon Chi (DEC) – was established in 1961 to meet the needs of students enrolled in marketing and distributive education programs in junior colleges, community colleges, technical institutes, and area vocational technical schools.

The mission of DECA and DEC is to enhance the education of students with interests in marketing, management, and entrepreneurship. The objectives of both marketing education and DECA is to teach marketing and management skills in such diverse career areas as food marketing, hotel management, restaurant marketing and management, department and specialty store retailing, industrial and international marketing, finance and credit, advertising, insurance, wholesaling, and entrepreneurship.

DECA and DEC is a business and education partnership; an integral component of marketing education, career oriented youth, meaningful marketing education to meet the needs of business--now and in the future, leadership development, competition and recognition, and free enterprise the American way. DECA and DEC utilize a program of competency-based competitive events in specific marketing occupational areas, as well as achievement/recognition activities on the local, state, and national level to meet goals of the organization (Vocational Student Organizations, "A Reference Guide," 1990; and *DECA is More Than You Ever Imagined*). Contact:

Distributive Education Clubs of America
1908 Association Drive
Reston VA 22091

Phone 1-703-860-5000 Fax 1-703-860-4013

Vocational Industrial Clubs of America (VICA)

The Vocational Industrial Clubs of America (VICA) was founded in May of 1965 to serve students enrolled in trade, industrial, technical, and health occupations at the secondary level. A postsecondary division of VICA was established in 1969. VICA is dedicated to providing experiences and opportunities for the total development of the individual through development of citizen and leadership qualities as well as through the development of occupational knowledge and skills. Today, VICA is the national organization for students enrolled in trade, technical, industrial, and health occupations programs in public high schools, trade and technical schools, junior and community colleges. VICA works directly with business and industry to maintain American productivity, quality, and competitiveness (*VICA Leadership Handbook*, 1989).

VICA programs and activities help students prepare themselves for the labor market and continuing education. VICA teaches the importance of developing leadership skills, positive attitudes, and pride in workmanship. The organization emphasizes respect for the dignity of work, high standards in trade ethics, superior workmanship, quality, and safety. VICA uses a coordinated effort between educators, administrators, corporate America, labor organizations, trade associations, and government to produce quality-trained, well-rounded, entry-level employees that can meet America's need for a globally competitive, educated, and skilled work force (*How Your Business Can Work with VICA*, 1994).

VICA students learn "quality at work" through participation in a number of programs and activities such as VICA's Total Quality Initiative, VICA's Skills USA Championships, leadership training, the Professional Development Program, and other chapter activities. Contact:

Vocational Industrial Clubs of America Inc
P0 Box 3000
Leesburg VA 22075

Phone 1-703-777-8810 Fax 1-703-777-8999

Technology Student Association (TSA)

The Technology Student Association (TSA), formerly The American Industrial Arts Student Association (AIASA), was officially organized in 1965 as a sponsored program of the American Industrial Arts Association (AIAA). It was officially incorporated in 1978 as the only national student organization designed exclusively to meet the needs of industrial arts students at the elementary, junior high and middle school, and high school levels. At the national conference in 1988, delegates voted to change the name to the Technology Student Association to reflect the commitment to the dynamic field of technology and the future.

Today, TSA is the national organization for elementary, junior high, and senior high school students who are enrolled in or have completed technology education courses. Technology education is a hands-on approach that teaches students about systems, problem-solving, and the decision making necessary for the use of complex technologies. Major subject areas include communications, manufacturing/construction, and transportation/power/energy.

The mission of TSA is to promote leadership and personal growth in a technical world. TSA students participate in a variety of projects and competitions that are challenging, educational, and inspiring. TSA students are provided with the opportunity to: participate in co-curricular and extra curricular activities, learn new skills through programs and competitions, develop leadership skills, earn recognition and prestige, meet and work with business and industry leaders, form new friends, and receive all national membership services. Contact:

Technology Student Association
1914 Association Drive
Reston VA 22091

Phone 1-703-860-9000 Fax 1-703-620-4483

Business Professionals of America (BPA)

The Business Professionals of America (BPA), formerly the Vocational Office Education Clubs of America (OEA) was founded in 1966 to serve secondary and postsecondary students enrolled in vocational office programs. In 1988, the name of OEA was changed to the Business Professionals of America with new logo, emblem, and colors. BPA is a national student association for students enrolled in business and/or office education. It is a co-curricular organization which is an integral part of the instructional program and is designed to develop leadership abilities, interest in the American business system, and competency in office occupations. The mission of the Business Professionals of America is to contribute to the preparation of a world-class workforce through the advancement of leadership, citizenship, academic, and technological skills (Vocational Student Organizations, "*A Reference Guide*," 1991; Vaughn, Vaughn, and Vaughn, 1993).

BPA goals has adopted the Secretary's Commission on Achieving Necessary skills (SCANS), has the strategic direction for competitive events, leadership direction for interaction with business, workplace competency development, and career preparation. Contact:

Business Professionals of America
National Center
5454 Cleveland Avenue
Columbus OH 43231

Phone 1-614-895-7277 or 1-800-334-2007
Fax 1-614-895-1165

Health Occupations Students of America (HOSA)

The Health Occupations Students of America (HOSA) was founded in 1976 to provide a student organization that exclusively serves secondary and postsecondary students enrolled in health occupations programs. HOSA was created to become an integral part of health occupations programs and to provide health occupations students with learning experiences that help to develop leadership, citizenship, and occupational knowledge and skills required to enter jobs and careers in the health occupations field. HOSA's two-part mission is to promote career opportunities in the health care industry and to enhance the delivery of quality health care to all people. Contact:

HOSA Headquarters
6309 N O'Connor Rd
Suite 215 LB-117
Irving TX 75039

Phone 1-214-506-9780 or 1-800-321-4672
Fax 1-214-506-9919

National Postsecondary Agriculture Student Association (NPASO) or (PAS)

The National Postsecondary Agricultural Student Organization (PAS) was founded in 1979 to serve students enrolled in agriculture/agribusiness and natural resources programs in postsecondary institutions. The broad purpose of PAS is to help students develop leadership management abilities, occupational knowledge, and skills required for careers in agriculture/agribusiness and renewable natural resources. Contact:

National Postsecondary Agricultural Student Organization
Box 34
Cobleskill NY 12043

Phone 1-703-360-3600 Fax 1-703-780-4378

INVOLVING STUDENTS FROM SPECIAL POPULATIONS IN VSOs

Students may need to be encouraged to become actively involved in VSO programs and activities. Given encouragement and assistance when necessary from support personnel, all students can be involved in VSO activities which will help them to develop the knowledge, skills, attitudes, and work habits needed for competitive employment and an independent, productive life in the community.

Students should be actively recruited by VSO members, the teacher/advisor, and support personnel. The teacher/advisor relationship and communication with students is often the determining factor of VSO involvement or rejection. Teachers can consult with staff or other school personnel, parents, and other advocacy groups to obtain information that might be helpful in attracting students to join a VSO.

Chapter Advisor Functions

The key to an effective VSO chapter/club that involves all students is a dedicated, informed, student-oriented vocational and applied technology teacher who is the chapter advisor. Since VSOs are an integral part of the educational program and curriculum, teachers should obtain materials from their national VSO headquarters to help them learn about the duties and responsibilities of chapter advisors and how to integrate VSO materials into the instructional program.

Almost all VSOs have materials for advisors such as the *VICA Teacher's Tool Kit* and a 21 chapter advisor's reference and training library entitled *The Art of VICA*. In addition to resources to train advisors, VSOs have curriculum materials such as the TSA *Technology Teacher's Guide*, HOSA's *A Guide for Integrating HOSA into the HOE Classroom*, and VICA's Professional Development Program and the *Total Quality Curriculum.*

The Vocational Student Organizations' "A Reference Guide" (1990) contained these functions of VSO advisors:

1. Understand the significance of the VSO in achieving the goals of vocational education.
2. Develop, refine, and evaluate materials, methods, and techniques used by local, state, and national organizations.
3. Be adaptive, innovative, and creative in management of the VSO.
4. Encourage all students to be active members of their respective organizations.
5. Allow chapter to be student-led rather than instructor-led.
6. Seek support groups that facilitate VSOs and vocational program activities.
7. Unite all students enrolled in a vocational program as members of a VSO chapter.
8. Actively promote vocational and applied technology education and VSOs in the community.
9. Provide a learning environment that will complement and reinforce rather than compete with or duplicate vocational classroom training.
10. Work cooperatively with students and academic teachers in developing skilled leaders.
11. Permit students to learn from both successful and unsuccessful activities.
12. Help chapter leaders administer the program of work.
13. Be current with all organization related policies, documents, publications, procedures, etc.
14. Assist with the fiscal management of the VSO chapter.
15. Review the vocational curriculum and determine how best to fully integrate VSO activities into the classroom.

16. Encourage members to elect an officer team that is able and willing to provide leadership for the chapter.
17. Assist in the development of an effective officer team.
18. Facilitate the development of a meaningful program of work that will guide the chapter for the membership year.
19. Encourage all members to participate in the local, district, state, and national competitive events program.
20. Facilitate participation in local, district, state, and national competition.
21. Help members plan, organize, and conduct fund raising projects to finance chapter activities not supported by school funds.
22. Use the chapter as an instructional tool to develop and refine leadership and followership skills.
23. Encourage parents to get involved in chapter projects and activities.
24. Secure approval from state and national agencies when appropriate.
25. Provide on-going counsel and advice to chapter members and officers.
26. Provide advice, support, and service to state and national VSOs.

The list of advisor functions presented can be useful in helping vocational and applied technology teachers provide leadership to VSOs. In order for students from special populations to be successfully integrated into a VSO, the advisor may need to make appropriate modifications in some activities. Sarkees and Sullivan (1985) presented the following suggestions for advisors to consider to encourage the integration of students with special needs into VSOs:

1. Assign students with special needs to committees and/or activities where they will experience success in order to build their confidence and self esteem.
2. Award certificates of merit or participation to students who are actively involved in VSO activities to the best of their ability.
3. Publicize the accomplishments of students who have special needs in newsletters, school newspapers, and local publicity (e.g., officers, committee members, competitors, and winners in contests, project leaders).
4. Set aside time to help students with special needs develop planning and decision-making skills. Be flexible and allow extended time limits for projects when necessary.
5. Use advisor-student contracts for project completion. Plan these carefully to meet the needs and ability levels of each student. Write in clearly defined goals, directions, and criteria. Reinforce this information periodically and share with support personnel.
6. Allow students to refer to notes or scripts when they address the large group. This will help to develop self-confidence.

7. Encourage students to become involved in community service projects such as sponsoring families in need, writing letters to shut-ins, or visiting nursing homes.
8. Work with local administrators to encourage a positive, flexible, supportive philosophy regarding the integration of students who have special needs in VSO activities. Close coordination may also be needed in order to provide appropriate support services for these students.
9. Reinforce the relationship between VSO activities and career goals.
10. Recommend resource materials for support personnel who can help to reinforce VSO information.
11. Invite support personnel to become actively involved in the VSO (e.g., club co-advisor, committee chairperson, chairperson, or judge for district or state contests).

One good technique for teachers in encouraging students from special populations to join VSOs is to find one particular talent that a student with special needs has and to encourage the student to apply that talent to a specific club activity.

VSO Support Team

VSO club advisors are often successful in involving students from special populations in chapter/club activities but it is helpful to build a support team. Collaborative efforts should be encouraged between the vocational and applied technology teacher/advisor and support personnel. Suggested team members might include special populations coordinators, special education teachers, English teachers, remedial teachers, administrators, peers, parents, community agencies, school psychologists, counselors, interpreters, and representatives from business and industry.

Examples of VSO collaborative team efforts were identified by Sarkees (1983) and Sarkees and Sullivan (1985) and include the following:

1. Conduct cross-training inservice sessions. Special education teachers can utilize vocational assessment information and share it with VSO advisors to assist in identifying appropriate modifications for activities, projects, assignments, and contests when necessary. They can also provide information to VSO advisors on preferred student learning style(s). VSO advisors can provide support team members with information about the role of the VSO in the instructional program including how and when club activities are implemented, the nature of activities and competitive events, and how team members can assist students from special populations in selected VSO activities. See Figure 7-1.
2. Jointly conduct leadership seminars for students from special populations that would help them develop participation skills and attributes such as the ability to speak in front of a group, accepting responsibility, delegating duties, accepting and giving constructive criticism, working together as a team, and executing the decision making

process through parliamentary procedure. Informal techniques such as simulation and peer tutoring could be used to deliver instruction in these seminars. For example, VSO advisors in a school or school district, and special education personnel could plan a leadership seminar to meet an evening during the week to focus on the topic of public speaking. Most VSOs have a prepared speech and an impromptu or extemporaneous speaking contest. These contests usually feature speeches on topics related to VSO goals and current programs and are supported with rating sheets which include specific criteria that can be used to evaluate speeches. In addition, some VSOs have materials on the topic of public speaking that can be used in a seminar.

VSO CROSS-TRAINING MEETING AGENDA

1. Introduction of participants (special educators/VSO advisor)
2. Overview of meeting purpose
   A. Share plans for building a VSO support team
   B. Discuss how special education personal can participate on a team
   C. Discuss how VSO advisors can give and request information
3. Show a motivational film on a VSO organization
4. Present brief overviews on each VSO in the school or district
5. Have a VSO advisor present a case study problem on a special needs student who has integrated into VSO activities
6. Have a special education teacher discuss his/her involvement in working with a VSO advisor regarding a special needs student
7. Present a summary of areas which call for VSO advisors and support team participants to work together such as tutoring, chaperoning, judging, co-advising, assisting in modifying materials, contests and rating devices, etc.
8. Develop a plan of action to establish VSO support teams
9. Summarize meeting
10. Share in refreshments

Figure 7-1. An example of a cross-training meeting agenda for special education professionals and vocational teachers serving as VSO advisors to follow in coordinating their efforts to enhance participation of learners from special populations in VSO activities.

Seminar content could include the following:

- An overview of the importance of public speaking skills.
- An example speech delivered by an experienced VSO student volunteer.
- An illustrated talk on each of the components of public speaking such as opening, voice quality, platform deployment, etc.
- Preparation of scripts for students to follow when speaking in front of groups.
- Assign students with special needs to work in small groups with VSO student volunteers, advisors, and special education personnel to develop and present components of speeches.
- Video-tape practice speeches given by students with special needs and review and critique them together.
- Award each participant a certificate of achievement for participating in the seminar.

3. Share vocational assessment information that may be relevant in the selection and modification of activities and competitive events for a given student such as manipulative skills, learning styles, perceptual impairment, and disability.

4. Incorporate VSO participation into the IEP for disabled students and IVEP for other students from special populations. Input should be provided by the VSO advisor, support personnel, parent/guardian, and student.

5. Jointly publicize and recognize students with special needs (without using labels) who have been successful in VSO endeavors such as club officers, project leaders, committee chairpersons, and participants in competitive events. The VSO advisor and support team can discuss ways to recognize the achievement of students with special needs in VSO activities. For example, special education personnel and vocational teachers can develop a VSO student recognition program such as the student of the week or month award and publicize this accomplishment on bulletin boards in the classroom and other appropriate locations throughout the school.

Newsworthy articles such as the election of officers, community and school service projects, and attending leadership conferences and meetings also provide excellent opportunities to list the names of students with special needs who are involved in these activities. First, second, and third place winners of competitive events receive recognition for their accomplishments but additional awards can be given to others who met high standards of performance such as the VICA certificates of honor, merit, and accomplishments.

Information about VSO activities and benefits need to be shared with parents and they should be encouraged to become actively involved when possible, even if it is only a "cheerleading" role. Every effort should be made to creatively think of ways to publicize accomplishments of students from special populations in VSOs since such recognition helps these students improve their self-concepts and build confidence in their abilities to succeed in other areas.

6. Work cooperatively to prepare students with special needs for competitive events and to modify contest directions, contest procedures, written test items, and response modes as necessary to compensate for disabilities while still adhering to the high standards of performance expected by other students. VSO advisors can inform other teachers who are working with a learner with special needs about the student's decision to enter a competitive event and provide these teachers with information and materials about the contest.

If needed, a VSO support team meeting can be conducted to explore ways to modify contests, materials, and procedures to allow full participation of a student with a special need. Such strategies as enlarging the print of directions and test items; providing an auditory tape of contest directions, test directions, and test items; allowing students to respond orally to test items; and substituting hands-on demonstrations when possible for written test items can be employed to enable students with special needs to compete in contests.

If there are students who are hearing impaired or speak limited English, interpreters can be arranged to provide assistance as needed. Practice sessions can be arranged to provide students with opportunities to rehearse their leadership and hands-on skills in simulated environments.

7. Encourage support personnel for students from special populations to become involved in chapter/club meetings and activities. The following are examples of the ways support personnel can be involved in VSO activities:

- Co-advisor of the chapter/club or section.
- Contest chairperson to plan and conduct a VSO contest.
- Interpreter for disabled students in contest setting.
- Judge of a VSO contest.
- Chairperson for field trips and overnight meetings.
- Speaker at VSO chapter/club meetings.
- Member of a Professional Development Program committee to interview degree-seeking students in VICA.
- Host or hostess at social or recreational events.
- Resource person to provide special services to VSO students such as remedial assistance in basic skills.
- Team advisor in civic and community service projects.
- Support observer when students from special populations are involved in contests.
- Co-teacher in the vocational and applied technology classroom and laboratory.
- VSO support team member.
- Recruiter and advocate for involvement of students with special needs in VSOs.

- Assist in leadership seminars for students from special populations.
- Assist in publicizing achievement of students from special populations.
- Assist vocational and applied technology teachers in integrating VSOs into educational programs.

8. Work cooperatively with administrators and other faculty to develop positive attitudes toward active participation of students from special populations in VSOs. Perhaps the greatest barrier to the involvement of these students in VSOs is the negative or indifferent attitude held by these students, vocational and applied technology teachers, academic teachers, administrators, and parents. These attitudes can only be changed by supplying information to these groups and by creating examples of students from special populations who have profited from involvement in VSO activities. This topic of negative or indifferent attitudes needs to be addressed in the IEP and IVEP planning process and specific strategies should be identified to make these attitudes more positive toward the involvement of students from special populations in VSOs.

VSO Activities

Vocational student organizations have many common programs and activities such as a program of work, chapter/club calendar, chapter/club section meetings, individual achievement/degree programs, leadership development programs, regional, state, and national conferences, competitive events, career development, community service, fund raising, social/recreation, communication/public speaking skills, public relations, and others. These activities and programs are interwoven into the regular educational program in such a manner as to make it difficult to tell what is vocational and applied technology program content and what is VSO program activities. These VSO programs and activities are supported with professionally prepared materials such as handbooks, guidebooks, workbooks, resource kits, secretary and treasurer's books, audio-visuals, instructional aids, awards, and certificates. These are available through the national organization or the organization's official supplier.

The opportunities for all students to become involved in VSO activities are limited only to the extent that the local chapter/club leadership and VSO advisor make opportunities available. There are so many possible activities that it is impossible for a chapter or club to engage in all of them in a school year. Therefore, VSO chapters and clubs usually use the national program of work major activities as a guide to developing their own program of work and program of work calendar.

Students with special needs, given appropriate support services when necessary, can participate in the mainstream of most VSO activities and it is important that they be encouraged to do so. A balanced VSO program of work contains the activities that students need to participate in to further develop their knowledge and skills required to prepare for satisfying employment and an independent, productive life in their family and community.

VSO Program of Work

The national VSOs have recognized the importance of well prepared, balanced programs of work and have developed them with major topics which are related to the goals of the organization. Examples of these major program of work topics include: personal growth, leadership development, social development, competitive events, community service, fund raising, and career development.

The chapter program of work includes all of those activities in which members want to participate. Members of VSOs can identify and select activities which meet their needs and the needs of the organization with consideration given to meeting the needs of the school and community. For example, one of the easiest topics to develop is the topic of social development. Examples of activities which could be selected by members are: skating party, swimming party, dance, talent show, cook-out, picnic, hayride, athletic activities, orientation of new members, school open house, and trip to an amusement park or other interesting sites.

Through active participation in the program of work planning process, students are provided with an overview of the broad range of opportunities they have to meet new friends and experience personal growth. Students have the opportunity to select those activities which are of interest and meet individual needs in such areas as community service, safety, public relations, social skills, recreational skills, and competitive events. These students are also provided with opportunities to improve their interpersonal and group participation skills and long range planning skills through active involvement in chapter/club meetings and committee assignments. Students can receive special assistance in developing long range and short term goals related to the program of work as well as effective strategies to meet these goals (e.g., time management, use of planning calendars).

The program of work serves as an outline of activities covering a definite time period – usually an entire school year. It should contain a listing of specific goals/activities, strategies for accomplishing them, persons responsible for each activity, and provisions for monitoring and evaluating each activity in relation to its goal.

In developing the program of work, it is good practice to prepare members for the planning meeting by providing before hand copies of last years' program and programs of work from other chapters if available. Students could be given exercises in developing the program of work by completing program of work worksheets.

See Figure 7-2. Vocational student organization advisors can also ensure involvement of all students by talking with those who will be presiding during the program of work planning meeting and asking them to call on as many students as possible, especially students with special needs.

EXAMPLE PROGRAM OF WORK WORKSHEET

VSO ____________ 19___ Program of Work Date ____________

School ____________ Program ________________ Advisor ____________

Major Topic: Activities/Projects	Date	Strategies for Accomplishing	Members Responsible	Evaluation Procedures

Figure 7-2. An example program of work worksheet for identifying VSO activities in which learners from special populations can participate and the support services they will need to complete activities successfully.

During the planning meeting all students are given an opportunity to brainstorm and identify possible activities under each major program of work topic. After the group makes tentative selection of activities, a program of work committee should be appointed and subcommittees formed to develop activities under each major topic area. All students should have the opportunity to learn how committees operate and how to actively participate in them.

The program of work committee presents the tentative program of work for review at a meeting of the entire VSO membership. Revisions and editorial work is performed on the tentative plan and it is sent on to the school administration for approval. Once the program receives administrative approval, the program of work is brought before the VSO members again for formal adoption and to assign permanent committees to further plan and conduct program of work activities.

The program of work activity provides many learning experiences for special needs learner and other students. These experiences should be identified by the VSO advisor and VSO support team and become short-term instructional objectives in the IEP and IVEP for special needs students.

Chapter/Club Calendar

VSOs carry on many activities during the year, but so do other organizations in the school and the school itself. It is important that a calendar of events be developed which allows adequate time for program of work activities to be planned and strategically scheduled to ensure their success. For example, early in the year organizational activities take precedence over other activities. Early activities include the VSO orientation meeting, election of officers, appointment of standing committees, training VSO officers and chairpersons, membership drive, planning the program of work, collecting dues, ordering needed supplies and materials, and sending reports and articles to the state association and national headquarters.

Planning the chapter/club calendar can be a valuable learning experience for students. Every student needs to learn how to develop a schedule of events and to establish realistic time frames for events to occur. Advanced planning is often one of the most important factors in whether an activity is effective or a failure.

VSO advisors and support team members can provide instruction to students about budgeting time and scheduling activities. VSOs have materials available to help students and VSO advisors plan chapter/club calendars. Examples of previous VSO chapter/club calendars can be presented and reviewed by students in preparation for a calendar of events planning meeting.

Chapter/Club Meetings

The majority of VSO activities which occur in chapters or clubs takes place at the local level. One of the most important activities is the chapter/club meeting. Members of VSOs are given the opportunity to make decisions and to see the consequences of those decisions. Some members will be elected to the leadership team to guide their class and chapter, while other members are able to experience first-hand the challenges that face leaders and their followers. Chapter meetings involve a type of "workforce team" that must work together to plan and implement a balanced program of work.

One of the most powerful instructional tools provided by VSOs is the chapter/club meeting. Many students have never participated in a formal business meeting of a group and they need to learn how. Our democratic society conducts business through millions of meetings everyday, and it is important that every student learn how to function effectively as leaders and/or members of all types of groups.

Most VSOs have excellent materials to help advisors and officers plan for and conduct effective chapter/club meetings such as the Meetings Kit available from national VICA and the Chapter Handbook available from national TSA. Advisors can use these materials to help members learn meeting skills such as planning agendas, preparing for meetings, using parliamentary procedure, making introductions, participating in committees, inviting and introducing guests, speaking in front of groups, and using effective team building and group dynamic skills.

Students with special needs can be prepared to effectively participate in chapter/club meetings if teachers and support team members follow some of the following strategies identified by Sarkees and Sullivan (1989):

1. Ask for volunteer "buddies" to accompany students from special populations to VSO meetings until they feel comfortable attending alone.

2. Involve support team personnel to work with the VSO advisor to design simulations, role-playing exercises, and other activities to practice essential meeting skills.

3. Encourage VSO officers to ask students with special needs to perform a specific, realistic duty to get them involved (e.g., setting up the meeting rooms, typing and reproducing the agenda, assisting in clean-up following the meeting).

4. Work with other individuals to solve specific problems such as transportation or providing interpretation services.

5. Provide written and mediated materials to students with special needs to individually review prior to meetings.

Membership Campaign

One of the first activities to occur in the beginning of a chapter/club year is the membership campaign. This activity is critical, for the purpose of VSOs is to involve all students in leadership and career development activities through the integration of VSO programs, events, activities, and materials with the regular vocational and applied technology education curriculum. While students do not have to be dues-paying members to benefit from classroom VSO activities, they can not experience everything offered unless they become members.

VSO advisors and leaders have a number of written and media materials available from their respective national organizations to help promote membership. All VSOs have magazines available for members as one concrete product they receive from joining. VICA has a 100% chapters program that allows chapters who enroll every eligible student in the instructional program national recognition with members receiving certificates, gold membership cards, and attractive 100% chapter pins to proudly wear on their VICA clothing.

TSA has a 30+ membership circle and a 300+ membership circle program that earns participants a special certificate and recognition through their national publication *School Scene*. Enhancing membership is a high priority with all the national VSOs and they are devising new ways to reach teachers such as the customer-based teams of FFA and the volunteer teams of teachers approach of VICA.

VSO chapters need to develop or adopt a membership campaign that includes some of the following activities identified by Sarkees and Sullivan (1989):

1. Daily announcements through available media
2. A central bulletin board with membership "thermometers"
3. Competitive sports events such as volleyball tournament for chapters with 100% membership, with the winning chapter challenging the teachers
4. Special fundraising activities to pay dues for those who are unable to pay them
5. Assembly programs for all students with guest speakers addressing school-to-work transition, followed by an announcement of the membership campaigns for VSOs represented in the school
6. A membership poster contest with a prize for the winning poster
7. A membership computer or videotape program contest with the winner receiving a prize

Officer Elections/Training

The elections of VSO section, club, and chapter officers is an exciting event in which all students can participate. It is a natural occasion to teach leadership skills. Most VSO organizations have materials that can be used by members and the VSO advisor to develop leadership abilities and to conduct the election of officers process. One excellent example of such materials is the Leadership Techniques booklet produced by Business Professionals of America. This source covers topics on: (1) what is a leader?, (2) opportunities for developing leadership, (3) the election and installation of officers, and (4) officer responsibilities and leadership training. The Teachers Tool Kit provided by VICA also has excellent materials for use in conducting the officer election process including large posters with descriptions of officer duties.

Budget Preparation and Fund Raising

All VSOs must develop a budget which is the plan for income and expenditures for the year, as well as identifying activities to generate income which is the process of fundraising. These two activities are important learning experiences for all students. Preparing budgets and planning for fundraising activities can reinforce math skills, personal finance concepts, and team work skills.

The VSO advisor must play a key role in helping students anticipate major VSO expenses and identify sources of income which will support chapter/club activities. Typical expense categories identified by Sarkees and Sullivan (1989) include state and national dues, VSO publications, conference registrations, office supplies, transportation, awards, VSO clothing, and committee funds. Income for these expenses is usually generated through membership dues, fundraising activities, and donations. A tentative budget is prepared by the VSO officers with input from the advisor and presented to and adopted by the membership at a chapter/club meeting.

Once a budget is adopted, the process of raising funds to generate income should begin. There are usually school policies that govern fundraising activities with some schools forbidding them entirely, while other schools allow as many as necessary to support the VSO if they can be scheduled without conflict. Fundraising activities are identified by the chapter/club but before they are accepted they should meet criteria such as meet school policy, has educational value, are profitable, involve all members, are short in duration, provide incentives and rewards for outstanding work, are not competitive with local schools and merchants, and have potential to start a tradition.

Students with special needs may need some assistance in understanding the procedures for preparing budgets and fundraising. Advisors, with assistance of special needs support personnel, need to work individually with students with special needs to solve specific problems such as money to pay dues or obtain VSO clothing (e.g., blazers, sweaters, jackets). It may also be helpful for advisors to employ the "buddy" system of having another VSO member work closely with students with special needs in performing their part of the fundraising assignment. Students from special populations can benefit greatly from the social interaction that is a natural outcome of total VSO member involvement in planning and preparing a budget and fundraising activity.

Achievement/Degree Programs

Vocational student organization activities are designed to function as an integral part of the regular instructional program. Several VSOs have provided a VSO integration tool, such as the VICA Professional Development Program (PDP) that has specific requirements in the regular vocational program as well as requirements of chapter/club knowledge and leadership abilities. Students progress through these programs on a self-paced basis and are recognized for their accomplishment by necessary degrees during degree ceremonies. Additional examples of these achievement/degree programs include: (1) the FFA Achievement Award Program, (2) the Degree of Achievement Program in FHA, and (3) the HOSA National Recognition Program. These programs provide structured learning experiences where individual students compete against predetermined standards, rather than against fellow classmates. Students are attracted to participate in these achievement/degree programs in order to earn certificates and the pins and stripes to wear on their VSO jacket and blazers.

Competitive Events

One of the most visible programs offered by VSOs is their competitive events. Every VSO has a competitive events program with events in leadership and occupational areas in individual and group contests. These contests take place in the local school and at the area, region, state, and national level. VSO competitive events are designed to provide opportunities for students to compete with themselves and others in demonstrating the leadership abilities and occupational skills they have received in their vocational programs. These competitive events provide a power incentive for students to excel in their occupational preparation programs.

VSO competitive contests are available as individual events or as team and chapter/club events. For example, most VSOs have an individual contest on extemporaneous speaking and a club business procedures contest for a group of members. The variety of competitive events available in each VSO should make it possible for every student to become involved in these incentive programs. Every student wants to be a winner--to receive recognition through compliments from parents and classmates, as well as through receiving medals, ribbons, trophies, plaques, and cash awards. Every student who participates is a winner, whether he or she receives top awards or not.

An example competitive event in which students have participated successfully is the VICA job skill demonstration contest. This contest involves demonstrating a skill and explaining the topic and process through the use of examples, experiments, and displays. The advantage that this contest offers is that contestants pick the content for the contest and have the opportunity to practice the actual contest many times before they are evaluated by competent judges. Another advantage of this contest is that it is only 5 to 7 minutes in length which requires much less physical stamina than other contests of a skill nature which may run 1 to 4 hours long.

Leadership Conferences

VSOs provide regional, state, and national leadership conference activities which are excellent opportunities for members to compete in leadership and occupational skill contests; participate in leadership skills and officer training workshops, serve as delegates representing their schools, districts, and states; travel to new cities and states and meet new friends; share ideas and develop new attitudes toward cooperation and national pride; and receive inspiration to further achievement in their VSO.

All students who serve as delegates should be prepared to represent their school or state on matters of common concern. If delegates are to introduce motions or make remarks they should be prepared to do so before arriving at the conference. Delegates and others attending leadership conferences should be reminded of expected behavior since the way they participate in these conferences reflects their chapter, district, or state association as well as their school. VSO advisors should share the conference agenda with students and prepare them for conference activities to ensure maximum participation.

Not every VSO member can attend leadership conferences, so students earn the right to represent their local chapter by actively participating in their chapter's activities. Some students may lack experience in traveling to conferences and spending nights away from home in hotels or at camps. VSO advisors should work with the students, parents, and appropriate support personnel to prepare these students for the trip. If these students are to participate in the conferences as a contestant or presenter, the IEP/and IVEP support team should prepare them thoroughly ahead of time.

The following suggestions and requirements should be given to all students who attend leadership conferences:

1. Obtain parent's permission and provide a liability release form.
2. Develop a list of clothing and other equipment and materials needed for each student to bring to the conference.

3. Go over expected conference behavior and regulations.
4. Go through a dry run of registering for the conference and conference lodging.
5. Upon arriving at the room, unpack clothing and organize it to avoid conflict with other students.
6. Check to see where emergency exists and fire extinguishers are located.
7. Review the conference agenda and mark those events you must be at and those you wish to attend.
8. Walk with friends or your advisor to the locations of meeting which you plan to attend.
9. Walk with friends or your advisor to the restaurants in or near the hotel where you plan to eat.
10. Be in your room when you are expected to be there.
11. Be prepared to report your activity to fellow classmates when you return from the conference.
12. Be sure you know what to do in the event that a roommate gets sick or another emergency occurs.

VSO Modification Ideas

One of the perceived barriers which inhibits the involvement of students from special populations in VSOs is insufficient and inappropriate activities. This barrier may well be more perceived than real since most vocational and applied technology instructors who have been successful in involving student with special needs in VSOs indicate that most aspects of the organization require little or no modification for these students. The following ideas may be useful in better meeting the unique needs of students from special populations (Sarkees and Sullivan, 1985; 1989):

1. Students with special needs may have difficulty reading VSO materials. These materials may be adapted for use by these students by rewriting them in simpler language, by recording them on tape, by presenting them in larger written type, or by scanning materials into the computer and presenting them in larger type fonts. For example, VSO materials that may be difficult to read include emblem ceremonies, officer installation programs, competitive events handbooks, and student handbooks.
2. Instructional strategies used in VSO activities may need to be carefully selected to meet the various learning styles of students. Students with special needs often profit more from action-oriented strategies such as role playing, video demonstrations of events, observing others, working one-on-one with students in the buddy system, etc.
3. Disabled learners may experience physical barriers in facilities where VSO meetings and contests are held. These facilities should be checked for barriers

before they are selected to accommodate VSO activities and events. Appropriate modifications may be needed to overcome a barrier in a facility should other facilities be unavailable.

4. VSO leadership activities, such as serving as an officer, often require memorization and oral recitation which may be a problem for some learners from special populations. These problems can be overcome by providing learning experiences on the trouble areas ahead of time and by working with support teachers to reinforce instruction in these areas. For example, FBLA student officers must learn their parts to participate in the emblem ceremony. Vocational teachers can video tape this ceremony ahead of time and use it to help students learn their parts. Special needs teachers could borrow the tapes and use them in their classes as a demonstration of public speaking skills. Overhead projection of officer speeches could be displayed on a screen until the officers learn their parts.

5. Many competitive events require students to read directions and other materials. Some students from special populations may be able to perform the contest activity well but cannot read the directions. Directions may need to be printed in larger type, be converted to a prerecorded audio tape, or be given orally. Directions can also be written in simpler terms and made more readable by drawings and illustrations.

6. Hearing impaired and limited English speaking students can participate in VSO activities and competitive events if the service of interpreters are provided. For example, interpreters have been provided at national VICA contests to enable hearing impaired students to participate.

7. Many students who compete in VSO activities and events experience high levels of anxiety and tension. Students from special populations may experience even higher tension and anxiety levels because of their low self-esteem and confidence. There is no substitution for preparation for competitive activities. Vocational and applied technology teachers and support personnel need to provide repetition and practice for all students to promote overlearning of the knowledge and skills required for a competitive task which usually results in lower levels of apprehension.

8. Participating as a contestant in an area, region, state, or national VSO contest is a new and stressful experience for most students. It is not uncommon for students to get lost in meeting facilities and to fail to attend required briefings for competitive contests. VSO advisors should arrive at the contest sites early and provide a dry run experience for students so they know where to go and what to expect. Contest designers can facilitate logistical concerns by using appropriately displayed posters and signs and by color coding contest signs, numbers, and materials.

9. Some contest judges may have no previous experience in judging student effort in competitive events. Contest judging can be made more objective if a contest rating briefing is conducted in which judges are informed about the nature of student contestants, the school programs (without naming schools) in which the students are enrolled, student learning characteristics, and student needs.

10. One of the logistical problems for all VSO advisors is providing transportation and supervisory services for students to meetings, conferences, and competitive events. Special consideration should be given to the unique needs of students from special populations in these two areas. For example, the VSO advisor may find it desirable to make room assignments so that one or more mature, responsible students are paired up with a student with a special need. Additional adult supervision may be required when bus transportation is provided to competitive events. Funds for travel need to be raised through club activities so all eligible students can participate in out-of-school activities.

11. Student from special populations often have low self esteem and self confidence. It is a good practice to encourage these learners to participate in committee work and group activities so they can experience success before they venture into individual activities. Another good practice is to encourage students who want to become committee chairpersons or officers to serve as an apprentice with past or present officers and chairpersons to "learn the ropes."

12. Students from special populations sometimes need more time to complete a project, activity, or contest because of disabilities. Special consideration should be given to time limits that would allow all students to participate, tempered with realistic work expectations.

13. Students with special needs may need more sequenced, structured activities and materials than other students. It is a good practice to plan meeting materials in advance by using a meeting agenda planning form which can be completed by participating students.

Students with special needs who are to present before the group should be provided with appropriate note cards and possibly scripts to reduce anxiety and ensure success. When planning VSO activities, the advisor should help students outline the steps required to complete activities. Contracts for project completion should be carefully prepared with clearly defined goals, objectives, steps, and directions that are appropriate to the unique needs and abilities of students from special populations.

14. Student from special populations often have trouble participating in meetings for a variety of reasons including poor self-image, lack of confidence, and lack of general meeting and leadership skills. VSO advisors, with assistance from special needs support personnel, should set aside time and present instruction to

help students develop these important meeting and leadership skills. Most VSOs have excellent materials to support instruction in this area, such as the VICA Meetings Kit.

15. Students from special populations, along with other students, can profit from individualized or self-paced instructional materials covering aspects of VSOs. Vocational and applied technology teachers can prepare individualized learning packages on a number of VSO topics such as chapter/club meetings, opening ceremonies, parliamentary procedures, preparing and presenting speeches, etc. Most VSOs have a variety of well prepared materials that can be used to support individualized learning.

16. Some competitive events employ written tests which may cause problems for some students from special populations. These written tests can be modified as needed by converting them to audio tapes, by reading the items aloud, by allowing oral responses instead of written responses, and by substituting hands-on demonstrations for written tests.

17. VSO activities and competitive events are an integral part of the instructional program. All students should be given the opportunity to compete in some portion of their instructional program as a learning experience at the local school level. The VSO advisor and VSO support team can plan and hold the local competition so that all students can participate. All students should receive some form of recognition and not just the winners. All VSOs have certificates and awards which can be given to those students who enter competition and do their best.

18. Students from special populations learn a great deal from other students. VSOs emphasize working together to accomplish goals and projects. VSO advisors should promote the buddy system (pairing a learner with special needs with a capable student) as a method of student development which helps build a sense of self-confidence for learners with special needs as well as increase their level of participation.

19. Many local schools have more than one vocational student organization. VSO advisors and support team personnel should plan and work cooperatively together to conduct leadership seminars for officers and committee chairpersons on such leadership topics as conducting chapter/club meetings, fund raising activities, etc.

20. Develop or secure certificates of merit or achievement for students who have actively participated in VSO activities to the best of their ability.

This list of ideas to increase the involvement of students from special populations in VSO activities and events is not exhaustive. Vocational and applied technology education teachers, with assistance from the special needs support team members, can come up with many more ways to improve the match between the capabilities of students with special needs and VSO activities. VSO participation should be a major component in the IEP for disabled learners and the IVEP for other learners from special populations and should be jointly planned by all parties involved.

Creative Activities

There is a tendency to duplicate national VSO activities, awards programs, and competitive events because these experiences are well established, organized, and supported with written materials such as handbooks, guides, rating sheets, and awards. There is nothing wrong with this practice, but vocational and applied technology education teachers and VSO support team personnel should consider other worthy activities to meet the unique needs of learners from special populations, while at the same time, providing benefits to other students.

One example activity that could be developed is to form or sponsor career or job clubs. This activity organizes students into a group that investigates all the factors involved in locating, obtaining, and making progress on a career or job. Activities may include members uncovering the hidden job listing through use of the telephone, direct contact with employment sources, and networking strategies with friends, parents, relatives, etc. Students role play how to open and close job bids, how to respond to tough questions in an interview, how to meet employer's expectations, how to work with other employees, and how to adjust to supervision styles. VSO materials such as job interview contest materials could be used to support this activity. National VICA has a job program that can be used as a source of ideas for this activity. In addition, there are many commercially available materials on the topic of finding and keeping jobs that could be obtained for this activity.

Another activity that could be developed is the creation of a futuristic community. Students could gather information from written materials and interview community leaders to determine what the community might look like 20 years in the future. Students could recreate the community in model form applying new technological advances in transportation, energy, communications, housing, agriculture, business, industry, government, and health care. All students would be actively involved in this project which provides opportunities for students to work cooperatively together and to use their creative talents.

A final example of creative activity is to implement a total quality management approach to classroom instruction and the organization and implementation of VSOs. An excellent source of information is the Total Quality Curriculum available from national VICA. This resource is composed of 17 chapters which begin with a discussion, followed by activities to put quality concepts into practice. Implementing a total quality curriculum will help students develop the new skills needed for tomorrow's workers such as creativity, problem solving, teamwork, and decision making.

These three examples are only sample creative, futuristic activities that could be developed which would capture student interest and provide opportunities for students to gain new knowledge and skills and to apply what they have already learned in an interest area.

VSO Advisor Functions for Students from Special Populations

Besides encouraging students from special populations to become active VSO members, advisors perform a number of other functions which are important for special population student growth and chapter/club success including the following (Sarkees and Sullivan, 1989):

1. Advise and guide students from special populations in selecting VSO activities in which they are interested and have a high probability of success in order to build self esteem and confidence. It is important for some of these students to engage in group activities first and advance to more demanding individual ones.
2. Provide supervision of activities that enables students from special populations to understand the interrelationship of vocational and applied technology education instruction and their VSO. All students need to receive reinforcement of the relationship between VSO activities and career goals.
3. Provide necessary instruction for students from special populations in management steps of planning, preparing for, executing, and evaluating VSO activities and projects.
4. Provide assistance to learners with special needs in developing and applying leadership, human relations, and communication skills in the classroom and in VSO activities.
5. Provide assistance in helping students from special populations set realistic goals for self improvement.
6. Provide assistance to students from special populations who are competing against standards in professional development and achievement programs and those preparing for competitive events.
7. Provide encouragement to students from special populations to run for VSO officer positions and volunteer to chair and/or serve on committees.
8. Provide specialized training for students with special needs who are serving as officers and chairpersons.
9. Recommend resources and resource materials that will help students with special needs to participate fully in VSO activities.
10. Suggest resources to finance and implement chapter and individual student

activities so that economically disadvantaged students can participate fully in VSO activities.

11. Coordinate VSO instruction with other school personnel to help students from special populations prepare for and participate in VSO activities.

12. Inform the school administration, faculty, students, parents, vocational advisory committee members, and the community about the involvement of student from special populations in individual and VSO chapter/club activities.

13. Arrange for transportation for students from special populations to and from VSO meetings.

14. Devote extra time to advise out-of-school VSO activities for all students.

15. Form VSO support teams to help students from special population benefit fully from VSO activities.

16. Promote the "buddy" system between students with special needs and other students in VSO activities.

17. Prepare special materials to help students with special needs succeed in VSO activities.

18. Invite support personnel to become actively involved in the VSO (e.g., club co-advisor, committee chairperson, chairperson, or judge for competitive events).

19. Work closely with administrators to secure positive support for integration of students from special populations into VSO activities and support of other school personnel.

20. Encourage all students to become involved in community service projects such as sponsoring families in need, writing letters to shut-ins, or visiting senior citizen homes.

21. Encourage students with special needs to refer to notes or scripts when they are addressing large groups if needed. This will help them feel more confident.

22. Employ advisor-student contracts for project completion. This will engage students in carefully determining realistic goals and developing directions, criteria, and time lines for project completion.

23. Set aside time to help students from special populations develop planning, problem solving, and decision making skills.

24. Publicize the accomplishment of students with special needs in newsletters, school newspapers, and local publicity (e.g., officers, committee chairpersons and members, competitive event contestants and winners, and project leaders).

25. Assist all students in learning from both successful and unsuccessful VSO activities.

26. Allow the VSO chapter/club to be student-led rather than instructor-led.

27. Facilitate the development of a meaningful program of work that will guide the chapter/club for the membership year and involve all members in VSO activities.

SELF ASSESSMENT

1. Identify and briefly describe the ten nationally recognized VSOs presented in this chapter.

2. What are some of the major advisor functions in implementing VSOs as an integral part of the instructional program?

3. What are some of the ways vocational and applied technology education teachers could involve support team members in VSO activities?

4. How can teachers or support people obtain additional materials to help organize and implement VSOs?

5. How can vocational and applied technology education teachers integrate VSO program, events, and activities into the regular instructional program?

6. What is the common organizational structure of the ten nationally recognized VSOs?

ASSOCIATED ACTIVITIES

1. Obtain films and other mediated materials on VSOs and use them in your classes.

2. Obtain VSO materials such as material on leadership skills, communication skills, and parliamentary procedures and incorporate them into your instsruction.

3, Volunteer your services to the state VSO advisor in your occupational interest area.

4. Become a professional or honorary member of a VSO in your vocational area.

5. Serve as a chaperon when VSO members travel away from the school.

APPENDIX

APPENDIX A – LEGISLATIVE REFERENCE INFORMATION
APPENDIX B – CHRONOLOGICAL CHART

APPENDIX A – LEGISLATIVE REFERENCE INFORMATION

ACT	DATE	PUBLIC LAW	CHAPTER	STATUTE	
				VOLUME	PAGE
Morrill Act of 1862	July 2, 1862	*	130	12	503
Hatch Act of 1887	March 2, 1887	*	314	24	440
Morrill Act of 1890	August 30, 1890	*	841	26	417
Adams Act of 1906	March 16, 1906	47	951	34	63
Nelson Amendments to Morrill Act of 1907	March 4, 1907	242	34	—	1281
Smith-Lever Act of 1914	May 8, 1914	95	79	38	372
Smith-Hughes Act of 1917	February 23, 1917	347	114	39	929
Smith-Sears Act of 1918	June 27, 1918	178	107	40	617
Smith-Bankhead Act of 1920	June 2, 1920	236§	219	41	735
Smith-Fess Act of 1920	June 2, 1920	236§	219	41	735
George-Reed Act of 1929	February 5, 1929	702	153	45	1151
George-Ellzey Act of 1934	May 22, 1934	245	324	48	792
George-Deen Act of 1936	June 8, 1936	673	541	49	1488
Servicemen's Readjustment Act of 1944	June 22, 1944	78-346‡	268	58	284
George-Barden Act of 1946	August 1, 1946	79-586	725	60	775
Health Amendments Act of 1956	August 7, 1956	84-911	871	70	923
Fishery Amendment, George-Barden Act of 1956	August 8, 1956	84-911	1039	70	1126

continued . . .

. . . continued . . .

ACT	DATE	PUBLIC LAW	CHAPTER	STATUTE	
				VOLUME	PAGE
National Defense Education Act of 1958	September 2, 1958	85-864	†	72	1580
Captioned Film for the Deaf Act	September 2, 1958	85-905	†	72	1742
Education of Mentally Retarded Children Act of 1958	September 6, 1958	85-926	†	72	1777
Area Redevelopment Act of 1961	May 1, 1961	87-27	†	75	47
Manpower Development and Training Act of 1962	March 15, 1962	87-415	†	76	23
Health Professions Educational Assistance Act of 1963	September 24, 1963	88-129	†	77	164
Higher Education Facilities Act of 1963	December 16, 1963	88-204	†	77	363
Vocational Education Act of 1963	December 18, 1963	88-210	†	77	403, 1-16
Civil Rights Act of 1964	July 2, 1964	88-352	†	78	241
Economic Opportunity Act of 1964	August 20, 1964	88-452	†	78	508
Elementary and Secondary Education Act of 1965	April 11, 1965	89-10	†	79	27
National Technical Institute for the Deaf Act of 1965	June 8, 1965	89-36	†	79	125
Higher Education Act of 1965	November 8, 1965	89-329	†	79	1219
Adult Education Act of 1966	November 3, 1966	89-750	†	80	1191
Elementary and Secondary Education Amendments of 1966	November 3, 1966	89-750	†	80	1191
Education Professions Development Act of 1967	June 29, 1967	90-35	†	81	81

. . . continued . . .

ACT	DATE	PUBLIC LAW	CHAPTER	STATUTE	
				VOLUME	PAGE
Elementary and Secondary Education Amendments of 1967	January 2, 1968	90-247	†	81	783
Vocational Education Amendments of 1968	October 16, 1968	90-576	†	82	1064
Nurse Training Act of 1971	November 18, 1971	92-158	†	85	465
Education Amendments of 1972	June 23, 1972	92-318	†	86	
Rehabilitation Act of 1973	September 26, 1973	93-112	†	87	355
Comprehensive Employment and Training Act of 1973	December 28, 1973	93-203	†	87	839
Education Amendments of 1974	August 21, 1974	93-380	†	88	484
Women's Educational Equality Act of 1974	August 21, 1974	93-380	†	88	484
Education of All Handicapped Children Act of 1975	November 29, 1975	94-142	†	89	773
Education Amendments of 1976	October 12, 1976	94-482	†	90	2081
Youth Employment and Demonstration Projects Act of 1977	August 5, 1977	95-93	†	91	627
Career Education Incentive Act of 1978	December 13, 1977	95-207	†	91	1464
Comprehensive Employment and Training Act Amendments of 1978	October 27, 1978	95-524	†	92	1904
Educational Amendments of 1978	November 1, 1978	95-561	†	92	2143
Department of Education Organization Act of 1979	October 17, 1979	96-88	†	93	668

. . . continued . . .

ACT	DATE	PUBLIC LAW	CHAPTER	STATUTE	
				VOLUME	PAGE
Job Training Partnership Act of 1982	October 13, 1982	97-300	†	96	1322
Education Handicapped Act Amendments of 1983	December 2, 1983	98-199	†	97	1357
Rehabilitation Act Amendments of 1984	February 22, 1984	98-221	†	98	17
Carl D. Perkins Vocational Education Act of 1984	October 19, 1984	98-524	†	98	2435
Handicapped Children's Protection Act of 1986	August 5, 1986	99-372	†	100	796
Education Handicapped Act Amendments of 1986	October 6, 1986	99-457	†	100	1145
Rehabilitation Act Amendments of 1986	October 21, 1986	99-506	†	100	1807
Technology-Related Assistance for Individuals with Disabilities Act of 1988	August 19, 1988	100-407	†	102	1044
Children with Disabilities Temporary Care Reauthorization Act of 1989	October 25, 1991	101-127	†	103	770
Americans with Disabilities Act of 1990	July 26, 1990	101-336	†	104	327
Carl D. Perkins Vocational and Applied Technology Education Act of 1990	September 25, 1990	101-392	†	104	753
Individuals with Disabilities Education Act of 1990 (Education of the Handicapped Amendments)	October 30, 1990	101-476	†	104	1103
Developmental Disabilities Assistance and Bill of Rights Act of 1990	October 31, 1990	101-496	†	104	1191

. . . continued

ACT	DATE	PUBLIC LAW	CHAPTER	STATUTE	
				VOLUME	PAGE
Technology-Related Assistance for Individuals with Disabilities Act of 1991	October 25, 1991	101-127	†	103	770
Job Training Reform Amendments of 1992	September 7, 1992	101-367	†	106	1021
Technology-Related Assistance for Individuals with Disabilities Act Amendments of 1994	March 9, 1994	103-218	†	108	50
Goals 2000: Educate America Act of 1994	March 31, 1994	103-327	†	108	125
School-to-Work Opportunities Act of 1994	May 4, 1994	103-239	†	108	568
Improving America's Schools Act of 1994	October 20, 1994	103-382	†	108	3518

[*] The first reference to a public law number and usage occurs on page 237, of the United States Code, 1988 Edition, Vol. 20, Statutes at Large (1789-1978), starting with the 57th Congress, January, 1902. Prior to this date, only statue and chapter locations were cited.

[†] Chapter designations were removed from reference citations after 1957.

[‡] Between the 57th Congress and the 85th Congress, public laws were referenced only by the public law number (i.e. PL 347). If a congressional session carried over into another year, the public law numbers were reset to 1. For example, if a particular session of the 57th Congress carried over from 1902 to 1903, on January 1, 1903, public law numbers would be reset to 1 for a new year. Because of this practice, several public laws in the same session of Congress could have identical numbers. Starting with the 85th Congressional session, one set of public law numbers were assigned per session regardless of the length. Citations and references to the laws were designated as PL 85-864, or 85th Congressional session, public law number 864. The first reference to this practice can be found on page 651, Vol. 20, of the 1988 United States Code, 85th Congress, 1957.

[§] Several citations listed may contain the same reference location in the United States Statutes. This is because a specific piece of legislation may contain amendments, enactments, or references to a number of bills and laws. The citation references the beginning of the legislation. As some statutes contain over 200 pages, some scanning of the sections of the legislation may be required.

APPENDIX B – CHRONOLOGICAL CHART	
2½ Million B.C.	In the Paleolithic Period, people learned to develop and use stone tools, learned to use fire and made weapons (bow and arrow, spears), developed bone needles, and invented the body parts system of measurement. Work education was provided through the father-son, mother-daughter trial-and-error system of learning.
9000 B.C.	People learned to improve stone and wood tools, domesticate animals, and plant and harvest grains. Crafts such as pottery making, spinning and weaving, basket making, brick making, boat and house building, and farming were practiced.
6000 B.C.	The great river civilizations developed along the Nile, Tigris, and Euphrates Rivers. Animals were domesticated for work and food. The ox-drawn wooden plow was invented, ushering in the agricultural civilization. People learned to irrigate fields and to grow grains like barley, wheat, and flax. A system of telling time was developed and by 4200 B.C. the Egyptians had developed a calendar and a form of picture writing from which an alphabet of letters emerged by 3500 B.C.
4200 B.C.	This period is known as the bronze age or age of metals when bronze drills and the bow-drilling technique were invented, and bronze axes, knives, files, scraping tools, adzes, and saws were developed. People learned to build large structures of stone, and molded kiln-dried bricks. New trades were developed including carpentry, masonry, brick making, pattern making, and boat building. Trades were learned through the trial-and-error method of passing along knowledge and skills from parents to children.
2000 B.C.	Egyptians developed an alphabet and recorded business transactions on clay tablets. Later a system of writing using a pen, writing fluid, and papyrus (crude form of early paper) was developed which led to the establishment of the first organized schools for scribes who recorded literature or served as clerks to record business transactions. Crafts became organized and a system of legalized apprenticeship came into being during the Babylonian Age.
1200 B.C.	The Hebrew people settled in Palestine and adapted themselves to new types of work in businesses and the trades. They held manual labor in high regard and established religious doctrine which required children to attend church school and learn a trade, thus establishing the earliest form of compulsory education.

continued . . .

. . . continued . . .

1000 B.C.	The discovery of iron making in Greece led to improved tools and weapons of war including drills, gouges, broad axes, knives, skews, files, scrapers, shaper-planes, metal-cutting saws, and calipers and dividers. The Greek civilization perpetuated a caste system with second class citizens and slaves performing the work and first class citizens holding and managing the wealth of the country. Greek schools were established in Sparta and Athens for children of first class citizens and a university system was established to prepare engineers and professionals. The dual system of education was born, one type of education for culture and another type of education for workers.
1000 to 200 B.C.	The Roman empire included the development of banks, currency, and shares in commercial enterprises. Roads, aqueducts, drainage systems, and massive structures were constructed using ideas borrowed from the Greek civilization, with new twists of their own. A system of public law and education was developed for Roman citizens and their children. The educational system consisted of the three levels of elementary, secondary, and higher education.
300 to 1300 A.D.	The Middle Ages constituted a period of nearly 1000 years when little progress was made to advance civilization, and the Christian monasteries carried the banner of education for culture and work. Manual labor was held in high regard, and monks were expected to work at a trade for seven hours each day.
1000 to 1100 A.D.	Merchant and craft guilds were formed to regulate the buying and selling of goods and to regulate the quality and quantity of goods produced. The guilds established the practice of indentured apprenticeship, which was both a way of life for a young person and a means of general education and preparation for skilled work. The indentured apprenticeship is considered the earliest form of vocational education which probably was initiated and refined during the Egyptian, Babylonian, Greek, and Roman civilizations and was reemphasized as an honorable form of education by the craft guilds.

. . . continued . . .

1300 to 1550 A.D.	The Renaissance and Reformation periods of history featured the rediscovery of great literature and the formation of a new spirit of human dignity which led to geographical and scientific discovery. Firearms and cannons were invented, and great ships were built both for commerce and for war through naval power. Most notably, this period produced great works of sculpture and art, and the printing of books written first in latin and later in the vernacular through the invention of the printing press. During this period, towns increased in size into small cities and the merchants' and crafts' guilds flourished. The Reformation brought on religious revolt leading to the establishment of protestant churches led by Martin Luther in Germany and a number of other religious leaders in other countries. The religious revolt included challenges to the type of education offered in church schools.
1483-1546	Martin Luther advocated that education should be the responsibility of the state and even recommended compulsory education for part of the day for both boys and girls, and the balance of the day devoted to learning a trade or occupation.
1483-1553	Rabelais advocated educational reform in the churches of France, which involved redirecting education away from a heavy concentration on the abstract to teaching subjects through natural events and situations of life. His ideas would be expanded by many other educational reformers centuries later.
1562	The Statute of Artificers was passed in England, taking the power away from guilds to regulate apprenticeship and placing it under government control, thus establishing a national apprenticeship system. This same type of action would occur in France years later.
1531-1611	Richard Mulcaster maintained that the hand and eye are the greatest instruments to receive learning. He is credited as being the first educator to make drawing one of the fundamental subjects of his Merchant Taylor's School in England.
1561-1626	Francis Bacon was the first educator to use the term "manual arts" in his theory of realism in which he advocated improving learning through the study of nature and involvement in experiments with common objects and real world experiences.

. . . continued . . .

1592-1670	John Amos Comenius introduced a practical method of education, and founded the sense-realism movement which emphasized that learning should be accomplished through experiences and investigation of objects according to the course of nature. He advocated formal schooling for both boys and girls in the form of infant schools in every home, a public elementary school, a gymnasium or secondary school, and a university. He is known as the "father of modern pedagogy" because of his work in forms of schools and teaching methodology.
1600-1670	Samuel Hartlib conceived the idea of agricultural colleges in England and the "office of address" which was an agency to help people find employment, an idea that has evolved into our labor departments and local employment service offices.
1601	English Poor Laws were enacted to place pauper children into apprenticeships, which gave apprenticeship a bad name.
1642	The Comprehensive Apprenticeship Law was passed in Massachusetts.
1642-1727	John Locke, a member of the Royal Society, presented his views on a new form of education that would fit youngsters for practical life. He advocated a dual system of practical training with poor children to receive occupational preparation and wealthy children to study the classics and engage in practical arts education in the mechanical trades as a form of physical activity and recreation. He strongly favored type of education that emphasized the development of thinking skills and discovery through the scientific method. Locke's *Essays on Human Understanding* is regarded as the "corner-stone of modern empirical psychology."
1647	Sir William Petty advocated the establishment of literary workhouses for children and guilds for tradesworkers in England. He recommended industrial education be made an integral part of school.
1647	Massachusetts passed a law requiring every town of fifty households to hire a school master to teach reading and writing. A town of 100 households was required to establish a Latin grammar school to prepare selected youngsters for college.

. . . continued . . .

1648	The Royal Society of London, a group of famous scholars of the day, expanded the philosophy of realism proposed earlier by Francis Bacon, which emphasized discovery of knowledge through methods of research such as observation, comparison, and experiment. This society included the study of manual arts in their writings. The creative works of these scholars was instrumental in opening a new age of scientific discovery.
1648	The French Academy of Painting and Sculpture was founded.
1663-1727	August Hermann Francke founded a school for poor children, a Latin school for the wealthy, a seminary for training teachers, and a publishing house to print copies of the Bible. He included instruction in several of the manual arts in his schools as a means of individual development and as a means of keeping students occupied in worthwhile pursuits.
1685	Thomas Budd proposed a plan of setting aside land to support public education in Pennsylvania and New Jersey.
1699	The Royal College of Art was established in Berlin.
1707-1768	Johann Hecker founded a new type of secondary school, the "realschule" in which he expanded Francke's school curriculum and methods of instruction to emphasize instruction in science, art, and the trades and industries. His school, and its practical curriculum, was the prototype for the non-classical secondary school curriculum in Germany.
1712-1778	Jean Jacques Rousseau rebelled against the classical curriculum and methods of education of his day and recommended that much of education should be taught through nature study and the manual arts. He advocated manual arts instruction as a means of mental training, which was in direct line with the tenets of faculty psychology of his day. He is known as the "father of Industrial Arts."
1738-1779	A number of inventions came into use such as James Watt's steam engine, which altered textile work forever and paved the way for the Industrial Revolution. With steam powered inventions, factory towns sprang up and the need for skilled workers emerged.

. . . continued . . .

1746-1827	Johann Heinrich Pestallozi, "father of instructional analysis and manual labor schools," introduced a number of educational principles and methods which have common acceptance today. He is believed to be the first to apply psychology to the learning process in his recognition of the stages of development of the individual. He used the technique of analysis to order learning tasks derived from the study of objects from the natural and humanmade environment. His principle of instruction was key to the establishment of manual training in Europe and eventually in America. His children learned by engaging in real-life activities around them, and the results of their learning helped to maintain their school and provide articles that could be sold to provide economic support which introduced the concept of manual labor schools.
1747	Moravians established a public school for children up to age 12 and a type of separate industrial school for boys and girls age 12 and over where common trades were taught.
1751	The Franklin Academy of Philadelphia was established to teach academic subjects as well as subjects of a practical nature, which served as a prototype for other academies. Soon afterwards, academies were established in other parts of the country.
1776-1841	Johann Herbart advocated the inclusion of workshops in elementary schools so that every youngster would learn to use their hands. He advocated manual training as a means of teaching other more abstract subjects.
1783-1852	Fredrich Froebel placed unity and interconnection at the center of his educational philosophy and maintained that the three elements of reception, reflection, and student response in the form of some creative activity with objects were critical in the learning process. His educational methods which involved the selection and construction of objects in a wide variety of mediums and according to the ability and interest level of the youngster, earned him the title "the father of the kindergarten."
1787	Cokesbury College in Maryland was one of the first manual labor schools in America to teach gardening and carpentry, which served as a prototype for other manual labor schools that emerged 40 years later.

. . . *continued* . . .

1787	The Northwest Ordinance authorized land grants for the establishment of educational institutions.
1791	The Constituent Assembly abolished the guilds in France and placed apprenticeship under government control.
1791	The Sunday School Movement, an idea borrowed from England, was introduced in Philadelphia. It brought children together from all classes, thus establishing the secular Sunday school which spread through the country.
1796	Thomas Jefferson's Bill for establishment of universal education at public expense was passed.
1799	The National School of Arts and Trades was established in France to train superior skilled workers and supervisors for manufacturing industries. This school was recognized by Napoleon Bonaparte, who championed other such schools in France.
1800s	The power age of machine tools began with the invention of the lathe (1800), planer (1817), milling machine (1818), drill press (1840), band saw (1853), grinder (1880), and first micrometer and master gauge blocks (1877).
1800s	The National Grange was formed to lobby for the interest of farmers at the state and national levels.
1800	Dr. George Birkbeck began his lectures in Glasgow, Scotland to adult mechanics. This evolved into the mechanics' institute movement, which made rapid progress in Britain and America during the next 30 years.
1805	The New York Free School Society was founded by Dewitt Clinton to provide education for poor children, calling attention to the need for free public education.
1807	Philip Emanuel von Fellenberg established his farm and trade school in Switzerland which utilized Pestallozian ideas of manual labor. His school was instrumental in the establishment of three other types of schools, agricultural, industrial reform, and the manual labor school.
1816	The Infant School, an idea of Robert Owens of Scotland, established in Boston to prepare children for grammar schools.
1818	Boston established a system of public primary schools.
1820s and 1830s	Some states appointed a chief school officer to monitor education in the state, and soon thereafter a State Board of Education was formed to develop school policy for the state.

. . . continued . . .

1820	The first mechanic's institute in America, the General Society of Mechanics and Tradesmen of the City of New York, was established. This school marked the beginning of the mechanics' institute movement in America.
1820	Girls were taught sewing in the primary grades of Boston schools.
1821	Boston established its first public high school.
1821	Emma Williard's Troy Female Seminary was established in Troy, New York to teach domestic or household duties along with academic subjects to female students.
1823	The Gardiner Lyceum, a type of manual labor school and full-time scientific and technical school, was established in Gardiner, Maine. This was one of the earliest American schools of applied science and engineering.
1823	Bookkeeping was included in the curriculum of the English high school of Boston.
1824	Rensselaer School was established at Troy, New York which was the second and perhaps most important of the applied science and engineering schools.
1824	The Franklin Institute of Philadelphia, the second mechanics' institute in America, was established.
1824	First girl's high school was opened in Worchester, Massachusetts.
1825	A mechanic's institute was established in Baltimore, Maryland.
1825	Robert Owens and William McClure established a new experimental school in New Harmony, Indiana which consisted of an infant school, elementary school, and secondary school for youngsters over age 12. This school employed a number of Pestallozian ideas including the concept of a manual labor school.
1826	Josiah Holbrook published a comprehensive plan for popularizing education to which he gave the title "American Lyceum of Science and Arts." He began to deliver a series of lectures on natural sciences in Worchester County, Massachusetts. This marked the beginning of the American Lyceum movement.

. . . continued . . .

1827	A mechanic's institute was opened in Boston.
1827	Massachusetts law required that bookkeeping be taught in selected high schools of the state.
1827	The Oneida Institute of Science and Industry, a presbyterian manual labor school, was established at Whitesboro, New York. This was one of the most famous academies because of its manual labor system.
1827	Massachusetts passed a law requiring the establishment of high schools in cities, towns, and districts of 500 families or more.
1833	Oberlin College was founded as one of the earliest coeducational institutions of higher learning.
1835	Girls were taught sewing in the grammar schools of Boston.
1836	Drawing was established as a required subject in the high schools of Boston.
1837	Horace Mann became Secretary of the Massachusetts Board of Education and emerged as a tireless leader in improving the conditions of schools and education in his state. He served as editor of the *Common School Journal* which presented educational ideas, described educational practices, and introduced innovation and improvements. He became a major leader in the development of free, public, universal education for all American youngsters.
1839	The first normal school for the training of teachers was established in Lexington, Massachusetts.
1841	Catherine Beecher published her *Treatise on domestic economy for the use of young ladies*, which covered nearly every phase of homemaking and paved the way for the development of home making education.
1842	The New England Female Medical College was founded.
1851	Massachusetts passed compulsory attendance laws for children until the eighth grade.
1855	Elmira College in New York was founded and became the first women's college to require young women to take domestic science and general household affairs courses. This was the first women's college to grant degrees.
1857	The National Education Association (NEA) was organized.

. . . continued . . .

1860	The first kindergarten in America was established in 1860 based on the kindergartens established in Europe by Froebel. The kindergarten was a school that stressed individual child development, motor activity as the primary teaching method, and social cooperation as its environment. Kindergartens were slow to evolve in America until after the Civil War, but by 1900 some 4,500 of them had been established in the United States.
1861	Oswego State Normal School was established to train teachers using teaching methods developed years earlier by Pestallozi and other European educators. The Oswego movement that followed brought much needed reform to the educational methods used in that time.
1862	The first Morrill Act was passed. This authorized public land grants to states for the establishment and maintenance of agricultural and mechanical colleges.
1868	Victor Della Voss established a new type of instructional program to teach the mechanical arts in the Imperial Technical School of Moscow in 1868. He developed eight principles know as the "Russian System" of manual training that incorporated job analysis for content identification, separate instructional shops, group instruction, and graded exercises to build skill competency. His system of instruction became the answer to instructional methodology for manual training in the United States and other countries.
1868	The Worchester County Free Institute, manual labor school, was established in Massachusetts to provide practical training and application of scientific principles in the mechanical arts. A number of these applied science and industry institutions became engineering colleges.
1868	The Hampton Institute, one of the first manual labor trade schools in America designed to provide specific trade training supplemented with directly related academic subjects, was established in Hampton, Virginia. This institution marked the beginning of the establishment of many private trade schools.
1868	A complete graded system of drawing was instituted in Boston schools. Drawing was a required subject in all grades of Cincinnati schools.
1872	The Kalamazoo Case established the right for states to collect taxes to support public education.

. . . continued . . .

1872	Massachusetts authorized schools to offer courses in sewing and other industrial education subjects.
1872	R. Hoe and Company, a manufacturer of printing presses, established one of the first corporate schools to train high quality employees for their firm.
1874-1907	Otto A. Salomon established a system of woodworking called sloyd in the elementary schools of Sweden to help children develop their mental and physical powers and to teach dexterity of hand and instill a general love of work. He is considered the father of the sloyd system of education, which influenced manual training and industrial arts in America.
1875	The Quincy Plan, developed by Francis Parker in Quincy, Massachusetts re-oriented the school system to an activity-centered curriculum based on the needs and interest of youngsters. This plan, based on the child-centered ideas of Pestallozi, changed the teaching methods of elementary education in America forever.
1876	Manual arts and arts and crafts were introduced into America from England and France. The name of manual training later changed to manual arts and then to industrial arts.
1876	Professor John Runkle, of the Massachusetts Institute of Technology, visited the Philadelphia centennial exhibition where he saw the Russian System of manual training. Professor Runkle established the School of Mechanic Arts as part of the Massachusetts Institute of Technology in Boston using some of the Russian System of manual training to educate and train qualified grammar school students.
1880	The first manual training high school was established in St. Louis, Missouri by Professor Calvin Woodward. This school borrowed some of the ideas of the Russian system, using the laboratory method of instruction and graded lessons in the use of common tools of the mechanical arts.
1880	Charles Leland introduced arts and craft instruction, which originated in England and France into the schools of Philadelphia. The arts and craft movement which followed led some manual training teachers to emphasize a wider variety of mediums for instruction and directed attention to artistic design.
1880	The Philadelphia High School for Girls offered courses in sewing and many other manual training school included courses in domestic science into their curriculums.

. . . continued . . .

1881	The New York Trade School was one of the first institutions established to offer specific trade training and supplemental studies for those preparing to enter employment as well as for those already employed. This was one of the first schools to utilize advisory committees.
1881	The Federation of Organized Trades & Labor Unions was formed and became the American Federation of Labor in 1886 consisting of 25 different unions and over 300,000 members.
1883	The Hebrew Technical Institute, a type of trade school, was established in New York City to provide general subjects and instruction in the mechanical trades for Jewish youngsters.
1884	The first public supported high school for manual training was established in Baltimore, Maryland.
1884	The Kitchen Garden Association was founded to deal with the problems of slum conditions in inner cities through education for household management.
1884	New York College for the Training of Teachers was established which later became Teachers College of Columbia University. Teachers College provided important leadership to the field of industrial arts. It was the first institution to offer professional coursework in the field; it was the first institution to confine its offerings in industrial education exclusively at the graduate level; it graduated the first doctorate in industrial education, and was the site of several important curriculum projects.
1887	The Hatch Act provided federal funds to establish and support agricultural experiment stations.
1888	Gustaf Larson established a system of sloyd instruction in Boston. Sloyd instruction emphasized developing the capacities of the child and the making of useful objects that were of interest to students. Sloyd also used only trained teachers rather than trained craftworkers. This experiment led the way to the establishment of "American sloyd" instruction in other schools of the country.
1890	The Country Life Movement began. This stimulated the development of general agriculture courses in elementary schools.
1891	The Williamson Free School Of Mechanical Trades, a trade school which was entirely free to those who could qualify, was established in Philadelphia to offer trade training that could match the best of apprenticeship programs.

. . . continued . . .

1893	Boston established its first public supported manual training high school.
1893	Professional courses for teachers of manual training were offered at Teachers College, New York.
1895	The American Correspondence School was established in Boston, Massachusetts by R. T. Miller, Jr. It moved to Chicago after the turn of the century.
1898	American Technical Society was founded in 1898 to publish books for use in courses offered by American Correspondence School.
1898	One of the first technical high schools was established in Springfield, Massachusetts.
1899	Ten annual conferences for home economics were conducted at Lake Placid and Chautauqua in New York under the leadership of Ellen Richards. These conferences provided organizational framework for programs of home economics education in schools of the late nineteenth and early twentieth century.
1900	Most states passed compulsory school laws and provided the final incentive to public-supported high schools throughout the nation.
1900	Beginning of the vocational education movement. Also, the beginning of the comprehensive high school that combined academic and manual training in one school facility.
1901	The Baldwin Locomotive Works of Philadelphia established a corporate school serving three levels of workers.
1902	General Electric Company established a corporate school which used an apprenticeship system that combined activities at the work site with classroom instruction for their employees.
1903	James Haney, director of manual training of the New York City public schools, introduced the term "manual arts" at the NEA convention.
1905	Governor Douglas appointed a Commission on Industrial and Technical Education, known as the Douglas Commission, that studied the need for some form of industrial education in Massachusetts and in 1906 reported a number of findings that sparked increased interest in establishing industrial education into schools to prepare individuals for vocations. The Douglas Commission Report attracted much attention to the need for public-supported programs of vocational education.

. . . continued . . .

1906	The National Society for the Promotion of Industrial Education was formed to promote the cause for industrial education nationwide and to assist in preparing draft legislation to be acted on by Congress.
1906	The Adams Act increased federal funds to states for operation of experiment stations established by the Hatch Act of 1887.
1908	The cooperative part-time plan of trade training was initiated by Professor Herman Schneider at Cincinnati, Ohio in connection with college engineering courses.
1908	Frank Parsons led the way for the establishment of the Vocational Bureau of Boston to deal with the problems of both youth and adults in finding suitable employment. He developed the concepts of vocational guidance and introduced the trait and factor theory of vocational guidance.
1909	The American Home Economics Association was founded.
1909	Charles Bennett, "father of manual arts" in America, outlined a classification system for elementary school manual arts to include the five areas of graphic arts, mechanic arts, plastic arts, textile arts, and book-making arts.
1909	Dean James Russell expanded the term "industrial arts" and recommended that industrial arts replace manual training in the elementary schools of the nation. Industrial arts was to be a study of the industrial processes by which raw materials are transformed into things of greater value to meet human needs and wants.
1911	Part-time cooperative courses were introduced into the high school of York, Pennsylvania.
1912	Charles Prosser became the Executive Secretary of the National Society for the Promotion of Industrial Education and was appointed to the Commission of National Aid to Vocation Education in 1914. In his leadership roles, Prosser was a strong advocate for public-supported vocational education that would prepare people to better serve the society. His ideas about vocational education were incorporated into the Smith-Hughes Act of 1917 and were dominant in vocational education for over 40 years.

. . . continued . . .

1914	The Commission on National Aid to Vocational Education was appointed by President Wilson to study the issue of federal aid to vocational education and to assist in drafting a bill to present to Congress. This Commission was instrumental in developing the language of the Smith-Hughes Act which was passed three years later in 1917.
1914	The Smith-Lever Act established cooperative extension programs in agriculture and home economics and initiated the concept of federal-state matching of funds.
1916	John Dewey published his book *Democracy and Education* in which he developed his ideas of progressive education. He was a strong advocate for vocational education of a broad nature that would help individuals understand the industrial nature of society and the nature of work as basic to social understanding. He was a strong proponent for an activity-centered program that featured problem-solving and doing activities.
1917	The Smith-Hughes Act was passed, authorizing federal funds for the establishment and support of secondary and postsecondary vocational training in the occupational areas of agriculture, home economics, and trades and industry. Federal funds could also be used to provide vocational teacher training.
1918	The Smith-Sears Act provided federal funds for establishing retraining programs for World War I veterans.
1918	The Commission on Reorganization of Secondary Education issued its famous "seven cardinal principles of education" with one of the principles being development of a vocation.
1920	The Smith-Bankhead Act provided for the establishment of rehabilitation programs for non-military disabled persons in civil employment.
1920	The Smith-Fess Act established rehabilitation programs for industry disabled persons.
1923	Gordon Bonser advocated the inclusion of industrial arts into the elementary school with a study of manufacturing industries as the curriculum base with the goal being to develop an understanding of the functioning of our industrial society. Industrial arts was to be a general education subject desirable for all to take.

. . . continued . . .

1926	The American Vocational Education was formed out of the merger of the National Society for Vocational Education (formerly NSPIE) and the Vocational Association of the Middle West.
1929	The George-Reed Act authorized additional funds for agriculture and home economics vocational programs funded by the Smith-Hughes Act of 1917, but no additional funds for trade and industrial education programs.
1934	The George-Ellzey Act increased supplemental funding for agriculture, home economics, and trade and industrial education programs authorized by the Smith-Hughes Act of 1917.
1936	The George-Deen Act increased federal support for vocational programs identified in the Smith-Hughes Act of 1917, and added the vocational area of distributive occupations and teacher education to receive federal funds.
1938	The Congress of Industrial Organizations (CIO), another large labor organization, was founded.
1940-1946	A series of ten Vocational Education for National Defense Acts were passed as war emergency majors to provide money for vocational education programs to prepare war industry workers.
1944	The Servicemen's Readjustment Act, commonly known as the GI Bill, authorized money to help World War II veterans make the adjustment to civilian life, and subsequent legislation allowed veterans of the Korean and Vietnam Wars to receive benefits.
1946	The George-Barden Act increased federal support for the vocational programs of agriculture, home economics, trade and industrial, and distributive education. It also added authorization for the Office of Vocational Education in Washington and vocational education for the fishery trades to receive federal funds.
1955	The American Federation of Labor (AFL) and the Congress of Industrial Organizations CIO) merged leadership to become the present AFL-CIO.
1956	The Health Amendments of the George-Barden Act added practical nursing and health occupations programs to the list of vocational programs eligible to receive federal funds.

. . . continued . . .

1956	The Fishery Amendments of the George-Barden Act further promoted vocational programs for the fishery industry.
1958	The National Defense Education Act provided federal support to state and local school systems for strengthening instruction in science, mathematics, foreign languages, and other critical subjects. In addition, it provided funds to support technical programs, vocational guidance and testing programs, training institutes, higher education student loans and fellowships, and statistical services.
1958	The Education of Mentally Retarded Children Act authorized federal assistance for training teachers of the handicapped.
1958	The Captioned Films for the Deaf Act authorized a loan service of captioned films for the deaf.
1960s	This decade marked the beginning of Manpower Legislation, and employment and training programs under the direction of the U.S. Department of Labor.
1961	The Area Redevelopment Act provided funds for retraining persons in defined redevelopment areas of the country that were severely economically depressed.
1962	The Manpower Development and Training Act provided funds for training in new and improved skills for the unemployed and underemployed.
1963	The Health Professions Educational Assistance Act provided federal funds to expand teaching facilities for health programs and for loans to students preparing for the health professions.
1963	The Vocational Education Act increased federal support for vocational education, but changed the way money was allocated toward serving people rather than occupational programs. This act authorized federal funds to support residential vocational schools, vocational work-study programs, and research, training, and demonstrations in vocational education. It also included business education as a program eligible for federal funds.
1963	The Higher Education Facilities Act authorized a five-year program of federal grants and loans to colleges and universities for the expansion and development of physical facilities.

. . . continued . . .

1964	The Civil Rights Act established basic human rights and responsibilities in the workplace and prohibited discrimination on the basis of race, gender, national origin, or handicap. Other issues addressed equal employment opportunities, voting rights, equal education, fair housing, and public accommodations.
1964	The Economic Opportunity Act of 1964 authorized federal funds to support college work-study programs for students from low-income families, education and vocational training for unemployed youth, training and work experience opportunities in welfare programs, Job Corps programs, and support for community action programs such as Head Start, Follow Through, Upward Bound, and Volunteers in Service to America (VISTA).
1965	The Elementary and Secondary Education Act (ESEA) authorized expenditure of federal funds for elementary and secondary school programs serving children of low-income families; for school library resources, textbooks, and other instruction materials; for supplementary educational centers and services; and educational research and development training.
1965	The Higher Education Act addressed some of the same issues that ESEA dealt with, only at the higher education level. Federal funds were made available to assist states and local school systems to solve educational problems through such programs as continuing education, student loans, and the establishment of the National Teacher Corp.
1965	The National Institute for the Deaf Act provided for the establishment and operation of residential schools for postsecondary education and training for the deaf.
1966	The Adult Education Act authorized grants to states to encourage expansion of educational programs for adults.
1966	The ESEA Amendments modified existing elementary and secondary programs and provided for state grants to initiate, expand, and improve programs and projects for handicapped children and youth.
1967	The Education Professions Development Act (EPA) provided federal funds to address the training of teachers in critical shortage areas, and provided fellowships for teachers and other educational professionals. This act was instrumental in providing a vital source of college and university vocational teacher educators.

. . . continued . . .

1967	The ESEA Amendments authorized federal support of regional centers for education of handicapped children, model centers and services for deaf-blind children, assistance in recruitment of personnel, and dissemination of information on the education of the handicapped, technical assistance for rural education programs, support for dropout prevention programs and for bilingual education programs.
1968	The Vocational Amendments broadened the definition of vocational education to bring it closer to general education and provided vast sums of money to address the nation's social and economic problems. The act established a National Advisory Committee, expanded vocational education services to meet the needs of disadvantaged students, and established methods of collecting and disseminating information about vocational education. This act placed more emphasis on vocational programs at the postsecondary level. It also added cooperative education as one of the vocational education programs eligible to receive federal funds.
1971	The Nurse Training Act provided funds for increasing and expanding provisions for nurse training facilities.
1972	The Education Amendments continued support for many of the programs established in the Vocational Act of 1963 and 1968 Amendments and introduced some new provisions important to vocational education such as special programs for the disadvantaged, and a broadened definition of vocational education to allow federal funds to be spent to support industrial arts programs and the training of volunteer firefighters. Postsecondary occupational education received more support in this act.
1973	The Rehabilitation Act reaffirmed the rights of handicapped persons in the work place. Section 503 established affirmative action programs to hire handicapped individuals and required employers to make reasonable accommodations, while Section 504 prohibited discrimination on the basis of handicap in any private or public program or activity receiving federal funds. This act was designed to allow handicapped individuals to enter the mainstream of American life.

. . . continued . . .

1974	The Educational Amendments encouraged the development of individualized education plans (IEPs) for children with special needs participating in Title I of the 1965 ESEA Act. These amendments also included the Women's Educational Equality Act of 1974 which was designed to assist states in bringing about educational equity for women. Other important provision of these amendments included support for career education, establishment of the National Center for Educational Statistics, and research into the problems of providing bilingual education.
1975	The Education of All Handicapped Children Act of 1975 launched an organized effort to provide a free and appropriate education for all handicapped children ages 3-21. This act spelled out the assurances for handicapped youngsters including due process, written individualized education plans, bias free testing and assessment, and measures to protect the confidentiality of records. In addition, a number of terms related to handicapped individuals were clearly defined. This act provided a number of grants to states and local school systems to improve vocational education and related services for handicapped individuals.
1976	The Education Amendments continued the trend of omnibus legislation to extend and revise previous legislation and to redirect American education in an attempt to correct some of the nation's problems including changing the public's attitude toward the roles of men and women in society. This act required the development of programs to eliminate sex discrimination and sex stereotyping. It also required the development of a national vocational education data reporting and accounting system and required states to develop an evaluation system. It established the NOICC and SOICC Occupational Information Coordinating Committees.
1977	The Youth Employment and Demonstration Projects Act established youth employment training programs that promoted education-to-work transition.
1978	The Career Education Incentive Act authorized the establishment of career education programs for elementary and secondary schools.
1978	The Education Amendments established the community schools concept to use existing educational facilities for instruction to adults and established a comprehensive basic skills program aimed at improving student achievement in reading, mathematics, and written and oral communication.

. . . continued . . .

1978	The Comprehensive Employment and Training ACT (CETA) Amendments revised existing manpower legislation to connect it with other related programs involved in preparing people for work including vocational education. Prime sponsors were required to identify the services to be provided to handicapped individuals in their five-year and annual training plans.
1979	The Department of Education Organization Act established the U. S. Department of Education.
1980s	Technology Education evolved from Industrial Arts.
1982	The Job Training Partnership Act (JPTA) significantly revised other manpower legislation to introduce a new era of collaboration between vocational education and the private sector to provide job training and related services to participants. This act provided funds to regional service delivery areas (SDAs) that used private industry councils (PICs) to determine what training programs were needed and how these programs were to be implemented. JPTA funds were not to be used for employment subsistence as was the case in previous manpower legislation, and 70% of funds were to be spent directly for training. Special Summer youth employment programs were established and the successful Job Corps program was continued.
1983	The Education Handicapped Act Amendments included a number of special provisions to support and coordinate education and service programs to assist handicapped youth in the transition from secondary to postsecondary education, employment, or adult services. The act also included support for expanding preschool special education programs and early intervention programs.
1983	The Rehabilitation Act Amendments authorized demonstration projects to address the problems encountered by youth with disabilities in making the transition from school to work.

. . . continued . . .

1984	The Carl D. Perkins Vocational Education Act continued the long-standing tradition of federal support for vocational education with two major goals in mind, one economic and one social. The economic goal was to improve the skills of the labor force and prepare adults for job opportunities. The social goal was to provide equal opportunities for adults in vocational education. This act had nine stated purposes including to expand, improve, modernize, and develop quality vocational education programs in order to meet the needs of the nation's existing and future work force marketable skills, and to improve productivity and promote economic growth. Educational services were to be provided to meet the needs of specific populations, including handicapped and disadvantaged individuals. The act spelled out the assurances that were to be provided to handicapped and disadvantaged individuals. This act was one of the most comprehensive in attempting to meet the vocational education needs of special populations.
1986	The Education Handicapped Act Amendments continued and expanded discretionary programs and transition programs. It established the handicapped infant and toddler programs, and changed the age of eligibility for special education services to age 3.
1986	The Handicapped Children's Protection Act provided monetary support for parents and guardian who found themselves in litigation over the rights of their children to receive a free, appropriate education.
1986	The Rehabilitation Act Amendments authorized funding for programs in supported employment services for individuals with disabilities.
1988	The Technology-Related Assistance for Individuals with Disabilities Act provided assistance to states in developing needed programs of technology-related assistance to individuals with disabilities and their families.
1989	The Children with Disabilities Temporary Care Reauthorization Act authorized funds to provide temporary care for children with a disability or chronic illness and provided crisis nurseries for children at risk of abuse and neglect.

. . . continued . . .

1990	The Education of the Handicapped Amendments, more popularly known as the Individuals with Disabilities Education Act (IDEA), combined many of the programs of previous legislation for individuals with special needs. It is the most important piece of legislation ever passed by Congress for educating disabled children and youth. IDEA includes many provisions such as requiring schools to provide assistive devices to increase or maintain the functional capability of individuals with disabilities and establishing special programs on transition. The list of persons who are eligible for special education and related services was expanded from nine to eleven. A new structure was provided for developing IEPs and ITPs.
1990	The Americans With Disabilities Act furthered the provisions began in the Rehabilitation Act of 1973 banning discrimination based on disability, and guaranteed equal opportunities for individuals with disabilities regardless of whether or not federal funds are involved in employment, public accommodation, transportation, state and local government services, and telecommunications. This act is the most comprehensive enactment ever written which identifies and protects the civil rights of Americans with disabilities.
1990	The Developmental Disabilities Assistance and Bill of Rights Act authorized grants to support the planning, coordination, and delivery of specialized services to persons with developmental disabilities.
1990	The Carl D. Perkins Vocational and Applied Technology Education Act amended and extended the previous 1984 Perkins Act authorizing the largest amount of federal funds ever for vocational education. The intent of this act was to assist states and local school systems in teaching the skills and competencies necessary to work in a technologically advanced society for all students. A major goal of this legislation was to provide greater vocational opportunities to disadvantaged individuals. The act provided funds for the integration of academic and vocational education and for Tech Prep programs, an articulated program between high schools and postsecondary institutions. The act eliminated set-asides for support services for special populations giving states and local agencies greater flexibility in how funds are best used to serve special populations.

. . . continued . . .

1992	The Job Training Reform Amendments revised the JPTA of 1982 to change the focus of manpower programs toward improving services to those facing serious barriers to employment, enhancing the quality of services provided, improving accountability of funds and the programs they serve, linking services provided to real labor market needs, and facilitating the development of a comprehensive and coherent system of human resources services. One of the new provision of special interest to vocational educators was the requirement for on-the-job training contracts and the development of individual service strategies (ISSs) which is an individualized employability development plan for each JPTA participant. This act is devoted to serving special populations who face the greatest employment barriers.
1993	The Family and Consumer Science became the new name for home economics Education.
1994	The Technology-Related Assistance for Individuals with Disabilities Act Amendments expanded the efforts to assist states in developing and implementing a comprehensive, consumer-responsive, statewide program of technology-related assistance for individuals with disabilities of all ages.
1994	The Goals 2000: Educate America Act was a blueprint for improving America's schools through the establishment of eight national goals and the development of voluntary academic and skill standards to assist state and local agencies in helping every child meet criteria that will ensure that youngsters are learning what they need to learn in order to function as a family member, involved community member, and competent worker. The act identified ten elements which constitute a suggested framework for developing a local Goals 2000 Plan.
1994	The Improving America's Schools Act was a reauthorization of the ESEA of 1965 which placed primary emphasis on serving disadvantaged students. The major goal of Title I has been revised to improve the teaching and learning of children in high-poverty schools to enable them to meet the challenging academic and performance standards being established by the Goals 2000 Act. This act increased opportunities for vocational and applied technology education to provide input into state and local educational plans and strengthened vocational and applied technology education in fourteen different areas.

. . . continued

1994	The School-to-Work Opportunities Act (STWOA) provided a framework to build a high quality skilled workforce for out nation's economy through partnerships between educators and employers. This act emphasized preparing students with the knowledge, skills, abilities, and information about occupations and the labor market that facilitated the transition from school to continuing education and work. Key elements of this act included collaborative partnerships, integrated curriculum, technological advances, adaptable workers, comprehensive career guidance, work-based learning and a step-by-step approach.

REFERENCES

Academic American Encyclopedia (Electronic data) (1994). History of Technology. Danbury, CT: Grolier Publishing Company.

Adams, D. A. (1993). The organization and operation of vocational education. In C. Anderson and L. C. Rampp (Eds.). *Vocational education in the 1990s, II: A sourcebook for strategies, methods, and materials* (pp. 35-59). Ann Arbor, MI: Praken Publishing Company.

Advisor's Guide to the Student Handbook (1986). Alexandria, VA: National FFA Organization.

Agricultural Proficiency Award Handbook. (1990). Alexandria, VA: National FFA Organization.

A Guide for Integrating HOSA into the HOE Classroom (1992). Irvin, TX: HOSA, Inc.

American Council on Industrial Arts Teacher Education (1981). *An interpretive history of industrial arts: The interrelationship of society, education and industrial arts.* (30th Yearbook). Bloomington, IL: McKnight Publishing Company.

American Home Economics Association (1989). *Home economics concepts: A base for curriculum development.* Alexandria, VA: Author.

American Home Economics Association (1994). *A conceptual framework for the 21st century.* Alexandria, VA: Author.

American Home Economics Association (1994). *Positioning the profession for the 21st century.* Alexandria, VA: Author.

American Society for Training and Development (ASTD) & U.S. Department of Labor (1988). *Workplace basics: The skills employers want.* Washington, DC: U.S. Government Printing Office.

American Vocational Association (1990). *The AVA Guide to the Carl D. Perkins Vocational and Applied Technology Education Act of 1990.* Author.

American Vocational Association (1992). American Vocational Association Annual Report 1991. *Vocational Education Journal, 67* 1, 31.

American Vocational Association (1993). *Vocational Education Today: Fact Sheet.* Alexandria, VA: Author.

American Vocational Association (1994). Working draft for the position statement of the American Vocational Association on the reauthorization of the Carl D. Perkins Vocational and Applied Technology Education Act of 1990. Alexandria, VA: Author.

American Vocational Association (1994, November). AVA amendments in ESEA win new funding sources for voc ed. *Legislative Update.* Alexandria, VA: Author.

American Vocational Association (1995). Inside AVA. *Vocational Education Journal. 70* 2, 13.

Ault, D. (1983). *There is room in VICA for special needs students. VICA Professional Edition, 18* (3), 1-2.

Barella, R. (1981). The vocational education movement: Its impact on the development of industrial arts. In T. Wright & R. Barella (Eds.) *An interpretative history of industrial arts: The relationship of society, education and industrial arts.* 30th Yearbook. American Council on Industrial Arts Teacher Education. Bloomington, IL: McKnight Publishing Company.

Barlow, M. L. (1967). *History of industrial education in the United States*. Peoria, IL: Chas. A. Bennett Co., Inc.

Barlow, M. L. (1976). 200 years of vocational education 1776-1976. *American Vocational Journal, 51* (5), 21-108.

Bennett, C. A. (1926). *History of manual and industrial education up to 1870*. Peoria, IL: Manual Arts.

Bennett, C. A. (1937). *History of manual and industrial education. 1870 to 1917*. Peoria, IL: Manual Arts.

Birchenall, J. & Wanat, J. (1981). Serving the handicapped in vocational student organizations. *Vocational Education, 56* (3), 51-54.

Boesel, D. & McFarland, L. (1994). *National assessment of vocational education: Final report to Congress volume I summary and recommendations*. Washington, DC: Office of Educational Research and Improvement, U.S. Department of Education.

Boesel, D., Hudson, L., Deich, S., & Masten, C. (1994). *National assessment of vocational education: Final report to Congress volume II participation in and quality of vocational education*. Washington, DC: Office of Educational Research and Improvement, U.S. Department of Education.

Brustein, M. & Mahler, M. (1994). *AVA guide to the school-to-work opportunities act*. Alexandria, VA: American Vocational Association.

Butler, T. (1981). What's in it for the teacher. *Vocational Education, 56* (6), 47-49.

Calhoun, C. C. & Finch, A. V. (1982). *Vocational Education: Concepts and Operations*. Belmont, CA: Wadsworth Publishing Company.

Carl D. Perkins Vocational Act of 1984 (PL 98-524). Washington, DC: Superintendent of Documents.

Carl D. Perkins Vocational and Applied Technology Act Amendments of 1990 (PL 101-392). Washington DC: Superintendent of Documents.

Cassidy, W. H. (1994). Youth apprenticeship programs–Business and school partnerships. In A. McEntree (Ed.). *Expanding Horizons in Business Education* (pp. 18-22). Reston, VA: National Business Association, National Business Education Yearbook, No. 32.

Chapter Action Kit (1991). Reston, VA: Future Homemakers of America, Inc.

Coleman, M. (1993). The thrill of victory. *Vocational Education, 68* (4), 30-32.

Cubberly, E. P. (1934). Public education in the United States. Boston: Houghton-Mifflin.

DECA Handbook (1995). Reston, VA: DECA, Inc.

DECA Inc. (1992). *Marketing education and DECA: Essential factors in creating a quality work force*. Reston, VA: A report prepared by the Corporate National Advisory Board of DECA, an Association of Marketing Students.

DECA Is More Than You Ever Imagined (1986). Reston, VA: DECA, Inc.

Dewey, J. (1916). *Democracy and education*. New York: Macmillan.

Dykman, A. (1993). Not just "seed and feed." *Vocational Education, 68* (4), 33.

Dykman, A. (1995). *On the Block. Vocational Education Journal. 70* (6), 26-31, 56.

Education of the handicapped (1991). Alexandria, VA: Capitol Publications Inc.

Edwards, N. & Richey, H. G. (1963). *The school in American social order* (2nd Ed.). Boston: Houghton Mifflin.

FBLA Advisor's Chapter Management Guide (1992). Reston, VA: Future Business Leaders of America, Phi Beta Lambda, Inc.

FBLA National Awards Program (1993). Future Business Leaders of America, Phi Beta Lambda, Inc.

FBLA/PBL National Handbook (1991). Reston, VA: Future Business Leaders of America, Phi Beta Lambda, Inc., Future Business Leaders of America-Phi Beta Lambda, Inc.

FFA Student Handbook (1991). Alexandria, VA: National FFA Organization.

FHA/HERO Chapter Handbook (1991). Reston, VA: Future Homemakers of America, Inc.

Fracaroli, M. (1981). How to become a better advisor. *Vocational Education, 56* (6), 50-52.

Georgia Department of Education (1988). *Home economics eonsumer home economics curriculum guide (grades 9-12).* Atlanta, GA: Author.

Georgia Department of Education (1990). *Georgia secondary vocational education.* Atlanta, GA: Author.

Georgia Department of Education (1992). *Business education computer applications volume IV: Electronic publishing curriculum guide (grades 10-12).* Ellijay, GA: Vocational Education Materials Center.

Georgia Department of Education (1993). *Home economics education exploratory home economics curriculum guide (grades 6-8).* Ellijay, GA: Vocational Curriculum Materials Center.

Georgia Department of Education (1994). *Agriscience in Georgia: An overview.* Atlanta, GA: Author.

Gray, K. (1993). Challenging an uncertain future. *Vocational Education Journal, 68* (2), 35-38.

Griffin, D. (1983). A new partnership becomes law. *Vocational Education Journal, 58* (1), 32-34.

Griffin, D. A. (1994). *North Carolina's first post-secondary technical institution: Past, present and future.* Unpublished doctoral dissertation, University of Georgia.

Hall, T. (1993) VICA goes to college. *Vocational Education, 68* (4), 28-29.

Hannah, G. (1993). Shift or drift. *Vocational Education, 68* (4), 21-25.

Harris, T. and Sweet, G. (1981). Why we believe in vocational student organizations. *Vocational Education, 56* (6), 33-35.

Herren, R. V. & Donahue, R. L. (1991). *The agriculture dictionary.* Albany, NY: Delmar Publishers Inc.

Home Economics Education Association (1991). *Coalition statement: Vocational home economics education.* Washington, DC: Author.

HOSA Handbook (1992). Irvin, TX: HOSA, Inc.

HOSA National Recognition Program (1991). Irvin, TX: Health Occupations Students of America.

How your business can work with VICA. (1994). Leesburg, VA: National VICA.

International Technology Education Association (1988). *Technology education: A national imperative.* Reston, VA: Author.

International Technology Education Association (1993). *Technology education: A global imperative.* Reston, VA: Author.

International Technology Education Association (1993). *Technology education: The new basics.* Reston, VA: Author.

In Touch With the Business of America-Chapter Organization Packet (1992). Federal Register. (1977). *42* (191).

Koeninger, J. (1988). *Value added vocational classrooms. Vocational Education, 63* (8), 38-41.

Learning Disabilities Research and Training Center (1994). What you need to know about the Tech Act. *The LD Link.* Athens, GA: Author.

Lee, J. S. (1994). *Program planning guide for agriscience and technology education.* Danville, IL: Interstate Publishers, Inc.

Marketing Education and DECA: Essential factors in creating a quality work force (1992). Reston, VA: DECA, Inc.

Marketing Education Resource Center (1987). *National curriculum framework and core competencies.* Columbus, OH: Author.

Martinez, R. L. (1992). Wanted: leadership qualities, *Vocational Education, 67* (5), 30-32.

Martin, G. E. (1981). Industrial education in early America. In T. Wright & R. Barella (Eds.). *An interpretative history of industrial arts: The relationship of society, education and industrial arts.* 30th Yearbook. American Council on Industrial Arts Teacher Education. Bloomington, IL: McKnight Publishing Company.

Morrissey, P. *The educator's guide to the Americans with disabilities act* (1993). Alexandria, VA: American Vocational Association.

National FFA Contests (1993). Alexandria, VA: National FFA Organization.

National Association of Trade and Industrial Education (NATIE) (1994). *Workforce 2020: Action report school-to-work opportunities national voluntary skill standards.* Leesburg, VA: Author.

National Center for Educational Statistics (NCES) (1992). *Vocational education in the United States: 1969-1990.* Washington, DC: Office of Educational Research and Improvement, U.S. Department of Education.

National Tech Prep Network (1992). *Tech prep/associate degree: Concept paper.* Waco, TX: Center for Occupational Research and Development.

National Tech Prep Network (1995). *Special Legislative Edition Connections.* Waco, Texas: Center for Occupational Research and Development (CORD).

Nelson, L. P. (1981). Background: The European influence. In T. Wright & R. Barella (Eds.). *An Interpretative History of Industrial Arts: The Relationship of Society, Education and Industrial Arts.* 30th Yearbook. American Council on Industrial Arts Teacher Education. Bloomington, IL: McKnight Publishing Company.

Nystrom, D. C. & Bayne, G. K. (1979). *Occupational and career education legislation* (2nd Ed.). Indianapolis, IN: Bobbs-Merrill.

Office of Educational Research and Improvement, U.S. Department of Education (1994). *National assessment of vocational education interim report to Congress.* Washington, DC: U.S. Government Printing Office.

Phillips, J. (1994). All business is global. In A McEntree (Ed.). *Expanding horizons in business education* (pp. 35-45). Reston, VA: National Business Association, National Business Education Yearbook, No. 32.

Policy of the United States Office of Education for Vocational Education Student Organization (1990). Washington, DC: U.S. Office of Education.

Policy statements: Statement No. 53. This we believe about the role of business education in technology (1993). *Business Education Forum 48* (1), 11-12. Authors.

Prosser, C. A. & Allen, C. R. (1925). *Vocational education in a democracy.* NY: Century Company.

PSA Handbook (1992). Alexandria, VA: National Postsecondary Agricultural Student Organization.

Roberts, R. W. (1971). *Vocational and practical arts education* (3rd Ed.). NY: Harper & Row.

Rumpf, E. L. (1971). *Vocational Youth Organizations.* Washington, DC: U.S. Office of Education.

Sarkees, M. (1973). Vocational student organizations: Benefits for handicapped students. *Teaching Exceptional Children, 16* (1), 60-64.

Sarkees, M. and Sullivan, R. L. (1985). Special needs students and vocational student organizations: A winning team. *Vocational Education, 60* (5).

Sarkees, M. D., and Sullivan, R. L. (1989). Learners with special needs in vocational student organizations. *The Journal for Vocational Special Needs Education, 12* (1), 21-26.

Savage, E. & Sterry, L. (1990). *A conceptual framework for technology education.* Reston, VA: International Technology Education Association.

School-to-Work Act-Overview (1994). Alexandria, VA: American Vocational Association.

Schultz, J. B. (1994). Facts of life. *Vocational Education Journal. 69* (4), 19-21, 41.

Secretary's Commission on Achieving Necessary Skills (SCANS) (1991). *What work requires of school: A SCANS report for america 2000.* Washington, DC: U.S. Department of Labor.

Secretary's Commission on Achieving Necessary Skills (SCANS) (1992). *Learning a living: A blueprint for high performance.* Washington, DC: U.S. Department of Labor.

Shephards Federal and State Acts and Cases by Popular Names Parts 1, 2, & 3 (1992). McGraw-Hill, Inc.

Skills USA Championships Technical Standards (1995). Leesburg, VA: National VICA.

Smith, D. F. (1981). Industrial arts founded. In T. Wright & R. Barella (Eds.) *An interpretative history of industrial arts: The relationship of society, education and industrial arts.* 30th Yearbook. American Council on Industrial Arts Teacher Education. Bloomington, IL: McKnight Publishing Company.

Stadt, R. and Washburn, J. (1993). We the pupils. *Vocational Education, 68* (4), 36.

Star Events Manual (1990). Reston, VA: Future Homemakers of America, Inc.

Stewart, D. (1994). Home economics division considers name change. *Vocational Education Journal 69* (6), 53-54.

Stonehouse, P. (1994). *Georgia department of technical and adult education standards and program guide development: A presentation.* Atlanta, GA: Georgia Department of Technical and Adult Education.

Teacher's Tool Kit (1991). Leesburg, VA: National VICA.

Technical Foundation of America (1989). *Industry & technology education: A guide for curriculum designers, implementors, and teachers*: Lansing, IL: Author.

The Art of VICA-Advisor's Reference & Training Modules (1992). Leesburg, VA: National VICA.

The AVA Guide to the Carl D. Perkins Vocational and Applied Technology Act of 1990 (1990). Alexandria, VA: American Vocational Association.

The Meetings Kit (1990). Leesburg, VA: National VICA.

The Student Bill Of Rights (1993). Leesburg, VA: National VICA.

The VICA Professional Development Program (1992). Leesburg, VA: National VICA.

Total Quality Curriculum (1993). Leesburg, VA: National VICA.

United States Code Congressional and Administrative News. 103rd Congress-First Session 1993, Vol. 1. West Publishing Co., St. Paul, MN.

United States Code, 1988 Edition. Containing the General Laws of the United States in Force on January 3, 1989, Vol. 20. United States Government Printing Office.

U.S. Department of Education (1994, May). Introducing goals 2000: A world class education for every child. *Goals 2000 Community Update.* Washington, DC: Author.

U.S. Department of Education (1994, November). The improving America's schools act passes, reauthorizes ESEA. *Goals 2000 Community Update.* Washington, DC: Author.

U.S. Department of Labor (1991). *Dictionary of Occupational Titles (DOT).* (4th Ed.) A complete reprint of the DOT as produced by the U.S. Department of Labor. Indianapolis, IN: JIST Works, Inc.

U.S. Department of Labor (1993). The American work force: 1992-2005. *Occupational Outlook Quarterly 37* (3) 2-44.

U.S. General Accounting Office (GAO) (1990). *Training strategies: preparing noncollege youth for employment in the U.S. and foreign countries.* Washington, DC: U.S. General Accounting Office.

U.S. General Accounting Office (GAO) (1991). *Transition from school to work: Linking education and worksite training.*
Washington, DC: U.S. General Accounting Office.

United States Statutes At Large (1994). Washington, DC: United States Government Printing Office.

Vaughn, P. R., Vaughn, R. C., and Vaughn, D. L. (1993) Handbook for Advisors of Vocational Student Organizations. Athens, GA: American Association for Vocational Instructional Materials.

VICA Leadership Handbook (1989). Leesburg, VA: National VICA.

Vocational Student Organizations, 7th Report (1972). National Advisory Council on Vocational Education. (1972).

Vocational Student Organizations – "A Reference Guide" (1990). National Coordinating Council for Vocational Student Organizations. (Available from National VICA, Leesburg, VA).

Walter, R. A. (1993). Development of vocational education. In C. Anderson and L. C. Rampp (Eds.) *Vocational education in the 1990s, II: A sourcebook for strategies, methods, and materials* (pp. 1-20). Ann Arbor, MI: Prakken Publishing Company.

West, L. & Meers, G. D. (1992). An introduction to the Carld D. Perkins Vocational and Applied Technology Education Act of 1990 for special Populations: Struggling to understand the reauthorized Perkins Act. *The Journal for Vocational Special Needs Education. 14* 2 & 3, 4-32.

Wilcox, J. (1991). The Perkins Act. *Vocational Education Journal.* 66 (2), 16-17.

Wright, T. (1981). Manual training: Constructive activities enter the public schools (1981). In T. Wright & R. Barella (Eds.). *An interpretative history of industrial arts: The relationship of society, education and industrial arts.* 30th Yearbook. American Council on Industrial Arts Teacher Education. Bloomington, IL: McKnight Publishing Company.

Wright, T. & Barella, R. (1981). Summary and Reflections. In T. Wright & R. Barella (Eds.) *An interpretative history of industrial arts: The relationship of society, education and industrial arts.* 30th Yearbook. American Council on Industrial Arts Teacher Education. Bloomington, IL: McKnight Publishing Company.

ABOUT THE AUTHORS

John L. Scott

John L. Scott is an associate professor in the Technological Studies Program, Department of Occupational Studies, College of Education, at the University of Georgia. He has taught at the middle school, high school, and university levels.

Dr. Scott consults with state departments of education and local school districts, is the chair of the Chapter Display Technical Committee for the VICA Skills USA Championships, and has served as president of the National Association of Industrial and Technical Teacher Educators and the National Association of Trade and Industrial Education.

Michelle Sarkees-Wircenski

Michelle Sarkees-Wircenski is a professor in the Department of Technology and Cognition, College of Education, at the University of North Texas. She teaches courses in vocational and applied technology education for educators as well as courses in training and development for individuals from business and industry.

A past president of the National Association of Vocational Education Special Needs Personnel, Dr. Sarkees-Wircenski has coauthored previous books in the area of vocational special needs education and a book in training and development. A variety of articles which relate to vocational/technical programs have been published by this author. She has delivered vocational special needs inservice and professional development sessions in forty states.

RELATED MATERIAL

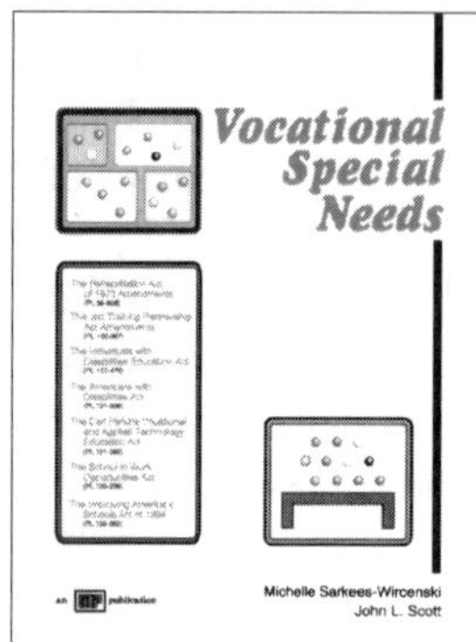

VOCATIONAL SPECIAL NEEDS

By M. Sarkees-Wircenski,
J. L. Scott

This professional text covers all aspects of dealing with special populations in vocational/technical education settings. Applicable legislation and its implications for instruction is emphasized. Case studies illustrate specific disabilities, legislative impact, and instructional strategies.

Contents include

- Foundations for Vocational Special Needs Education
- Overview of Vocational and Applied Technology Education
- Individuals with Disabilities
- Vocational Assessment
- Individualized Education
- Curriculum Modification
- Instructional Strategies
- Evaluation Strategies
- Vocational Student Organizations
- Coordinating Support Services
- Transition Programming

INSTRUCTORS AND THEIR JOBS

By W. R. Miller

This important textbook can help achieve goals through its valuable suggestions on how to plan, prepare for, and conduct classes. It explains how to measure and evaluate student achievement and get the most from instructional aids. Relates theoretical and practical aspects of the psychology of education to common problems faced every day in the classroom.

Contents include

- Learning Process
- Influences on Learning
- Instructional Planning: Designing Courses and Lessons
- Discussion and Other Group Participation Methods
- Computers: An Aid to Learners and Instructors

For more information call TOLL-FREE 1-800-323-3471 or Fax 1-708-957-1100.

WRITING FOR PUBLICATION

American Tech books are written by skilled people who know their trade and are willing to invest their time and effort to develop learning material designed to help your students learn that trade. *Trade experience is the most important author qualification at American Tech.* Teaching experience, while not an absolute requirement, is a definite asset.

Our editorial staff is experienced in working with tradesworkers to develop comprehensive learning material. Technical editors, copy editors, artists, and our printers use current technology to transform your trade experience into well-organized, heavily-illustrated, attractive books, workbooks, activity manuals, and instructor's guides.

If you would like to consider becoming an author for American Tech, request a complimentary copy of *Author's Guide.*

This 42-page booklet is filled with specific guidelines and examples that show how to organize and develop a proposal that will receive serious consideration by our publishing staff.

To receive a copy of *Author's Guide* or a four-color catalog of our publications, contact:

American Technical Publishers, Inc.
1155 West 175th Street
Homewood, IL 60430

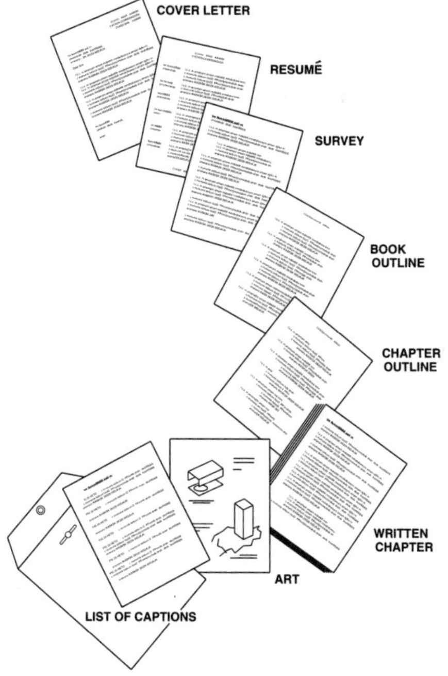